ABOVE
the
GROUND

A
TRUE STORY
OF THE
TROUBLES
IN
NORTHERN
IRELAND

DAN LAWTON

WILDBLUE
PRESS

WildBluePress.com

ABOVE THE GROUND published by:
WILDBLUE PRESS
P.O. Box 102440
Denver, Colorado 80250

WILDBLUE PRESS is registered at the U.S. Patent and Trademark Offices.

ISBN 978-1-960332-25-7 Trade Paperback
ISBN 978-1-960332-27-1 eBook
ISBN 978-1-960332-26-4 Hardback

Interior Formatting and Cover Design by Elijah Toten
www.totencreative.com

ABOVE *the* GROUND

TABLE OF CONTENTS

FOREWORD

Why should I want to go back
To you, Ireland, my Ireland?
The blots on the page are so black
That they cannot be covered with shamrock.
I hate your grandiose airs,
Your sob-stuff, your laugh and your swagger,
Your assumption that everyone cares
Who is the king of your castle.
Castles are out of date,
The tide flows round the children's sandy fancy;
Put up what flag you like, it is too late
To save your soul with bunting.

—Louis MacNeice (1938)

PROLOGUE

I hope to . . . prove my innocence, to bring into focus the English judicial system in Northern Ireland and methods of persecution and a better understanding world wide, of what is actually going on, [so] that in turn, God willing will result in investigation, and possibly leading to a solution. I think everyone is ready for peace and harmony. I have been through these experiences for a reason, not what the British would have you believe.

—Kevin Barry John Artt, letter from Santa
Rita County Jail (June 10, 1992)

In 1983, at age twenty-three, Kevin Barry Artt was falsely convicted of the murder of Albert Miles, a British prison official, on behalf of the Irish Republican Army. His conviction, rendered under emergency laws in one of Northern Ireland's juryless courts, came at the end of the longest trial in Irish legal history. Seven weeks later, Kevin escaped from the notorious Maze prison. The escape made headlines around the world. Afterward, Kevin became Britain's most wanted fugitive.

Kevin made it to the U.S. in 1985 and settled in San Diego, where he lived quietly underground until the long arm of the British government caught up to him in 1992. An epic extradition battle followed in the federal courts in San Francisco. The case endured in the federal courts in

California for over eight years. To read the record of the case is to learn about the darkest and most disturbing episodes of that time from men who contributed to its making.

Kevin Barry Artt is an innocent man, convicted in an unjust and discredited legal system.

Kevin's life offers a metaphor for the life of Northern Ireland during the period spanning 1969 and today. The country in which Kevin grew up was one in which a Unionist majority and its British sponsors controlled all the levers of power—courts, laws, police, jails, guns, and the permits thereto, the allocation of good jobs and decent housing. As a Catholic, Kevin belonged to a minority for whom equal rights were unthinkable to the state and those who ran it. As the minority became ever more insistent on its rights during the late 1960s and 1970s, a dirty war unfolded metastatically in Northern Ireland. For Kevin and other Catholics in Belfast, there was no winning that war. There was only outsmarting it or escaping it unless a person was to resign himself to a lifetime of second-class citizenship and suffering.

Kevin did not wish to resign himself to such a life. Nor did he wish to become another statistic, one more name on the long list of lives suddenly ended or ruined by the Troubles. His is a tale of survival.

It is also a story with a happy ending. A children's book inspired by Kevin's life would feature as its protagonist a boy who passes unharmed through a dark forest inhabited by monsters. He emerges safely, miraculously, out the other side, despite the monsters' best efforts to destroy him. And destroy him they nearly did.

Kevin Barry Artt's story offers a vehicle for trying to answer some zoom-out questions. *How did courts in Northern Ireland treat defendants accused of terrorist offenses during the early 1980s? Why did they treat them that way? In trying to crush terrorism, what price do governments pay when they abandon traditional limits on what police and courts can do to their citizens? Is it possible for a man to survive assassination attempts, cruel and prolonged interrogation and trials, and the best efforts of police, intelligence services, and paramilitaries to ruin his life without becoming embittered and angry at the world? To the refugee, is America still a refuge from foreign oppressors?*

And, most of all, these: *Who was it who killed Albert Miles? Was it Kevin Barry Artt? If not, why did he falsely confess to a crime he didn't commit? Why did thousands of people do that in Northern Ireland during the Troubles?*

On my first visits to Northern Ireland during the 1990s, my sense of being a stranger in a strange land was acute. For a deracinated American of the baby boomer generation, trying to comprehend the history and hatred that spanned centuries was both daunting and humbling. I had never before seen army troops patrolling country roads in full camouflage, armored personnel carriers rumbling down city streets, fortified police barracks with radio antennae so tall they could be seen from a mile away. In a country slightly smaller than the state of Connecticut, there were over a hundred fixed military installations and thousands of heavily armed soldiers. The fear and dread in the air were disguised but pervasive. I understood California, where I had grown up, and where Kevin Barry Artt had wound up. Northern Ireland was a world for which I was not prepared. To start to understand Northern Ireland, I needed a glossary. (One follows this prologue.)

When it comes to the Troubles, I have no ideological axes to grind, but I do not pretend to be a journalist who is impartial about his subject. I served as a part of Kevin Barry Artt's legal team from 1992 to 2000 and Kevin and I grew close during that time. I hope the reader will find I have not let that closeness interfere with my duty to tell the truth even though it may disappoint some interested parties, including Kevin himself.

I have had the good fortune of hundreds of interviews with Kevin Barry Artt, as well as access to the records of Kevin's trials and appeals in Belfast and San Francisco. Within them were thousands of pages of transcripts, notes of witness interviews, police reports, and photographs. There were also reams of private communications between Kevin and his lawyers. Kevin could have insisted on the secrecy of that material. He decided to waive his privileges in the interest of telling the whole truth. His former lawyers allowed me access to their files and work product for the sake of this book. No reader can wonder what I or he might have selectively concealed.

As I write this, Kevin lives openly in America. The British and American governments have long since given up trying to return him to prison in Northern Ireland. Like millions of Irish immigrants before him, he has made a life here, started a family, and put down roots. He has peace and security, things he never experienced in his native country. For the moment, he has the life we all want, all the elements of the California Dream.

One might ask, *Why this book? Why now?*

My answer to these questions would be that truth does not get old. In 1975, Irish poet Seamus Heaney described his country as a land of password, handgrip, wink and nod, silenced by the tight gag of place. Northern Ireland remains so at this writing, twenty-five years after the conflict between the IRA and the British government ended with the Good Friday Agreement. This book tries to pierce that silence, expose the lies that ruined much of the lives of Kevin and his family, and tell truths which are distasteful to both the British government and the men of what used to be the IRA.

Kevin's answer might resemble what 25-year-old Irish patriot Robert Emmet said to a British court on the day before his hanging and beheading for high treason on September 29, 1803:

I have much to say why my reputation should be rescued from the load of false accusation and calumny which has been heaped upon it.
This is his story.

Dan Lawton
San Diego, California
April 19, 2023

GLOSSARY

Ace Taxi: Unlicensed taxi service which operated in Belfast during the 1970s and 1980s. Security forces suspected Ace of connections to the IRA, who supposedly used Ace vehicles to transport personnel, firearms, and explosives.

Ardoyne: Working-class residential area of north Belfast with strong Catholic and Irish nationalist tradition.

Article 3(a): Clause in U.K.-U.S. supplementary extradition treaty which came into effect in 1986. The clause authorized American U.S. courts to deny extradition of persons to the U.K. where the extradition request was based on "trumped up" charges or would subject the person sought for extradition to prejudice on the grounds of his race, religion, nationality, or political opinions. Article 3(a) was intended to give American courts limited power to inquire into the fairness of the Diplock court system in Northern Ireland.

British Army: Land warfare force of the British government first deployed to Northern Ireland during the modern Troubles in Operation Banner in 1969. The highest number of British troops stationed in the north at any one time was 25,700, in 1972, the deadliest year of the Troubles.

Castlereagh: Fortified interrogation center operated by the RUC in east Belfast from 1977 to 1999. Castlereagh was the principal place of interrogation of terrorist suspects and arrestees in the eastern part of the six counties. Torture and coercive interrogation practices employed by RUC detectives in Castlereagh drew international condemnation.

Catholic: Person who is an adherent of the Roman Catholic Church. Catholics comprised a minority in the six counties during the Troubles and suffered discrimination in employment, housing, and policing. Catholics comprise a majority on the other side of the border, in the Irish Republic.

Collusion: Active and illicit participation of British security forces, including the RUC and the British Army, in the killing of suspected Irish Republican enemies by Loyalist paramilitaries, and the deliberate refusal to investigate or prosecute those responsible afterward. Collusion often took the form of security forces' illegal sharing of personal details of suspects with Loyalist groups and illegal supply of firearms and ammunition to them. Much of the content of official British government reports concerning collusion remains secret to this day.

Crown: Metonym referring to the crown of the British monarch, the constitutional head of the British state. Used as shorthand reference to the British government and all of its organs, including military forces, courts, and public agencies.

Crum: Nickname for Crumlin Road Jail, a jail on the Crumlin Road in Belfast, first opened in the Victorian era. During the Troubles, the Crum held many defendants charged with terrorist offenses pending their trials in the courthouse across the street.

Diplock courts: Special courts created in Northern Ireland under emergency laws enacted by the British Parliament in 1973. Named after the British law lord William Diplock, who delivered a report recommending enactment of the laws to the British government in December 1972. Persons accused of terrorist offenses were tried in these courts by judges sitting without juries. Diplock courts operated continuously in the six counties from 1973 until their abolition in 2007.

DPP: Department of the Director of Public Prosecutions, the public agency responsible for the prosecution of crimes in Northern Ireland during the modern Troubles.

Emergency laws: A series of laws enacted by the British Parliament beginning in 1973. The laws vastly expanded the powers of security forces to effect stops, arrests, searches, detentions, and interrogations of terrorist suspects in Northern Ireland. They also created novel rules which eliminated jury trials for defendants accused of terrorist offenses curtailed due process protections for those defendants, and eased the admission of confessions into evidence in the Diplock courts.

Extradition: A combined judicial and diplomatic process whereby a person deemed a fugitive by the *requesting* country (such as the U.K.) is transferred involuntarily by authorities in the *requested* country (such as the U.S.) to the *requesting* country in order to face prosecution or serve the remainder of a sentence previously imposed. Extradition is a product of a treaty between the requesting country and the requested country, whose governments typically give reciprocal treatment to one another's extradition requests.

Fenian: Term which originated with the founding of the Irish Republican Brotherhood (IRB), a secret revolutionary society which favored Home Rule for Ireland and was hostile to the British Crown, in 1858. The IRB's members were known as Fenians. During the modern Troubles, members of the security forces (and others) in the north used the term Fenian as a slur denoting Catholics and Irish nationalists.

GFA: Good Friday Agreement, an agreement brokered by U.S. Senator George Mitchell and approved by voters in

Northern Ireland and the Republic of Ireland in 1998. The GFA is thought to have marked a formal end to the modern Troubles.

H-Blocks: Shorthand reference to the Maze (Cellular) prison, whose buildings housing cellblocks resembled a capital letter "H" when seen from above. Notwithstanding the prison's modern features, the term became a code word understood to epitomize British oppression of Irish nationalism during the 1970s and afterward. Each H-Block had four wings, with one segment of each letter "H" forming one of the wings, and a central area (known as the "circle") located at the crossbar of the "H."

IRA: Shorthand for the Provisional Irish Republican Army or PIRA. Known by the Irish name *Óglaigh na hÉireann*. The IRA was a nationalist Irish paramilitary force which sought the forcible expulsion of Britain from Northern Ireland and the establishment of a new, independent, democratic socialist republic consisting of all thirty-two counties of Ireland united under a single government and flag. The IRA is said to have disbanded in 2005 after decommissioning its weapons under the Good Friday Agreement.

Long Kesh: British internment camp opened in 1971 outside Lisburn, Northern Ireland, on the site of a disused RAF aerodrome. Initially used by the British government as a site for the indefinite detention of Irish Republican internees without charges or trial.

Loyalist: Label which describes a person who believes Northern Ireland ought to remain a part of the United Kingdom and not unite with the Republic of Ireland. Some understand the term to imply a willingness to use violence to achieve that end, distinguishing Loyalists from Unionists. Most Loyalists are likely to be of a Protestant religious denomination.

Maze: Her Majesty's prison, the Maze prison. A maximum-security cellular prison located near the town of Lisburn, about nine miles southwest of Belfast, in Co. Down, Northern Ireland. It was the principal prison for prisoners convicted of terrorist offenses in the north during the period spanning 1976 and mid-2000.

Nationalist: Label which describes an Irish person who believes in a united Ireland consisting of all thirty-two of its counties, free of British control, and governed by a single national government. Most nationalists are likely to be Catholic. The term is sometimes used interchangeably with the term "Republican," including by nationalists and Republicans themselves. The term does not imply willingness to use violence, though there were and are Irish nationalists who believe in the use of violence to achieve a united Ireland.

New Lodge: Working-class residential area in west Belfast, predominantly inhabited by Catholic residents. The area has a history of Republican activism and paramilitary violence.

Northern Ireland: The six counties of Antrim, Armagh, Down, Fermanagh, Derry, and Tyrone which are part of the United Kingdom and which are located in the northeast part of the island of Ireland. Sometimes referred to as a "statelet" or "province" of the U.K. Northern Ireland came into being in 1921 as the result of the Anglo-Irish Treaty. The treaty formally ended the Irish War of Independence, in which the Irish Republican Army had sought to drive Britain from the island and create an independent nation consisting of all thirty-two of Ireland's counties. At that time, most of the population of the six counties were Protestant descendants of English and Scottish planters. They considered themselves British subjects loyal to the British crown. The parliament which their representatives controlled formally declared Northern Ireland's allegiance to King George V in 1922.

For most of Northern Ireland's existence, the Protestant majority dominated the government, politics, and economy of the six counties, to the exclusion of the Catholic minority which suffered discrimination in housing, employment, education, and policing.

Orange Order: Anti-Catholic fraternal organization founded in 1795 and dedicated to the maintenance of Protestant supremacy in the six counties.

Peelers: British and Irish slang term for police.

Protestant: Adherent of any non-Catholic Christian denomination in Northern Ireland. Protestants have comprised the majority of the north's population from 1920 to this writing. In the Irish Republic, Protestants are a minority.

Provisionals, Provies, Provos: Slang reference to members of the Provisional IRA.

Republic of Ireland: Country consisting of twenty-six of the thirty-two counties of the island of Ireland. The Republic had its genesis in the treaty which settled the Irish War of Independence in 1922. The treaty resulted in the partition of Ireland into Northern Ireland (the six counties in the northeastern part of the island) and the Irish Free State. The latter had the status of a British Dominion, a part of the British Commonwealth akin to Australia and Canada. In 1949, the Irish Free State declared itself an independent republic, formally ending the state's affiliation with the British Commonwealth. Its name since then has been the Republic of Ireland.

Republican: Label used to describe an Irish nationalist who believes in a united Ireland, consisting of all thirty-two counties of Ireland, and free of any British control. The term is sometimes used as a synonym for nationalist, as both Republicans and nationalists aspire to the same thing, a united Ireland. The term does not imply willingness to use violence, though there were and are Irish Republicans who believe in the use of violence to achieve a united Ireland.

RUC: Royal Ulster Constabulary. Heavily armed national police force in Northern Ireland first established in 1922, with personnel of largely Protestant denomination and Unionist political opinion. In 2001, under the GFA, the RUC was renamed the Police Service of Northern Ireland (PSNI) and reformed. During the Troubles, many Irish nationalists and Catholics deeply resented the RUC and its methods.

Screw: Slang term used by Republican prisoners in the Maze to describe prison guards.

SCS: Special Category Status, a special status afforded by the British government and Northern Ireland prison service to Republican internees and prisoners during the period between 1971 and 1976. The term was viewed by the British government as preferable to the terms "political status" and "political prisoner."

Sinn Féin: Irish Republican political party founded in 1905 and active in both the Republic and in the north. The party is dedicated to the reunification of Ireland and an end to British jurisdiction in the north. Often described as the "legal political wing of the IRA." Translated from the Irish, the party's name is Ourselves or We Ourselves. Pronounced, "shin fain."

Six counties: Alternative name for Northern Ireland, favored by Irish nationalists who do not recognize the state's legitimacy and refuse to call it Northern Ireland.

Supergrass: Nickname for government-sponsored witnesses who testified in mass trials brought against mostly Republican defendants in the Diplock courts in the early

1980s in Northern Ireland, derived from the slang term grass (informant).

Taig: Derogatory nickname for a Catholic or Irish nationalist, used as a slur by Unionists and members of the police and British Army in Northern Ireland during the 1970s and 1980s.

Troubles: Unconventional conflict among (1) the British government and government of Northern Ireland, (2) Irish Republicans who sought a united Ireland free of British sovereignty, and (3) Loyalists who opposed a united Ireland and wished for the six counties to remain a part of the U.K. The modern Troubles began in 1968 and are thought to have ended in 1998. The Troubles manifested themselves sporadically, in a variety of ways: murders, riots, civil disturbances, hijackings, bombings, punishment beatings (or "kneecappings"), and otherwise. The IRA pursued a bloody guerrilla war aimed at British security forces. Other combatants included Loyalist paramilitary groups who opposed Britain's withdrawal from the six counties. Violent killings attributed to the Troubles exceeded 3,700. Most of those killed were civilians. The number of injured topped 47,000. The other human and economic costs of the Troubles are impossible to calculate with precision.

UDA: Ulster Defence Association, a violent Loyalist paramilitary group formed in September 1971. Declared a proscribed organization by the British government in August 1992. Largest Loyalist paramilitary group in the north.

UDR: Ulster Defence Regiment. An infantry regiment of the British Army, formed in 1970. Viewed by Irish nationalists as a Protestant militia.

UFF: Ulster Freedom Fighters (UFF). Pseudonym for death squads consisting of UDA men.

Unionist Label used to describe a person who believes the six counties of Northern Ireland ought to remain a part of the United Kingdom, separate from the Republic of Ireland, and not to be united with the remaining twenty-six counties of Ireland. The term does not necessarily imply belief in the use of violence as a proper means for maintaining union with the British Crown.

UVF: Ulster Volunteer Force. Violent Loyalist paramilitary group first formed in 1913. During the Troubles, the UVF declared a motto of war on the IRA and executed IRA men "mercilessly without hesitation."

SECTION I

COLD NOVEMBER NIGHT

ONE

Butler, from Across the Road

In 2019, the Troubles were over, supposedly, the killing mostly stopped. But the ghosts remained, hovering, in a land long roamed by ghosts and riven by old hatreds and bitter memories passed down like poisoned family heirlooms. Albert Miles is one such ghost. Trying to know him is like trying to know any other ghost. What we have are the memories of aging men and a few old photographs. It is precious little.

I have an old photograph of Albert and his wife, Florence, taken by their son, Alan, while the family was on holiday in 1976 in Godalming, Surrey, England. The photo shows Albert and Florence in a happy pose, dressed in their Sunday best. Albert is forty-seven, Florence fifty. Florence looks younger than that. She beams, a coquettish smile. Her arm is around Alan's waist, her head cocked gently inward, nearly resting on Albert's shoulder. Albert looks straight into the lens of the camera. The carefree air of a content married couple on a well-earned vacation suffuses the photograph.

Albert's face is handsome in a craggy way: aquiline nose, strong jaw, a gently lined broad forehead, deep-set brown eyes, large ears. One light crease descends around each side of the horizontal line of his mouth. He resembles Sid James, the handsome British comic actor. His brown hair has begun to recede but is still thick at the top and sides. He wears a gray suit, white dress shirt, and striped tie. One who didn't know him might figure Albert for a kindly, small-town family doctor. To Albert and Florence, in Surrey in 1976, the Troubles were a world away.

Albert had grown up in England, in the town of Fleetwood, in the Lancashire in northwest England, after being born out of wedlock. His father had been a fisherman and a native of Dublin. Albert grew up working class. As a young man, he was athletic. He had enjoyed a short but successful career as an amateur boxer and played rugby for Fleetwood's rugby union club. He had met Florence while on holiday in Blackpool, a Lancashire resort on the Irish Sea. After a brief courtship, the couple wed, then relocated to Belfast. There Albert worked as a welder before eventually joining Northern Ireland's prison service.

By age forty-nine, Albert had been promoted rapidly through the service, rising from prison officer, to chief officer, to assistant governor. His duty stations had included Belfast's Crumlin Road Jail, the British prison ship HMS *Maidstone* moored in Belfast Harbor, and the Borstal in Millisle on the Ards Peninsula. For a time, he ran the prison service's training college. Tonight, he held the title of Deputy Governor of Her Majesty's Prison Maze—the Maze prison, about nine miles southwest of Belfast. Albert was second-in-command of the prison, reporting only to Stanley Hilditch (the governor). In that role, he had direct command of the H-Blocks. There hundreds of Irish Republican prisoners were serving time for murders, possessing explosives and firearms, detonating bombs, shooting British soldiers and police. Some of them were the most dangerous and notorious men in the IRA—Seamus Clarke, Gerry Kelly, Brendan McFarlane, and Bobby Storey.

They and the other IRA men housed at the Maze viewed themselves as political prisoners. Albert had no use for that notion whatsoever. The IRA men in his custody were terrorists. They were prisoners who had to follow the rules. They were entitled to no special prerogatives. They were no more political prisoners than rapists or burglars, the so-called ODCs (ordinary decent criminals). Albert was old school. Rules were rules. He believed in discipline.

Beginning in 1976, Albert had seen the worst of the blanket and no-wash (or "dirty") protests, in which Republican prisoners protested the British government's new policy of treating them as common criminals inside the Maze. The protests had begun when the men refused to wear prison-issue uniforms and went around clad only in blankets. There were hundreds of them. When guards began beating the protesters during their trips to and from the toilets, the prisoners refused to leave their cells, which lacked toilets. And now hundreds of them were serving their sentences without clothing, washing, or using toilets. They were smearing their excrement on the walls, pouring their urine out into the corridors from underneath the cell doors, waking up each morning covered in maggots that infiltrated their nostrils and ears overnight.

The protests were extreme, disgusting. But, however sickening the conditions the prisoners' protests forced onto his men during their shifts in the H-Blocks, Albert, like Margaret Thatcher herself, believed there could be no compromises with terrorists.

***

Florence and Alan didn't know it, but in the superheated atmosphere of the H-Blocks at the time, Albert was not well-liked by the Republican prisoners in his charge. They blamed him for the worst of their suffering, which they suspected Albert either ordered or tolerated. Beginning in November 1978, his guards had begun forcibly washing the blanket men, using stiff deck brushes to scrub their armpits and genitals, leaving them bloody and raw. For the last two years, his guards regularly beat the prisoners, both in their cells and outside them. There were Loyalist prisoners in the Maze, but none of them received any such abuse from the guards, who were uniformly Loyalists as well.

1978 was a dangerous time in Belfast. Bombs were going off. British Army helicopters hovered overhead at all hours of the day and night. The IRA was shooting police constables and British Army soldiers. Heavily armed troops patrolled Catholic areas of Belfast around the clock. And the IRA had started going after prison officials on the outside, assassinating them while they were off duty, in their homes, leaving church with their families on a Sunday. Some of them had been Albert's friends who had come up alongside him in the prison service. Conscious of the hazard of his profession, Albert had talked of moving to a safer neighborhood and arming himself.

But he had done neither.

On November 26, 1978, on a Sunday night in Belfast, the Miles family had just finished dinner. The house at 8 Evelyn Gardens was a modest two-story brick row house with a small garden in the back. It sat at the end of a quiet, U-shaped residential street, Evelyn Gardens, just off the Cavehill Road, west of the Antrim Road in north Belfast. Outside, the temperature was about 37 degrees, just above freezing. There was no noise outside except for the wind. It blew in gusts this night. Albert was dressed in a brown shirt, blue vest, and grey pullover. He had taken off his shoes, the hush puppies he routinely wore. A pair of black slippers lay near, in the ground floor front hallway. The strains of "Half Way There," by the English pop duo Splinter, played on the downstairs radio. The small television in the front living room was tuned to the BBC, which was airing an episode of "A Horseman Riding By," a new series set in Devon and focused on the traditional English society blown apart by the First World War. Alan, age twenty-one, was in the downstairs hallway, on the telephone with a friend, Lorna Humphreys, who was at home in Bangor, County Down.[1]

At about 8:20 p.m., three knocks at the front door pierced the warm, placid scene.

At that moment, Albert was in the kitchen, on the first floor. Florence was in the breakfast room, at the rear of the house. Albert heard the knocks first. He shouted to Florence that there was someone knocking at the front door. Alan did the same.

"Who would it be at this time?" Florence wondered aloud. Alan thought it was a neighbor, Marion Brown, who often visited.

Florence walked down the hallway, past Alan, toward the vestibule, but stayed in the hallway, on the inside of the closed vestibule door, and shouted through the two doors: "Who's there?" Albert emerged from the dining room into the hallway, also approaching the vestibule.

"Butler, from across the road," came the mumbled reply from outside. The voice was male.

There was no Butler who lived in Evelyn Gardens.

Puzzled, Florence thought it might be a neighbor wanting something.

She opened the vestibule door, which swung inward. Again, from behind the closed front door, she asked who it was. The same voice replied. "Butler," it said. She cracked the outside door open, leaned to her left, peered out, and saw a strange man standing there. Florence did not recognize him. He looked to be in his early twenties. He had black curly hair, was about five-foot-ten in height, and had a mustache. He wore a knit wool "bobtail cap," what Americans might call a stocking cap.

"Yes?" Florence said.

---

1. Bangor is a seaside resort town on the southern side of Belfast Lough, about thirteen and one-half miles east of Belfast.

The front door burst inward, *ka-bam*, kicked open by the man just outside.

The man swiftly clapped a gloved left hand over Florence's mouth and pushed her up against the wall, on the left side of the vestibule as one faced out toward the front door.

Florence screamed. She realized what was happening, *doorstep murder*. She thought Albert and Alan might realize it too and escape out the back door if she could only hold the intruder at bay for a few seconds.

But it all happened too fast.

Albert had heard the commotion and dashed forward, toward the half-open vestibule door, behind Florence.

He could not have realized that his life would come to an end here, now, in his own house, on the hallway rug, on a quiet Sunday evening, in a short fusillade of bullets that would tear apart his insides.

The man in the bobtail cap pressed Florence up against the wall, clearing a line of fire for a second man just behind. The trailing man had a .38 caliber pistol. Alan glimpsed it. It was dark in color. While the first man struggled with Florence in the vestibule, the trailing man strained to aim at the shadow he saw behind the vestibule door. Not wanting to shoot the first man accidentally, he fired a round, high and left.

It ricocheted, *thock*, off the top of the concrete pillar just to the left of the front door, leaving a divot.

As Albert rushed forward, he neared the vestibule door. It was ajar. Albert caught a glimpse of the man in the bobtail cap struggling with Florence up against the wall on the left-hand side of the vestibule.

Now the trailing man stepped just inside the threshold of the front door, into the vestibule. He leveled the .38, holding it with one hand, aiming dead center, while the first man held a screaming Florence up against the wall to his right.

His next three rounds found their target. *Bam! Bam! Bam!* Florence saw flashes go past her eyes, through the vestibule.

The trailing man's second round hit the glass pane that formed the top part of the vestibule door, shattering it and showering Albert with glass. After hearing the first shot, Albert had raised his right forearm in an instinctive, defense motion. The lead bullet holed the right sleeve of his sweater at the cuff, pierced the skin, traveled up the arm, and lodged beneath the skin on the inner side of the upper arm, about four inches below the elbow. A tiny fragment of broken glass, turned into shrapnel by one of the bullets, slashed his right forefinger.

The trailing man's third shot struck Albert in the right temple, just behind the eyebrow. Miraculously, it perforated the skin, then bounced off, without entering the skull. The force of the round spun Albert around, so that he was facing the rear of the house, with his back to the vestibule door.

The trailing man's fourth round struck Albert in the back of the head, just to the left of the midline, spinning him around and knocking him unconscious. The bullet traveled downwards and left, under 1 ½ inches of scalp, then exited after cutting a groove in the subjacent skull.

To Alan, everything was happening in slow motion. He had known it was bad when he saw the man in the bobtail cap holding his mother against the wall. Then he had seen flashes, heard shots. Alan had seen the trailing man, just inside the front door, in the vestibule, with the dark gun in his right hand, held out at arm's length. The man's position would have put him less than five feet away from Albert. Alan had seen his father falling to the floor in the hallway, onto his left side.

Alan dived for cover, to his left, into the living room. He had seen both the intruders' faces for a few seconds. In 2019, he still remembered their eyes. They looked focused, intent. The second man had large eyebrows. His facial expression looked evil.

Albert lay sprawled on the floor, face down, his left side against the inside of the vestibule door, unconscious, insensate.

It had all happened in less than five seconds.

Now the first man extended his arm through the empty space where the glass pane in the vestibule door had been. It was time to finish the business, with a coup de grâce. He pointed a Colt .45 caliber revolver downward, at a forty-five-degree angle, aiming for the middle of Albert's back, just between the shoulder blades. He fired, *BAM!* In the small space of the vestibule and front hall, the gunshot was near-deafening.

On the phone in Bangor, Lorna Humphreys had heard the doorbell ring at Alan's end, then heard either Alan or Albert shout "The door," before continuing her conversation with Alan. Then she heard a crashing sound, about four or five gunshots, and screams. After a moment Alan returned to the telephone. Then he told Humphreys to call the police. She dialed 999. The two gunmen had fled, as speedily as they had barged in.

Now the house was still.

It had all happened so fast, "Half Way There" was still playing on the radio. The only other sound was Florence's screams. All she could think was, *close the front door.* She slammed it shut.

Alan sprang from his hiding place in the living room. He rushed toward the vestibule. There he found his father lying face down on the floor, against the inner part of the vestibule door, the weight of his prone body trapping his mother in front of it, between the two doors. Shards of shattered glass lay on the floor. Florence, frantic, was trying to escape the vestibule, by pushing inward on the vestibule door, but it wouldn't budge. Florence called to Alan to move his father so that she could get inside. Alan did it, rotating

Albert forty-five degrees. Florence pushed the door open and came into the hallway. She shouted to Alan to call the police.

Alan ran out into the street. "They've shot my dad," he shouted. Neighbors had begun emerging from their houses. Among them were the Thompsons, and James Townsley, the next-door neighbor. They had heard the shots.

Townsley followed Alan inside. There they found Albert face down, motionless, not breathing, with Florence kneeling alongside. Townsley turned Albert over and checked for a pulse. There was none. Two pints of blood had hemorrhaged into his abdominal cavity. Townsley started mouth-to-mouth resuscitation. Except for a small bloodstain on the right sleeve of Albert's shirt just below the elbow, there was little blood visible.

Of at least five rounds fired by the two gunmen, four had hit Albert Miles.

It was the fourth round, a copper-jacketed .45 caliber bullet, which was killing him now.

It had struck Albert in the back, between the shoulder blades, after he had collapsed onto the floor and lay prone and unconscious. It passed just to the right of the spine, then spiraled downwards and slightly forward into the trunk. There it had lacerated the left atrium of the heart, pierced the lower lobe of the right lung and liver, and perforated the small intestine. It had come to rest in a muscle forming the right side of the pelvic floor. Albert had begun to bleed out internally. Blood was pouring into his right chest cavity and abdomen. Albert vomited his partly digested dinner, aspirating some of it into his lungs, as his life ebbed away.

The sounds of gunshots and a car being driven at high speed toward the Cavehill Road had roused everyone in Evelyn Gardens.

Charles Robinson, of 28 Evelyn Gardens, had emerged from his house after hearing the sound of "wood smashing." He saw a dark sedan with a "long bonnet" turning right (north) onto Cavehill Road, swerving to avoid a Northern Ireland Electricity Service van parked at the intersection of Evelyn Gardens and Cavehill Road. Other neighbors, James and Marion Brown, of Flat 3, 18 Evelyn Gardens, had seen the same car through their living room window after being roused by the sound of three "bangs," zooming out of Evelyn Gardens, accelerating toward the Cavehill Road.

Summoned by a radio call while on patrol in their car nearby, RUC officers Watson Giffen and Samuel Barry arrived at 8:29 p.m., only nine minutes after the gunmen had first appeared. At the same time, the RUC was rapidly throwing up vehicle check points in north Belfast, hoping to intercept the shooters in flight.

Townsley had propped Albert's head on a small sofa pillow and was still giving mouth-to-mouth resuscitation. Albert Miles lay on his back on the rug amid shattered glass, with his left arm resting on his abdomen just above his belt buckle, his right hand resting on his sweater over the right side of his ribcage, his eyes half-open but sightless, and the vomit of his dinner drying on his face, dead on the floor of his home.

An RUC medical officer, Dr. Kelly, pronounced him dead at 9:24 p.m.

A team of scene-of-crime officers (SOCOs) had arrived. They began photographing and mapping the scene. Top RUC brass started crowding into the little house.

About a mile and a half away, at 11 Sheridan Street in the New Lodge ward, a Catholic enclave in north Belfast, sat Kevin Barry Artt, a nineteen-year-old taxicab driver, with his girlfriend, Lorraine Keenan, and her brother and parents in the Keenan home. It was "just the usual Sunday, . . . messing about watching TV" after having had dinner at around 7 p.m., Lorraine would testify later. After dinner, Lorraine's brother, Stephen, departed for a pub, the Felons Club, at the top of the Falls Road. Kevin and Lorraine went into Lorraine's bedroom. There they listened to records for an hour or so before joining the rest of the family to watch television in the living room.

At some point between 9 and 10 p.m., the channel they were watching interrupted its programming to broadcast a news bulletin. It announced that Albert Miles, the deputy governor of the Maze prison, had been shot and killed in his home earlier that evening. After talking Lorraine into giving him permission to go out and have a drink without her, Kevin left at around 10 p.m. to join Stephen at the Felons Club. Kevin drove his car, a brown 1973 NSU Ro 60, a four-door sedan. Once Kevin arrived there he went in and found Stevie.

Someone came in and said a man had been shot dead near the Cavehill Road.

Meanwhile, about nine miles away, news of the killing had spread to the Republican wings in the H-Blocks of the Maze, via a smuggled-in transistor radio. The word spread rapidly via the prison's coconut telegraph. The men shouted it from cell to cell down the wings, in Irish, the language they used when the guards, who understood only English, were listening. Some of the men started cheering. One, Kieran Nugent, had been the first man on the blanket protest, in 1976, four years before the first of two hunger strikes which culminated in the deaths by starvation of ten Republican prisoners.

"I remember Governor Miles," Nugent would say years later. "He said, 'we are going to break you.' He stood there shouting at me. Gave me a slap in the face and then he stood back and watched the other warders beat me up. When he was shot . . . that was a great morale booster."

By 1:30 a.m. on the morning of November 27, the last of the detectives cleared out of 8 Evelyn Gardens. Before they did, one of the detectives showed a series of mugshots to Alan Miles. Alan did not recognize any of the men pictured as the men who had killed his father.

Alan helped his stricken mother into bed. He downed a dose of sedatives and went to bed himself. Before everything went black, he wondered what his father's killers might be doing.

At the ensuing inquest, the coroner received the sworn written statement of RUC detective Constable Thomas Patton. It read in part:

> On 26th November 1979 [sic] I identified Mr. Mile's [sic] body to Professor Marshall at the Mortuary where a Post Mortem examination was carried out. Although nobody has been made amenable enquiries would indicate that this murder was the work of the Provisional IRA.

TWO

The Car

Earlier that evening, Eamonn Sweeney, a young resident of Ardoyne in north Belfast, drove his four-door sedan, a Ford Cortina Mark III, to the Shamrock Club in the company of his girlfriend, Leanna. The color of the car's body was dark blue, the canvas top black. Its license plate bore no. GIA 1905. The couple arrived sometime after 7:30 p.m. and before 8:00.

Sweeney parked the car near the rear entrance to the club, close by a parking space reserved for the band, and noticed that the band's space was vacant. Sweeney figured that the musicians had not yet arrived. He and Leanna entered the warm club and soon recognized friendly faces. There was the smell of cigarette smoke, the odor of Guinness, the sounds of laughter and friendly conversation, promising an evening of socializing with friends.

Soon after arriving, Sweeney heard an announcement over the club's PA system. The speaker said someone's car was blocking the rear entrance, read the license plate number, and asked the owner to please move it. Sweeney recognized the license plate number as his own. He walked to the door, feeling suspicious. He had just parked his car and knew it wasn't blocking the rear entrance.

When Sweeney got outside, a pair of men greeted him. It was between 7:50 and 8:00 p.m.

Sweeney recognized the two right away. One was Maurice Gilvarry, age twenty-two, known to Sweeney to be an IRA man, from Ardoyne. The second man was Tommy Allsop. He was from New Lodge. Allsop stood about 5'9", had a round face, and was a bit chubby. Both men had mustaches and black hair.

"We're taking the car," said Gilvarry.

"You can't take it," replied Sweeney, startled.

"You know what'll happen if you don't do as we ask," Gilvarry answered.

Sweeney knew what was happening. He knew who they were. Gilvarry and Allsop had not displayed a firearm. They had not needed to. Sweeney did what most others in that situation would have done. He handed over the keys.

"I knew the score," remembered Sweeney in 1996. "This was the first time this had ever happened to me. But I knew what my options were."

In parting, Gilvarry offered a warning.

"Don't do anything inside," he told Sweeney. "You'll be under observation in there."

Sweeney turned and went inside, where he did his best to act naturally, like nothing had happened.

Around forty-five minutes later, Sweeney spied Gilvarry at the front door of the Shamrock. It was about 8:40 p.m. Sweeney walked toward him. Allsop was there too, along with a third man who had long, fair hair.

"Let's take a walk," Gilvarry said.

The men walked Sweeney back to his car, covering the distance from the club to the car in three or four minutes. The vehicle was parked on Etna Drive. Gilvarry handed the keys to Sweeney.

"Has this car been used for anything?" asked Sweeney.

"If it had, we'd have torched it," said Gilvarry. "Don't bother reporting anything to the police. Say nothing."

Gilvarry was lying. The practice of using a hijacked car in an operation and returning it to the owner was uncommon but hardly unheard-of. IRA men often used cars on operations, then returned them, sometimes with a stern warning and a few pounds for the owner's trouble.

Gilvarry and his two companions disappeared into the night.

Sweeney went back inside, collected Leanna, and drove her home.

Sweeney felt torn.

Turning in an IRA man to the police was dangerous to a man's health. Sweeney believed that his girlfriend's brother, Sean Madigan, was a member of the IRA. He contemplated approaching him to ask him if he knew whether Gilvarry and his compatriots had used the car for anything.

He opened the driver's side door. Under the dome light, he inspected the interior. He looked for bullet casings, blood, a glove, or balaclava left behind.

There was nothing. "No telltale signs whatsoever," Sweeney remembered.

In the morning, Sweeney awoke to the news that Albert Miles had been shot dead in his home in Evelyn Gardens the night before. In an instant, a wave of something like nausea washed through his body.

Miles had been murdered at about 8:20 p.m., twenty minutes after Gilvarry had relieved Sweeney of his car, and ten minutes before Gilvarry had returned it. Sweeney knew Gilvarry was with the Provisionals, and Gilvarry's statements to Sweeney had been unmistakably menacing.

It seemed hard to believe that the events at the Shamrock Club and Evelyn Gardens were mere coincidence. On a Sunday night, a driver could cover the distance between the Shamrock Club and Evelyn Gardens in five minutes without stopping or with a short stop along the way.

Soon afterward, Sweeney visited Sean Madigan at his home. Madigan lived nearby, around the corner. He had recently come out of jail after serving some time.

Sweeney told Madigan what had happened in the Shamrock, then said he wanted some answers from Gilvarry.

"Go and see what the bloody hell happened here," Sweeney pleaded. "I need some peace of mind."

"All right," Madigan said. "Wait here."

After Madigan departed, Sweeney waited. After about thirty minutes, Madigan returned. He told Sweeney that Gilvarry had denied using the car to do anything. There had been another operation going on that night. It had taken precedence over anything Gilvarry and Allsop would have done with Sweeney's vehicle. Madigan added that, if Gilvarry and Allsop had used the car in an IRA job, Sweeney would never have seen his car again.

Sweeney decided not to go to the RUC. His conversation with Madigan had left him a little uneasy but still reassured. Gilvarry or Madigan might be lying. But the chance Gilvarry had used the car in the Miles murder seemed low. What IRA man would be dumb enough to use a car to murder a prison official, return it to the owner, personally escort him to it, leave a trail of clues behind in the car's interior, and trust him not to tell the RUC about it?

"I kept my head down and said nothing," recalled Sweeney in 2019.

Weeks later, at 3 a.m. one morning, Sweeney awoke to the sound of boots kicking in the front door of the family home on Newington Avenue. His first thought was of his parents. His mother had no time for the Republican movement, which was all around them every day. A young woman who lived nearby had blown herself up with a bomb which detonated prematurely. Another neighbor, Mario Kelly, had been shot dead within a hundred yards of the house. The neighborhood was close by the New Lodge district. Everybody in it was somehow involved in the IRA.

Sweeney was not. But he did not want his mother thinking he was. He feared the raid would plunge her into a state of complete distress.

Within moments, RUC men were flooding into Sweeney's bedroom, blinding him with flashlights pointed at his face, shouting, brandishing pistols. They dragged him out of bed, arrested him, handcuffed him, bundled him outside and into a Land Rover, and transported him to Castlereagh Interrogation Centre in east Belfast. Another team of constables impounded the Cortina. They towed it to the RUC's Tennent Street station.

Inside the fortress-like compound of Castlereagh, Sweeney sat in a seven-by-seven-foot holding cell.

"I didn't want to be thought of as a tout," said Sweeney. "Therefore, I wasn't going to tell them a thing in the first interview. There were touts who got shot dead. I was going to sit this out for at least twenty-four hours."

At first, Sweeney told detectives nothing.

As time passed, he began to speak but denied knowing anything. The detectives' mode of presentation was telling Sweeney what had happened rather than asking.

Ye were approached. Yer car was taken. It was used in the Miles shooting.

The detectives implied they knew Sweeney was involved in the murder of Albert Miles. The detectives were describing the events exactly as they had occurred. Sweeney could not fathom how they knew.

"They started saying to me they knew my car was taken," remembered Sweeney. "They knew the call came in the club. They knew where the car was parked, that it was left back at Etna Drive. They told me all that. I had no idea how they knew it."

The detectives started showing Sweeney photographs. There might have been about ten or fifteen of them. Sweeney recognized several faces as belonging to men who were prominent in the Republican movement. Some of them were known to Sweeney, and everyone else in his neighborhood, as IRA men. None of the photos showed the faces of Maurice Gilvarry, Tommy Allsop, or anyone else Sweeney had seen at the Shamrock that night.

There were three photographs in which police seemed particularly interested. Sweeney recognized the men pictured as Kevin Barry Artt, John Campbell, and a "fattish man in his 20's from Spamount Street." They were especially interested in the fat man. The detectives told him the fat man had taken the keys and driven the car to a house. There had been a girl there. The girl had given them the information.

Sweeney felt scared of the detectives. But the IRA scared him more than the police did. Initially, he told the detectives as little as possible. Coming home too soon from a spell in Castlereagh sent a bad message to neighbors and friends, that one had talked a little too soon and too much.

After four sessions spanning twenty-four hours, Sweeney agreed to sign a statement. It read:

"On Sunday 26th November, 1978, I went to the Shamrock Club with my girlfriend at about 8 pm. Shortly after arriving there, I was requested to come to the door of my car as it was blocking the band from unloading their instruments.

"When I got outside, two men approached me and took my car keys off me and threatened to shoot me if I told anyone. I handed over the keys to one of the men and was told to go back into the club. I told my girlfriend about this and shortly afterward looked at my watch. It was 8:20 pm.

"About 30-40 minutes later I was again requested to come outside and, on this occasion, I was taken to Etna Drive where my car was returned to me. I was again threatened not to tell anyone about this or I would be shot. I returned to the club, collected my girlfriend, and took her home.

"When I got to my own home sometime around midnight, I was taken into an entry by two men. There were two other men already in the entry. I was told to keep my mouth shut about what had happened that night otherwise me and my girlfriend would be shot. I gathered that this threat applied to my whole family. I was afraid to mention this to anyone for fear of the threat being carried out."

Sweeney made up the part about having been threatened at his house, so as to make his failure to report the episode to the RUC seem forgivable to friends and neighbors.

Sweeney went to the RUC station at Tennent Street, signed some forms, and retrieved his car.

As he drove home, he wondered how detectives knew what they had told him in Castlereagh.

How could they have learned it? Who could have told them?

THREE

All Right-Minded and Christian People

News of the Miles killing reverberated throughout the north. Roy Mason, the pipe-smoking, beetle-browed Secretary of State for Northern Ireland, denounced the murder.

"The hypocrisy of the Provisional IRA has been clearly and unequivocally exposed," said Mason. "Prisoners and relatives of prisoners must now realize how callously they are being used."

"All right-minded and Christian people," he said, "must deplore the murder of Mr. Miles, the latest in a long list of atrocities," said Rev. Dr. William Philbin, the bishop of Down and Connor. Philbin questioned whether those responsible for the killing were "the same people who plead for special consideration for those they have made the agents of their savage policies."

The Northern Ireland Office and prison service announced an immediate ban on visits, letters, and parcels at all Northern Ireland jails and prisons until after Miles had been buried. The governor of the Maze prison himself, Stanley Hilditch, visited Florence and Alan at 8 Evelyn Gardens to express his condolences. So did the local member of Parliament, Anne Dickson, a representative of Her Majesty's Northern Ireland Office, and five prison service officers.

Broadcast outlets and newspapers gave the news heavy coverage. *The Irish News* noted condemnation of the killing (the seventh of a prison official during the Troubles) by religious and political leaders throughout the province.

The headline above the statement published in the Republican newspaper *An Phoblacht* on December 2, 1978, read, "LONG KESH TORTURER EXECUTED."

"One of the persons most to blame for the torturing of the prisoners of war in the H-Blocks of Long Kesh Concentration Camp, Co. Antrim, was executed by an active service unit last Sunday night, according to a statement supplied to us," the statement read.

"He was the deputy governor, Albert Myles [sic] (50). The execution took place in his home in Evelyn Gardens, North Belfast, a cul de sac in the Cavehill area.

"It is understood that the ASU went right up to the front door and knocked on it for admission. The knock was answered by the man's wife. ASU members then pushed past her and, seeing Myles through a glass panel, fired at him, killing him instantly.

"Óglaigh na hÉireann [the IRA] warned prison officers years ago because of their collaboration with the Crown forces in the torture and degradation of the prisoners of war. . .

"Albert Myles . . . is believed to be the most senior officer in the prison service to fall in recent years in the war in the north-east.

In another statement published in *The Irish News*, the Provisionals justified the killing of Miles by pointing to his supposed complicity of abuses of prisoners in the Maze.

"This man was fully aware of the beating and torture of the men 'on the blanket,' and was in fact instrumental in sentencing political prisoners to solitary confinement and dietary punishments. . .

"We justly executed Miles for his responsibility over H-Block."

In the New Lodge and other Republican strongholds in Belfast, a sort of euphoria prevailed. Hundreds of men in the Maze were on the blanket and dirty protests. The guards were torturing them. There was seething hatred over the rampant abuse of fathers, sons, husbands, and brothers by the screws. The buck stopped with Albert Miles. He was either ordering his men to commit the abuse or tolerating it.

Inside the Maze, Miles' killing only caused the abuse to escalate. The guards were enraged.

"The screws just went nuts, so they did," remembered former Republican prisoner Gerard McConville in 1996. "You know, the hatred became more intense from their quarter."

FOUR

Section 12, You're Under Arrest

Kevin Barry Artt had his own flat, at 371 Antrim Road in north Belfast. On the night of December 11, 1978, he had stayed overnight at the Keenans', in the little house at 11 Sheridan Street in the New Lodge district, as he often did.

At 4:20 a.m., British soldiers and RUC constables shattered the predawn quiet of the Keenan house by kicking down the front door. The thump of boots on the stairs heralded the charge of two constables into the bedroom of Gladys and Brian Keenan, who squinted against the flashlights pointed in their faces.

Is Barry Artt here?

"Yes," Gladys answered.

What room?

"I'll get him up," she said.

Before she could do so, constables swept out of the bedroom, down the hallway, and into another bedroom, with Gladys trailing behind. The constables, accompanied by two British soldiers, unholstered their weapons and pointed them at the two bedraggled young men who lay in a bed that lay against the wall. One, Gladys and Brian's son Stevie, was closest to the officers. Kevin was closest to the wall.

Stevie Keenan, blinking, rose with his hands up. A constable put his pistol to Stevie's head. The tiny room was crowded with shouting men in green uniforms.

Soldiers jerked Stevie out and into the street, swiftly slapping handcuffs on him.

You're under arrest, section 12– a soldier began to say.

Another soldier interrupted him. *No, that's Keenan*, he said.

Off came the handcuffs. *It's not your turn this time*, said the first soldier.

In the bedroom, another constable had put a gun to Kevin's head as another constable and two soldiers stood by.

Get up, you bastard, and get dressed, said the officer.

Lorraine and her parents were huddled in the hall just outside the bedroom. They watched as Kevin dressed at gunpoint.

Using plastic zip ties, the constable bound Kevin's hands behind his back.

"Hey mate, that's too tight," said Kevin. The constables ignored him and dragged him out to the street. Stevie lit a cigarette and put it in Kevin's mouth.

On the street, a soldier greeted Kevin. *Section 12, you're under arrest*, he said.

The constables put Kevin in a Jeep and sped off to Castlereagh Interrogation Centre.

The printed form signed by the arresting officer recited the short piece of boilerplate which sufficed for the arrest:

> I arrest you under Section 12 of the Prevention of Terrorism (Temporary Provisions) Act 1976 on reasonable suspicion that you have been concerned in the commission, preparation or instigation of acts of terrorism.

The RUC's intake form appended the mugshot of a sleepy-looking Kevin. In the photo, Kevin's hair is long and bushy. He wears a mustache. The eyebrows arch slightly upward toward the midline, a slight look of dazed concern on his face as he grips the placard listing his name, address, date of birth, and date of arrest. It noted his occupation as "dumper driver." Next to the box which listed how any relatives were notified of his arrest, an officer wrote, "father being informed by girlfriend."

Two days later, Kevin's mother, Maeve Artt, visited Gladys at the little house in 11 Sheridan Street.

"They're trying to blame Barry in some murder," said Maeve. She mentioned Albert Miles' name.

"Sure, Barry was sitting here when that came over the TV," replied Gladys.

FIVE

Welcome to the Romper Room

Castlereagh Holding Centre resembled a fortress, with a ten-foot-high stone wall clad in red brick and topped with barbed wire surrounding its two-story, rectangular buildings, which sat on Ladas Drive in east Belfast. One building housed thirty-eight cells measuring seven feet by seven feet square, for holding suspected terrorists in between interrogations. In the back was a second building which housed what the RUC referred to as "interview rooms." There were twenty-one of them.

Kevin had never visited Castlereagh before. Like many other young Catholic men, he knew of it by reputation.

Castlereagh was more than a police station. It was a confession factory, a snake pit, a windowless clockless concrete maw where the police took you after they kicked in your front door at four in the morning and rousted you from your bed and hauled you in the back of a Jeep before you had a chance to put on your shoes. They took your photograph and your particulars and your shoelaces and your watch and isolated you from your lawyer and your wife and everyone else for days and nights on end in a tiny holding cell with walls painted dull yellow and no toilet or sink. The constables kept hauling you out of there, to be grilled by detectives in session after session in cramped interview rooms lined with acoustic tile. Team after team of cops rotated in and out in waves and didn't stop. They yelled and screamed and told you they had the goods on you, and it was all over for you, and your wife was going to leave you, and you were *going down for all day*, you were *absolutely fucked* unless you played ball. Sometimes they took notes of what you said and other times they didn't but often they beat you with their fists until you finally broke down and said whatever it was they wanted you to say so that they would *just stop* and you could have some peace at last instead of hanging yourself in your cell.

Just the name, *Castlereagh*, was scary, a code word for every bad thing police could do to you without shooting you or hitting you with a baton. A man went in there and if he came out again it was to go home like a whipped dog until the next time. Or he went to the Crum to wait for a trial where the evidence against him was going to be whatever they'd got him to say when he was at the end of his rope in the interview rooms with the detectives shouting and sneering. The place was a hellhole, a real-life version of George Orwell's Ministry of Love, the one place you never wanted to go.

Its namesake was an Anglo-Irish statesman, Robert Stewart, better known as Lord Castlereagh, possibly the most hated man in the history of Ireland. As Chief Secretary for Ireland, he had helped put down the Irish Rebellion of 1798, seeing to it that one of the rebels, Reverend William Porter, was hanged in front of his own church. Later, Castlereagh had lobbied in the Irish and British parliaments for the passage of the Act of Union of 1800, which incorporated Ireland into the United Kingdom. In 1822 he had committed suicide by slitting his own throat in his dressing room. The mocking epitaph composed by Byron read:

> *Posterity will ne'er survey*
> *A nobler grave than this:*
> *Here lie the bones of Castlereagh:*

Stop, traveler, and piss.

Some gave it a sardonic nickname, *the Romper Room*, a moniker that bespoke a grim Belfast joke. The joke, like other grim Belfast jokes, was that the nickname connoted the polar opposite of everything the place really was. Bad things happened in there, all of it out of the sight of everyone in the world except the police who dished it out and their captives who took it.

The interrogations went on day and night, for hours on end, punctuated by spells in the prisoner's holding cell. Steam pipes ran beneath the beds in the holding cells. They radiated heat during summer, winter, spring, and fall, keeping the ambient temperature high year-round. A prisoner would sweat around the clock, dehydrating all the while. Punches were administered close to the center of the abdomen, lessening the chance of leaving bruises which might be noted by a doctor later.

During their breaks, some detectives drank whiskey or vodka. Severe beatings sometimes followed these alcoholic interludes. Despite the acoustic tile lining the ceiling and walls, the interview rooms weren't soundproof. A man undergoing interrogation in one interview room could hear the sounds of slaps, screams, and blows thudding into the body of the prisoner in the next room.

At night, sleep was impossible. The ventilation ducts along the wall hummed constantly. Overhead, the fluorescent lights burned around the clock, flooding every square inch of each cell with bright light 24/7. The guards never turned them off. Any prisoner who managed to doze off, if only from exhaustion, would soon be jarred from his sleep by the racket of guards banging on the cell door as they passed by on their hourly rounds. Sometimes, the guards amused themselves by shouting out the home addresses of Republican detainees in the corridors outside the holding cells, broadcasting the information within easy earshot of Loyalist prisoners who occupied nearby cells.

When it was time for interrogation, uniformed warders escorted prisoners from their cells to the interview rooms. Inside each was a table and three chairs. Two chairs sat on one side, for detectives. One sat on the other, for the prisoner. Detectives in plain clothes did the questioning. Detectives ordered some captives to do push-ups to accelerate their thirst, then denied them water. No bathing or washing was allowed.

Asking for one's lawyer was mostly pointless, though occasionally one was allowed in days after the prisoner first asked for one. The routine on what detectives called a "seven-day lift" was to deny the prisoner access to any lawyer, family, or other visitors for the duration of his stay. Detectives often told the prisoner who refused cooperation, complained, or threatened to file a complaint that his stay at Castlereagh would certainly last for seven days.

The verbal abuse was pervasive, with the terms *Fenian bastard* and *lying cunt* being favorite phrases. Detectives hated their Republican captives. They made no bones about it. Female prisoners could expect no better treatment than males, and, in some cases, worse. Republican prisoner Liam Maskey, an internee and frequent guest at Castlereagh, had a sister who was arrested and questioned there in 1975.

"They beat her with a chair, and stuck part of it up her," remembers Maskey. "It fucked her up." After her release, she left the country and relocated to the Netherlands. During one five-day spell in Castlereagh, Maskey recalls, he lost fourteen pounds.

The RUC's most senior detective, chief superintendent Bill Mooney, was said during one briefing to have exhorted his men like a football coach.

What are ye, men or mice? Get in there! Have I got to get in there and do it meself? I! Want! Results!

Results, he added, would enhance the chances of promotion of those who delivered them.

The driving force behind Mooney's zeal was easy to understand. In 1978, the state was at war with the IRA. It would turn the tide in the Maze prison and the Diplock courts and on the conveyor belt that led to and through them. The Crown wanted convictions. Confessions, true or otherwise, were the key. That was all there was to it.

Now, in the early morning hours of December 12, 1978, as police booked in their newest detainee, Kevin Barry Artt felt a sense of dread. Uniformed constables photographed him, removed his watch, took hair samples and fingerprints, probed his ears and nostrils, took swabs from them, scissored clippings from his eyebrows and eyelashes. The detectives carefully noted Kevin's scars and tattoos—a one-inch scar in the center of his forehead, an eagle tattoo on the right forearm, a bird (a swift) on his left forearm. They escorted him to his tiny windowless cell. Kevin felt scared to death.

After a couple of hours, Kevin heard the jangling of keys, then the clack of the bolts in the lock as a uniformed constable opened the cell door.

"Let's go," he said. "Time for your first interview."

The man led Kevin into an interview room. To Kevin, it looked not much bigger than his cell. There was a table, two chairs, and two unsmiling detectives. They glared at him. Kevin nodded at them, then looked at the walls and ceilings. They were covered in acoustic tile, punctuated by thousands of uniform round holes.

One of the detectives asked Kevin, "Do ye know why ye are in here?"

"No," he replied.

For the next seven days and seven nights, Kevin Barry Artt would leave the cell only to be interrogated and use the bathroom. No visits or exercise were permitted. Outside, constables paced up and down the corridor, twenty-four hours a day. Sometimes they rapped on the metal cell door with a baton, seemingly just to create a racket and jar Kevin out of any short sleep that might have overtaken him. The temperature was very warm. No clocks were visible anywhere, and, stripped of his watch, a haggard and dehydrated Kevin soon lost track of time.

SIX

Gilvarry

Detectives had combed through Albert Miles's neighborhood, interviewing sixty-nine neighbors. They searched vacant houses in the area, to see if they might yield any clues. They reviewed property records to ascertain who owned each vacant house, then contacted all workmen they might have employed in the recent past. On the Sunday following the shooting, they set up vehicle checkpoints nearby, at Salisbury Avenue, Evelyn Gardens, and Cavehill Road, stopped motorists on their way through, asked them about their movements on the preceding Sunday, and inquired whether they had seen anything unusual.

None of it had yielded anything.

The only real lead in the case came from Maurice Gilvarry, a twenty-two-year-old IRA man from the Ardoyne district.

His fellow volunteers did not know it, but Gilvarry was a traitor, secretly working as a double agent for the RUC's Special Branch.

The hijacking of a dark blue Ford Cortina belonging to Eamonn Sweeney on the night of the murder had drawn the attention of police. The site of the hijacking was within a few minutes' drive of 8 Evelyn Gardens. Sweeney had not reported the hijacking to police. But someone else had.

The only person in any way associated with the car's hijacking who was known to be a double agent was Gilvarry.

Like many a double agent before and after him, Gilvarry was a mixed bag. He grew up as one of eleven children in a big Catholic family crammed into a two-bedroom house in the half-square-mile-sized district known as Ardoyne, home to over twelve thousand other Catholic residents. As a schoolboy athlete at Holy Cross Primary School, he excelled at Gaelic football despite being nearsighted, a condition which required him to wear glasses. At age twelve, he had seen rows of houses burned to cinders by Loyalist mobs as the RUC stood by passively, tasted the CS gas that permeated hundreds of homes, watched as local residents hijacked buses and made makeshift barricades out of them, in 1969, when the modern Troubles first metastasized into violence and chaos.

Afterward, Gilvarry attracted the attention of the British Army. In 1973, its troops delivered him to the Cages of Long Kesh, a sort of POW camp for men suspected of terrorist activity, for indefinite detention without charge or trial. At age sixteen, Gilvarry was one of the youngest men interned.

By the time he emerged, Gilvarry was angry and determined to do something. He returned to Ardoyne and joined the IRA's Belfast Brigade.

To friends and neighbors, Gilvarry made little secret of his involvement.

"He strutted about the place," remembered Eamonn Sweeney in 2019. "He seemed to relish that sort of reputation."

Whatever Gilvarry's ideals when he first joined the Provisionals, they appear to have been compromised as time passed.

By age twenty-one, Gilvarry was an informant and double agent, in the pay of Special Branch, a unit of the RUC whose men gathered intelligence, handled informants, and worked undercover in plain clothes. He supplied information, sabotaged IRA operations, set up IRA men for assassination. At his handlers' direction, on the street Gilvarry received extra hassle from RUC men and soldiers, in full view of his friends and neighbors. Gilvarry participated in several IRA operations during the time the RUC employed him, the better to maintain credibility vis-à-vis his Officer Commanding (OC) and fellow volunteers. Police questioned Gilvarry in connection with at least some of them. No charges ever resulted. To an observer, he was the last man one would expect to be a turncoat.

Sometimes, what Gilvarry supplied was pure gold.

In June 1978, he reported an imminent IRA operation which would take place in the Ballysillan area of Belfast. Three IRA men, Dennis Brown, James Mulvenna, and Jackie Mailey were to firebomb a post office depot. Acting on Gilvarry's tip, a team of heavily armed British Army Special Air Service men in plain clothes, accompanied by RUC men, lay in ambush. The group surprised the three Provisionals after they emerged from a hijacked Mazda and shot them all dead. Gilvarry later romanced the widow of one of his dead colleagues, and eventually moved in with her, to the shock and revulsion of every decent person in Ardoyne.

As time passed, Gilvarry grew more brazen. On a Sunday night in February 1979, Gilvarry and two other IRA men broke into the home of Patrick and Violet Mackin, at 568 Oldpark Road in north Belfast, close to Ardoyne. Mackin, age sixty, had recently retired from the prison service. Gilvarry shot them dead where they sat watching television. Later, he telephoned his Special Branch handlers, omitted any mention of his role in the killing, and named his accomplices and a third man. The third man was innocent. The RUC arrested him, found no evidence of his involvement, and released him without charge.

SECTION II

THE FACTITIOUS STATE

SEVEN

1969

A history of the six counties is beyond the scope of this book. By the summer of 1972, more than 30,000 British troops occupied the six counties, concentrated in Catholic ghettoes. There, the troops looked like an army of occupation. Their appearance aroused seething resentment in the minority population.

A resurgent IRA emerged from somnolence and penury, and declared itself a revolutionary, irredentist guerrilla army. Its goal was driving the British from the island, unifying all thirty-two counties of Ireland into a single independent socialist republic, and thus enabling the Irish people to realize the vision proclaimed by Patrick Pearse on the steps of the General Post Office in Dublin that day in 1916.

New recruits were told they could expect either imprisonment or an early grave. The leadership established training camps for them in the Irish Republic. There, trainees learned the fundamentals of handling firearms and explosives.

It was a war, pitting the IRA against the enemy, British security forces—the Army, RUC, UDR, and military intelligence services who operated in the north. Funerals of dead Volunteers featured paramilitary pageantry, with honor guards of uniformed men who fired volleys of shots over the coffin before it was lowered into the earth. To IRA men and their sympathizers, civilians were not legitimate targets. Harming them was strictly discouraged. But soldiers and policemen were fair game. Their deaths could be justified as a means to the worthy end of a united Ireland. Judges, prison officials, prison guards, and Loyalist paramilitaries later became targets too. In war, people got killed. The state was killing, and the Republican and Loyalist forces were killing. That was what war was.

For youths, there was the Irish National Boy Scouts (Na Fianna Éireann), known as the Fianna, to which many IRA men belonged as boys. Their oath committed them to work for the independence of Ireland, never join the armed forces of England, and obey superior officers. One who took the oath was a skinny, bookish teenager named Gerry Kelly.

Kelly grew up in north Falls area in a Catholic home. He attended St. Finian's, a De La Salle Brothers school on the lower Falls Road. There was no hate taught or allowed in the house.

"I was taught to be a product of your religion and to be proud to be Irish," Kelly recalled in 2019. "It was a simple thing. My mother said, 'Never betray your religion.' Because of the history of what had happened to Catholicism in Ireland, that was powerful to me."

Before 1969, the Kelly household was not very political. But what Kelly saw all around him began to politicize him.

"The pogroms that happened in the early days in 1968 and 1969, it was the beginning, if you like, of the televised arena," Kelly said. "I had some relatives who were interned. I knew fairly quickly that the majority of those who were interned were actually not involved in Republican activities. Internment radicalized me. It was a huge thing. On the street there were obviously civilians shot.

"I remember being moved by the B Specials opening fire on cars in the lower Falls, the shooting of Patrick Rooney, Loyalists burning houses in west Belfast. I became determined to fight back. 'My community shouldn't be taking this,' I thought.

"My view became there was a military presence that was oppressive, and it couldn't be spoken to. You had to fight back against it. I wasn't born political, but I became political.

"There's nobody born to be a soldier. I wasn't wed to violence. I stepped into it reluctantly. But, like everything else, when I stepped into it, I did wholeheartedly. But the issue of taking up arms had to be one of last resort. It certainly was for me."

1972 was the most violent year of the Troubles. To many it seemed the province was on the brink of a civil war. Four hundred sixty-seven people were killed, over 10,000 shootings were recorded, and nearly 2,000 bombs were planted. Of those killed, 321 were civilians. Dividing the number of dead into a population then approximating 1,536,065 yields a ratio which, if applied to the population of California during the same year, would have meant 4,118 civilians would have been killed in the state during those twelve months. The killing of 103 British Army troops meant that a soldier had a 1 in 250 chance of being killed while on his tour of duty in the six counties. The numbers were worse for the RUC and UDR, whose members stood a 1 in 145 chance of violent death during that year.

By 1973, barracks, vehicle checkpoints, and watch towers proliferated throughout the six counties. Radio antennae, visible from miles away, climbed skyward from behind the heavily fortified walls of barracks. Thousands of infrared-sensitive cameras mounted on walls and poles kept watch around military and police installations around the clock. High metal grills and anti-mortar netting surrounded the tops of watch towers. The number of British troops serving in Northern Ireland swelled to 16,500.

By the time he was seventeen, Gerry Kelly shared one thing in common with thousands of other young Catholic men in Belfast. He wanted to do something.

In 1970, when Kelly joined the Fianna Éireann, he did not look the part of an urban guerrilla. He was built like a beanpole. He wore glasses.

"I was a bit of a geek," he recalled in 2019. "I didn't get into fights a lot. I was the last person my mother would have expected to become involved."

At seventeen, Kelly felt inwardly unsure of whether he could measure up. By the time he was eighteen, he had gotten a job as a civil servant with the city electrical utility, a good position for a Catholic at the time. After earning a couple of pay raises, his salary enabled him to purchase a used car, a Ford Anglia, for forty pounds. Kelly soon used the car to travel south of the border. There, he had his first run-in with security forces.

Aiming to raise funds for the Fianna, Kelly and a couple of accomplices embarked on an impromptu operation south of the border, robbing a bank in Co. Louth.

"Frankly, it was stupid. But you're young," Kelly recalled in 2019.

For the failed heist, Kelly drew a two-year sentence in prison. During a visit with his father while incarcerated, Kelly said, "I just want to be part of this."

Five months later, in January 1972, Kelly began what would become an illustrious career as an escape artist, absconding from Mountjoy Prison in Dublin. It was shortly before Bloody Sunday.

Kelly hid for about a week in Dublin in a safe house before being brought up to Belfast. Immediately he went to the family home, in the north Falls. He walked in the back door and greeted his astonished mother and father. The three sat close together for an hour or so, drinking tea and talking quietly.

Suddenly, an Army Saracen hove into view, visible through the window, just outside the front door. Kelly bolted out the back door and ran.

As it turned out, the soldiers had no idea Kelly was there. In trying to make a right-hand turn, the driver had cut the corner too close and accidentally put the Saracen up on the sidewalk.

Kelly joined the IRA. He was nineteen years old.

EIGHT

Fenian Bastards

In 1976, Her Majesty's Prison, Maze (Cellular), was a brand-new state-of-the-art maximum-security prison, under the ultimate authority of a prison minister who held a seat in the cabinet of the British government in London. The Maze sat on three hundred sixty acres inside a British Ministry of Defence base outside the town of Lisburn, about ten miles southwest of Belfast. British Army soldiers manned watchtowers which dotted the eighteen-foot-high perimeter wall at 200-foot intervals.

The new prison would be home to all men convicted of terrorist offenses committed after March 1, 1976. No longer would IRA men be treated like POWs or reside in the Nissen huts of Long Kesh, the disused RAF base which had been converted into a catchment for them in 1971. The British Parliament had seen to that, erasing "special category status" (SCS) from the books in 1975. IRA men would be treated as what Margaret Thatcher said they were: convicted criminals. At the Maze, they would inhabit separate, brick-and-mortar units, soon known as H-Blocks, numbered 1 through 8. Each H-Block was shaped like a large letter H.

One of the first IRA prisoners to arrive at the Maze and be denied SCS was Kieran Nugent, a young IRA volunteer convicted of having hijacked a van. He soon became a celebrity inside and outside the H-Blocks.

On September 14, 1976, Nugent refused a prison-issue uniform. He told prison officers that if they wanted him to wear it, they could nail it to his back.

The prison service swiftly revoked fifty percent of his remission, effectively doubling his sentence, confined him to his cell twenty-four hours a day, removed his mattress and all other furniture from his cell, impounded his reading material, and reduced his statutory visits to one per month. Guards took away Nugent's clothes, forcing him to go naked. Other prisoners soon followed Nugent's example. The guards impounded their clothes and took away their visits too.

To ward off the chill and cover their nakedness on their way to and from the visiting area, Nugent and the others resorted to the only other covering available to them, the blankets in their cells. Each protester cut a hole in the center of his blanket, making a poncho out of it.

Without knowing it, Nugent had started a movement.

Whenever new prisoners arrived, guards escorted those who refused to don uniforms to the circle. There they made the prisoners strip naked and subjected them to slaps and verbal abuse. *Provie cunts. Fenian bastards.*

To Republican prisoners, the protest was simple. They viewed themselves as political prisoners. It was the British who had bestowed SCS in the first place. Rescinding it and classifying them as common criminals delegitimized their cause and its noble history. They wanted to draw the attention of the world to their plight. Then everyone would see the British government for what it was: an oppressor of the Catholic minority, an illegitimate occupier of Irish soil, an imperial power bent on crushing Irish nationalism.

The blanket men vowed to end their protest only upon restoral of SCS. By 1978, four hundred Republican prisoners were on the blanket. Most were men housed in the

Maze. To the prison service, there was no going back and no cognizable protest. There were only prisoners who refused to follow the rules. They had to be punished.

On the wings, guards started beating the protesters daily and severely. Prisoners got beatings on the way to the lavatory, returning from the visiting room, going to and from Mass in the chapel. Leaving one's cell to go for medication or a visit with one's lawyer meant a beating on the way back. Every blanket man was beaten, every single day of the week.

To the blanket men, it seemed the prison administration had embraced a simple policy: beating them off the blanket.

The guards were overwhelmingly Protestant and Unionist. They did not care for Catholics or the cause of Irish nationalism. Some moonlighted as Loyalist paramilitaries. Many had tattoos featuring the Union Jack and Loyalist slogans and symbols. Around the twelfth of July each year, some could be seen donning orange sashes and marching up and down the wings in front of the prisoners, openly drunk while on duty.

Outside the walls, news of the abuses of Republican prisoners arrived in Catholic neighborhoods via secret communiques, known as comms, smuggled out of the Maze by visitors. Comms were tiny handwritten messages scribbled onto cigarette papers with a pencil or pen. Prisoners wrote comms surreptitiously and often at night, then rolled them up and clad them in cling film, known to Americans as Saran Wrap. Transport of the tiny packages inside and outside the prison was via the mouth, the nose, underneath a man's foreskin, the rectum. Once outside, the comms made their way to families and the IRA.

The comms told the story: prison officers and guards were torturing and abusing Republican prisoners inside the Maze.

NINE

I Want to Hit a Blanket Man

By March 1978, the guards' beatings of blanket men neared a crescendo. No blanket man could leave his cell for a trip through the circle or to the lavatory without being beaten by guards. The more a man left his cell, the more beatings he took.

Oh, is that a blanket man? I want to hit a blanket man, a guard would say. Then he would do it. As with many tales of the Troubles, accounts of what, exactly, sparked the next stage of the protest vary depending on who is telling the tale.

Some versions have it that prisoners, afraid of being beaten after leaving their cells, started refusing to use the lavatories. They demanded wash basins for their cells. The guards brought in wash basins with just enough water in them to cover the bottom of the basin, making the exercise pointless.

"We refused to wash in our cells in a plastic basin consisting of two inches of water," remembered Gary Roberts in 1996.

Another version has it that the guards denied the blanket men use of the lavatories, forcing the men to relieve themselves in their slop buckets.

What no one disagrees about is the upshot: there was no way for prisoners to empty slop buckets outside the cells which was either allowed by the guards or agreeable to both guards and prisoners.

A series of reactions and counterreactions by guards and prisoners sent the Republican wings of the Maze sliding toward a kind of abyss.

At first, guards removed the prisoners' slop buckets from the cells and emptied them in the lavatories. The guards, "dressed up like spacemen with bloody big gloves," came around with trolleys bearing big black buckets. The prisoners were told to empty their slop buckets into them. But some guards were unable to resist a bit of torment. When the big black buckets got full, guards began emptying them into the next prisoner's cell. They also began up-ending and kicking over the slop buckets, dumping the contents on the cell floors or onto the prisoners' bedding or the prisoners themselves. Both guards and prisoners blamed one another for hurling buckets of urine and feces at the other.

Eventually, the guards removed the buckets entirely. Without slop buckets, and confined to their cells, the prisoners began throwing their excrement and urine out the windows.

Guards threw the excreta back in again.

Prison authorities installed thick glass on the cell windows, disabling the prisoners from throwing anything out. Prisoners broke the glass and resumed throwing their excreta out. The urine they poured out under the cell doors or threw out of the slots in the doors.

The prison administration installed fine mesh grilles over the cell windows (in lieu of glass which could be broken), making it impossible to throw excrement out. So, the prisoners began smearing it on the walls, doors, and floors of their cells, using pieces of their foam mattresses. The cells' walls, which had originally been painted white, darkened with surrealist frescoes of dark brown swirls and weird patterns.

So began the second phase of the prisoners' campaign for restoral of special category status: the no-wash, or dirty, protest.

Brendan Hughes, the Republican OC at the Maze, ordered the escalation. No one was forced to go on it, and not all Republican prisoners joined. But all Republican prisoners in H-Blocks 3, 4, and 5 participated. They comprised a majority of the Republican prisoners in the Maze at the time. "It had become an arms race," remembered former Republican prisoner Anthony McIntyre in 2019. "They did one thing, we did another. It was escalation or capitulation."

As time passed, the no-wash protest descended into part-standoff, part-nightmare.

Protesters' cell furnishings dwindled to a mattress, a small sponge, three rough blankets, no sheets, and one pillow. Flies attracted to the food and smells laid eggs. These produced maggots which soon swarmed the cells of the protesters, many of whom already suffered from diarrhea and dysentery. In the mornings, prisoners awoke to the sickening sensation of maggots crawling over and into their hair, noses, and ears.

Because haircuts could only be gotten by exiting one's cell, something the prisoners refused to do, the prisoners began growing long hair and beards. Guards hauled more and more men off to punishment cells known as "the boards," beating them with fists and batons and dragging them by their matted, dirty hair along the way.

Republic prisoner Gerard McConville arrived at the Maze in 1977, freshly convicted of possessing a firearm after having signed a confession in Castlereagh. He described the guards' behavior in one such instance, which happened three months into the no-wash protest, during June or July of 1978.

"The only way I can describe it is they were in a frenzy," he said. "They were like lunatics. They were fighting each other to get hitting us. They were shouting, you know: 'Let me get at that Fenian bastard. I haven't kicked a Fenian yet. I want to kick him. I want to hit him. Let me at him.'

"All this is all happening. All the voices are flying past you. I got dragged in. I can just remember thinking: Watch your head and watch your face. I actually thought during that beating—it was the worse [sic] beating that I got. I thought I was going to be killed. And if they had of—if they hadn't of just ran into a wall, I probably would have.

"We ran in and came to a wall, and they threw me against the wall, and I put me hands up to stop. And I stopped myself about, I would say, six inches, eight inches away from the wall. The wall was covered in blood. I immediately thought Brendan [Lynch], my mate, I thought he had got that—the bad beating. I was saying: 'Jesus, poor Brendan. I wonder how bad he is.' Got dragged down into the cell, thrown into the cell. There was bedding in the cell, in this one, in the boards. My head hit the pillow and I looked up and the pillow was covered in blood.

"So I got up, started examining myself, and realized that I had been opened from the front of the head . . . right across to the back of the head. I mean the scar is still very visible, even now . . .

"I shouted and I said . . . 'You better get me a doctor down here.' I was told, 'Fuck off and die, you Fenian bastard, it's one less to feed.'"

Afterward, McConville spent three days in the prison hospital.

For guards, every shift meant being confronted with sickening sights and smells. They reacted as one might expect. They took out their frustrations on those who made their daily shifts so nasty. The word that best described the guards' treatment of the protesters was brutal. Human nature and testosterone were at work. The frequency of beatings went up. So did the severity. The guards inflicted most of these with boots and fists. Sometimes they used batons.

To the British, the situation was incomprehensible, disgusting. In design and amenities, the Maze represented the state of the art in Europe. The most irredeemable terrorist had access to ball fields, classrooms, handicrafts, ping-pong tables. Now IRA men were befouling it.

In November 1978, prison authorities decided on a new tactic: forced washes of prisoners, starting in H-3.

Guards forcibly removed prisoners from their cells and dragged them to the lavatories, punching and kicking them along the way if they resisted, then threw them into washtubs. There the guards put the prisoners in chairs, held them down, and cut off their long hair and beards. The newly shorn men were then dumped into tubs full of disinfectant. There the guards scrubbed them down with large deck brushes designed for scrubbing floors. The bristles were hard and stiff. The guards made sure to scrape them on the prisoners' genitals, underarms, and ankles, scrubbing them until they were bloody and raw. Every prisoner on the protest endured it. The chronic verbal abuse rained down all the while.

After one forced wash of an entire wing's worth of Republican prisoners in H-1, every single prisoner had been beaten and needed medical attention. On seeing them, the medical officer sat with his feet on the table. There was a "body sheet" displaying a schematic of a man's body, intended to allow the medical officer to note the places of bruises, abrasions, and lacerations. The medical officer refused to fill it out for anyone.

Someone was going to have to pay—the men in the H-Blocks, the British government and its prison service, or both of them.

The IRA decided it would be the prison service.

The IRA started assassinating prison officials and guards on the outside.

To Kieran Nugent, the man who had initiated the blanket protest in 1976, the assassination campaign seemed like no more than self-defense.

"We would have been murdered in our cells only that the IRA started shooting the screws outside," Nugent said.

Of the six prison officials who came to 8 Evelyn Gardens to pay respects and comfort Florence and Alan Miles on November 28, 1978, five would be shot dead by the IRA.

TEN

Hairy Shoes

Albert Miles' friends in the prison service knew him as Bert. To them, he was affable. Unlike some of his officer-colleagues, he had not attended a university. He had come up through the ranks.

To the outside world, Miles appeared to be an enlightened and respectable prison official, not a thug. During the late 1970s, he had appeared on national television, where it was said Miles "expressed a humane and professional attitude toward the prisoners . . ."

But in dealing with Republican prisoners in the Maze, Miles presented a different face. To them, in a world where everyone had a nickname, Miles' was "hairy shoes," connoting the hush puppies he often wore while on duty. Miles had sneered at the first man to have gone on the blanket, Kieran Nugent, in 1976, slapped him, told him they were going to break him, then stood by and watched as the guards beat him up.

While undergoing medical treatment in custody at Lagan Valley Hospital in Lisburn, Gerry Kelly had tried unsuccessfully to escape, by trying to take a gun off an officer who was guarding him. Prison officers subdued Kelly and transported him back to the Maze.

"I got the usual beating, kicked all around the cell," Kelly remembered later.

"I said, 'I'm goin' on hunger strike.' There were two purposes to it. One was I wanted to show them that I wasn't going to lay down for this. The other was I wanted to force their hand."

During the beating, Kelly sustained a broken finger. After transport to the prison hospital, Kelly underwent an x-ray. During the procedure, Miles surprised Kelly by entering the room.

"Well, Kelly," Miles said. "You think you're gonna affect me? The only way you'll get out of here will be in a brown box."

"Fuck off," Kelly replied.

Years later, Kelly recalled Miles as a "hard Charlie, a screw's screw."

In 1995, Republican prisoner Gerard Loughlin's memories of Miles were uncomplicated and still vivid.

"He was a scumbag," Loughlin said.

Another prisoner with no fond memories of Miles was Gerard McConville.

"He was notorious for endorsing beatings," said Gerard McConville, at his deposition in Belfast in 1996.

During the protests, Miles had told the protesters, *I'm going to break yese and I don't care what it takes to get it done.* He personally visited the cell of blanket man and IRA member Jimmy McMullan in 1977. He told McMullan he was Fenian scum, that he would break McMullan's protest, and that he could guarantee that all Republican prisoners would be wearing prison uniforms.

McMullan made no reply.

Miles lifted McMullan's slop bucket, took the lid off, and made like he was smelling the contents. "This smells better than you," he said, putting the bucket back down.

Miles ordered guards to beat a prisoner, Martin Hurson. The beating dislocated a disc in Hurson's back and broke one of his toes. Hurson later died during the second hunger strike, in July 1981.

In November 1978, on the first day the guards employed the deck brushes, the IRA green-lighted the killing of the prison official who had put the brushes in his men's hands. It was Albert Miles.

ELEVEN

At the King's Threshold

By 1980, the blanket protest was approaching four years' duration, and the no-wash protest was in its second year. The number of men on the blanket and dirty protests exceeded the number of all internees that the British had swept up in Operation Demetrius in 1971. The protests had achieved exactly nothing. All the suffering had yielded no concessions from the British. Conditions on the wings were abysmal. The beatings from the guards were daily, constant, unremitting, pitiless. Men had been living in their own filth for over two years. Many had not left their seven-by-eight-foot cells for any reason for three years. More and more men were getting ill. Some were going insane. Some felt detached from the cause and from Ireland itself.

Outside the walls, the IRA seemed in a steep decline. There were more IRA men inside the Maze than there were on active service on the outside. To many who sympathized with the Republican cause, including Kevin Barry Artt, the movement was falling apart. The Republican prisoners needed a breakthrough, a way to smash the status quo and force the British to buckle. There was no other way to regain SCS and end the brutality on the wings. It was time for a game-ender: a hunger strike, in which the strikers would dare the British either to back down or watch the strikers starve to death.

The hunger strike was a time-honored tactic in the history of Irish resistance to British rule. During the pre-Christian era, Irish poets and tradesman who had gone unpaid stationed themselves outside the homes of their delinquent clients until they either obtained payment or starved to death, tarnishing the reputation of the deadbeat. The lore had inspired Ireland's Nobel Prize-winning poet and senator, W.B. Yeats, to write a play, "The King's Threshold," in which the protagonist starves himself to death.

In the 1940s, IRA men had starved themselves to death over the political status issue, which Eamonn de Valera had refused to concede to them. Republican prisoner Billy McKee had pushed the British to create SCS in the first place, with his own hunger strike in 1972.

On October 27, 1980, Brendan Hughes announced a hunger strike, defying the wishes of the IRA's Army Council, who feared a hunger strike would ingloriously fail, as it did, on December 18, 1980.

Afterward, the new OC, Bobby Sands, a handsome, shaggy-haired twenty-seven-year-old IRA man from west Belfast, met with prison governor Stanley Hilditch. Hilditch was eager to avoid a second hunger strike, he told Sands. But he had his orders. All he could offer was "prison-issue civilian-type clothes," to be worn during non-working hours. The prisoners would have to work and wear prison uniforms, he said. He stared at Sands over his desk.

Sands said the deal was unacceptable. The prisoners would soon escalate the blanket and dirty protests with new actions, he said.

What actions? asked Hilditch.

"Ye'll find out," said Sands.

The new hunger strike would begin on March 1, 1981, the anniversary of the British withdrawal of SCS five years earlier. Sands would be the first to go on it. A second man would follow a week later. After that, the pattern would repeat.

The logic was simple: there was no other way to win.

The rights demanded were the same as those demanded by the blanket men in 1976: to wear one's own clothing, associate freely, have normal visits, letters, and parcels, not do prison work, and have remission lost by prior protests restored. During Sands' hunger strike, Brendan McFarlane took over as OC.

Outside the Maze, the IRA's leadership disapproved of another hunger strike. In a comm smuggled out to the Army Council, Sands told them it was happening anyway. The prisoners wanted to do it. The blanket protest would continue, but the no-wash protest would end. The hated wing moves would end with it, relieving the suffering of men who had taken daily beatings and lived in filth for several years.

On March 1, 1981, Sands started refusing meals.

Two days later, the Secretary of State for Northern Ireland, Humphrey Atkins, told the House of Commons that there would be no political status for prisoners, hunger strike or no. The men could starve themselves to death. Thatcher declared it the IRA's "last card," played in desperation in the face of the imminent and total failure of a discredited cause.

On March 6, 1981, an unforeseen event set in motion an astonishing political event that would further elevate Sands in Irish history. Frank Maguire, a member of the British parliament who represented Fermanagh and South Tyrone, died suddenly of a heart attack at age 51. His death left his seat in Parliament vacant, triggering a by-election, what would in the U.S. be called a special election.

No Sinn Féin candidate could stand for the seat. The party's policy required a boycott of all elections in the north.

Republicans speedily organized a new party, the Anti-H-Block party, and made Sands its candidate for the seat. Whether Sands liked it or not, he was now running for public office from inside the Maze. Someone smuggled a radio into one of the Republican wings, enabling Sands' colleagues to monitor broadcasts of the latest news of the campaign being conducted on his behalf outside the walls.

On election day, April 9, 1981, whoops and cheers erupted on the Republican wings. Sands had won, polling 51.2 % of the vote. Second place went to Ulster Unionist Party candidate Harry West, who tallied 48.8% of the total. Nearly 87% of the voters had cast votes. Soon afterward, a guard seized the smuggled-in radio during a cell search; the men replaced it with a new one brought in two days later.

There was open jubilation in Catholic areas, outrage in Loyalist ones. Severe riots rocked Belfast, Lurgan, Cookstown, and Derry.

On April 25, 1981, Sands, nearly blind, issued a statement explaining his position. "The British government has the ways and means to grant the demands of the Republican hunger strikers. Until they do so, the hunger strike will continue."

Sands, an amateur poet, penned these lines during the protest:

There's an inner thing in every man,
Do you know this thing my friend?
It has withstood the blows of a million years,
And will do so to the end. . .
It died in blood on Buffalo Plains,
And starved by moons of rain,
Its heart was buried in Wounded Knee,
But it will come to rise again . . .
It lights the dark of this prison cell,
It thunders forth its might,
It is "the undauntable thought," my friend,
That thought that says, "I'm right!"

Outside the prison walls, scores of Loyalist picketers, supporters of Paisley, rooted openly for Sands' death. Some carried signs reading, "Let Sands Die." On May 5, 1981, Bobby Sands, MP, age 27, blind, emaciated, and unconscious, died of starvation in the Maze's hospital. He had gone sixty-six days without food.

Republican prisoner Jimmy Smyth recalled the morning:

> The news came from the fellow with the radio before the screws came around with the breakfast. That had to be the first morning there was not a thing said to any of the prisoners by the screws. I think when they opened the door and saw everyone's face[s] they must have known what mood the men were in. We wouldn't have taken any of their shit. Our friends were now starting to die, what fucking more can they do to us.

TWELVE

Their Last Card

News of Sands' death ignited riots across the six counties and even south of the border, in Dublin.

In the House of Commons, the British prime minister, Margaret Thatcher, dismissed Sands as a convicted criminal who chose to take his own life.

"It was a choice," said Thatcher, "that his organization did not allow to many of its victims."

There would never be political status for IRA prisoners, Thatcher declared, no matter how many hunger strikes there might be. Restoring SCS, she said, was out of the question. It would be like giving the IRA a license to kill.

Sands' death reignited the Republican movement. The British Foreign Secretary, Peter Carington, had proclaimed that the IRA lacked status and was accepted by no one in the north. The solemn throng of 100,000 mourners which trailed the hearse bearing Sands' skeletal remains to Milltown Cemetery in Belfast seemed to belie that.

By now, the hunger strikes were both a global *cause célèbre* and inspiration for a mass movement in the north. Public sympathy for militant Republicanism reached its all-time high. The images of emaciated hunger strikers, both living and dead, broadcast on the airwaves and printed on the front pages of newspapers and magazines, shocked and angered millions. In the U.S., media coverage of the strikers stirred an interest in the Troubles among Americans who had previously known little about them.

Overnight, Sinn Féin, which had been seen by some as a sort of Rotary Club for retired IRA members, had been transformed into a potent political party in the north. For the first time since 1969, Irish Republicanism had political muscle which translated into elections of Sinn Féin candidates to public office. H-Block committees formed. A broad front assembled, uniting left-wing, humanitarian, and liberal organizations in the cause of Irish Republicanism.

Prisoners' letters started reaching newspapers, elected officials, even the Vatican.

"I wrote a letter to the Pope which he answered," former Republican prisoner Jimmy Smyth recalled in 1992. "My mother has it at home."

The guards remained as they had been during the blanket and dirty protests. They were furious, hostile, full of hate. They despised the Republican prisoners more than ever. They showed it every day, with batons, fists, boots, curses, abuse of a hundred varieties. They joked loudly about the starving men in front of their Republican comrades in the wings. Within the prisoners' earshot, some guards openly made wagers on which striker would die next and when.

"They hated our guts, and they showed it," Brendan Hughes remembered in 1996. "They detested everything that we represented. . . We didn't hate them. And we couldn't understand it, often, that hatred, why they hated us so much."

As malnutrition set in, the men noticed the physical changes to the strikers. Francis Hughes, the second man to go on the strike, looked like he was disappearing in slow motion, slowly getting smaller. His movements slowed down. He struggled to wash himself. After three or four weeks, guards took him out of the wing and put him in the prison hospital. He died on May 12, 1981, just seven days after Sands took his last breath. While army helicopters hovered over mourners' heads, an IRA honor guard fired a volley of rifle shots over his coffin outside the family home in Bellaghy, County Derry. Sinn Féin leader and former IRA man Martin McGuinness gave a graveside oration, pledging that the British would never break Irish Republicanism.

As the months passed, eight more hunger strikers followed Sands and Hughes into the grave: Raymond McCreesh, age 24; Patsy O'Hara, age 23; Joe McDonnell, age 30; Martin Hurson, age 24; Kevin Lynch, age 25; Kieran Doherty, age 25; Thomas McElwee, age 23; and Michael Devine, age 27.

The atmosphere in the north became explosive. People felt rage over the British government's dogged refusal to yield to men whose protest was non-violent and political. In Ardoyne, rioting and petrol-bombing went on nearly non-stop from August through October. The rioting which followed the deaths of McElwee and McDonnell seemed on par with 1969. Masked men openly carrying weapons appeared in the streets. There was non-violent political action too. People walked in protest marches and registered to vote.

For hunger strikers' families, there was only sorrow and anguish. They struggled to intervene in the medical care of their dying sons, fathers, and brothers as their sight gave way to blindness and their organs failed.

In October 1981, their frantic efforts succeeded at last.

On October 3, 1981, a defiant statement smuggled out of the H-Blocks said continuing the strike had become a "physical and psychological impossibility."

Three days later, James Prior, the new Secretary of State for Northern Ireland, announced the new rules, softening the hated criminalization policy that had ignited the protests five years earlier.

Prisoners would be allowed to wear their own clothes at all times, subject to certain limits. They could receive parcels, letters, visits. There would be the chance to earn back 50% of the remission time previously lost due to the protests. Some inter-wing associations would be allowed for prisoners in adjacent wings of the H-Blocks. As for unfettered free association and the right not to work, the British did not budge.

Five years of protests and privation in the Maze were over at last. Many prisoners felt devastated at the loss of ten comrades. Some felt bitterly that the strike had not achieved all its goals. Others felt the strike had succeeded and restored their privileges.

Whether the strike had truly succeeded or failed, the Provisionals knew a juicy propaganda tool when they saw one.

To young Catholics, the names of Pádraig Pearse, Michael Collins, James Connolly, and the other martyrs of Irish Republicanism were familiar. But the decades-old black-and-white photographs of their faces seemed like relics of another time, as images of George Washington and Frederick Douglass did to American schoolchildren during the 1970s.

Now the IRA and Sinn Féin had new heroes to hold up: Bobby Sands and his nine dead comrades. They were Irish patriots, prisoners of a just war, who had starved themselves to death rather than be treated as common criminals. The grainy color photograph smuggled out of the Cages in 1975 made Sands look like a rock star or heartthrob professional soccer player. The image became a new icon in the north and around the world, the fresh face of Irish Republicanism, gracing wall murals and posters.

Outside the Maze, the IRA was resurgent, and the British were seemingly backpedaling.

Inside the Maze, many wings were occupied solely by Republican prisoners by the summer of 1982.

Among them were Gerry Kelly, Larry Marley, and Brendan McFarlane.

They were plotting a new move against the British. It was a mass escape.

SECTION III

KEVIN

THIRTEEN

Kevin Barry

Teresa McLoughlin, the second eldest of four daughters, was born in Belfast in 1940 to Catholic parents, Theresa and John McLoughlin. She and her sisters grew up in the Catholic enclave of Andersontown in west Belfast. As a teenager, Teresa had dark red hair and stunning good looks.

In 1956, when Teresa was sixteen, a doctor looking at an x-ray saw a small shadow on her lung. It was a possible sign of tuberculosis. TB was a nasty and fast-moving disease. During the first half of the twentieth century it had killed thousands of Irish children.

The family had Teresa admitted to a sanatorium for patients with tuberculosis and respiratory ailments, Forster Green Hospital in south Belfast.

The hospital had another patient, an eighteen-year-old male named Charlie McNutt, a Protestant from the Ormeau Road in Belfast.

One day, Charlie heard the rumor of a beautiful new girl on the women's ward.

The name of the formidable matron who ran the ward has been forgotten. But her nickname has survived: Big Aggy.

Charlie managed to get under Big Aggy's radar and infiltrate the women's ward. One morning he appeared at Teresa's bedside with a bag of candy in hand. Out of modesty, the startled young girl drew the covers up to her shoulders. Charlie introduced himself without fanfare. He proposed a straightforward transaction: a piece of candy for a kiss. Teresa accepted. Charlie kissed her on the lips just as Big Aggy appeared. Charlie fled down the corridor.

When Charlie's sister Mavis visited him later that day, Charlie told her he had just met the girl he was going to marry.

During weekly screenings of films in the hospital cinema on Wednesday nights, Charlie and Teresa began sitting together. Flashing some of the resourcefulness that his son Kevin would display later, Charlie soon wangled a key to the hospital's back door from a friendly nurse on his ward. Out of Big Aggy's sight, he used the key to pass in and out of the hospital clandestinely with Teresa, whom he escorted into town on dates. Transportation was supplied by friends who had access to vehicles. Charlie enlisted them to pick the couple off and drop them off at a side gate.

Neither of the two young patients ever developed tuberculosis.

Following their discharge from the hospital, Teresa returned to school. After completing her senior certificate, she got a job as a clerical worker in the civil service at Stormont. Her romance with Charlie continued, to the disapproval of many who frowned on romantic relationships between Catholics and Protestants.

By the end of March 1959, Teresa was pregnant. She was nineteen.

Following the norms of the time, the family sent the frightened young girl to Kinturk convent near a tiny village, Castlepollard, to avoid the shame and scandal of an out-of-wedlock birth. The convent was about fifty miles south of the border, in County Westmeath.

Charlie tried to find out where Teresa was. The unwritten rules of the time forbade anyone from telling him. Her whereabouts remained unknown to him for the duration of her pregnancy.

The sisters of Kinturk placed many of the babies born in the convent with married couples who adopted them, some in the United States. Other babies went unadopted. The nuns kept them there "until a suitable occupation was got for them." The property could accommodate about fifty such girls.

On September 18, 1959, Teresa gave birth to a healthy baby in the convent.

Teresa and Charlie were unmarried teenagers. To make matters worse, she was Catholic and he was Protestant. For them to raise a son together was out of the question. The boy would need adoptive parents.

Teresa's eldest sister, Maeve, and her husband, John Artt, were willing candidates. They had married two years earlier, in 1957, and were childless.

"I was nearly dead for a baby," remembered Maeve in 2019.

Teresa and Maeve's mother, Theresa McLoughlin, was married to John McLoughlin, an inspector for the telephone company. He had pro-British views. Theresa's political opinions were Republican. Her grandmother had lived on Albert Street, off the Falls Road. The grandmother had been friends with the late Irish patriot, Kevin Barry, whom the British had hanged in 1920 at age 18 for his part in an IRA ambush of British soldiers in Dublin.

"She was very politically minded," Maeve recalled in 2019. "My father was civil service, and he wasn't too much inclined. But my mother definitely was."

John Artt owned a small business just outside Belfast. It was a full-service automobile repair shop with an adjoining gas station, grocery store, car wash, and diner. John, a teetotaler, was a kind and gentle man. Maeve was a loving wife if a bit "high-strung."

They learned of the boy's birth at 6:00 a.m. the same morning he was born, via a telephone call from Kinturk convent. Maeve decided on the spot that their new son should be named after her great-grandmother's friend, Kevin Barry. It was a good, strong, patriotic name. The boy's name would be Kevin Barry Artt.

FOURTEEN

Awakening

Maeve and John chose to raise their new son in the Catholic faith. Maeve and John were delighted to adopt the blond-haired baby. When he was six weeks old, they took him into their home at 37 Abbey Crescent, off the Doagh Road in Whitehouse, a small, predominantly Protestant village northeast of Belfast, where John had been born and raised.

The customers of John Artt's garage, known as Whitehouse Service Station, were mostly Protestant. Several were RUC men.

John had inherited the service station from his own father, George, who opened it in 1914. George started out selling petrol from tins before installing pumps. John had been one of five sons. The others were Cromac, Ralph, George, and Fergus.

John went into business with his father at age fourteen, expanding the station to include seven pumps, a store selling car accessories, a car wash, a repair shop with three ramps, a light grocery store, and an authorized Rootes-Chrysler dealership, selling both new and used cars. The light grocery store made Whitehouse Service Station unique in the Belfast area. Under John's ownership, the business prospered.

The Artt family had no history of membership in the IRA. Neither Maeve or John Artt, Charlie or Teresa McNutt, nor any aunts and uncles expressed support or sympathy for the IRA. No one in the family had ever associated with any militant group. Police had never raided the family's house.

Kevin grew up sheltered from politics and the Troubles. At home, there was no talk of Sinn Féin, the Troubles, religion, or politics. Kevin enjoyed the comforts of a middle-class life and the company of a stay-at-home mom. Maeve was graceful and vivacious. She enjoyed hosting friends in her home with gourmet cooking and music. Musically gifted, she played the piano and taught Kevin how to sing. Maeve and John did their best to give their boy as much love as they could.

Beginning at age nine, Kevin worked for John on the weekends and after school. He helped operate the car wash. He watched John's mechanics do automotive repairs, studying them. Kevin figured he would take over Whitehouse Service Station someday, so he made little effort to succeed as a student.

Maeve and John sent Kevin to a private Catholic elementary school, Park Lodge Christian Brothers in Belfast. Each day one of John Artt's employees dropped Kevin off and picked him up from school.

It was while he was attending Park Lodge that Kevin heard the word *bastard* for the first time.

He was playing with some other kids in a field, across the street from the Whitehouse Service Station.

Ye're a bastard, said the boy.

His name was Tony Thompson. His father worked for John Artt at the service station.

Kevin was ten, perhaps eleven. He had never heard the word before. Curious, he asked Thompson what it meant.

Ask yer mother, said Thompson.

After he arrived home, Kevin asked Maeve about the word, not knowing it was profane. He could see the hurt and sadness which overtook Maeve's face in the moment.

Maeve broke the news to him: she and John had adopted him. His birth parents were his aunt, Teresa McLoughlin, and her husband, Charlie McNutt. They had given him up soon after he was born in Castlepollard.

The news turned Kevin upside down. He knew Maeve and John loved him, but the questions that swirled in his mind were the same questions that have bedeviled countless adopted children. *Why would my parents give me away? Did they not love me? What was wrong with me? Why has no one ever told me this before now?*

Kevin's hatred for the word *bastard* endured in him for years afterward.

Maeve felt fierce anger over the episode. It boiled over soon afterward, when she spied Tony Thompson from behind the wheel of her car not far from the house.

"Maeve tried to nail the kid with the Jaguar on this little lane that cut from the Antrim Road to Shore Road through a golf course," Kevin remembered in 2019. "He had to jump in the bushes to avoid getting run over. Of course, his dad got fired."

Kevin's first glimpse of the Troubles came in August 1969, during a trip back across Belfast to Jordanstown from his grandmother's.

Maeve was driving Kevin home in the family's Daimler sedan after a visit to his grandmother's in Andersontown, in Catholic west Belfast. In the aftermath of the Battle of the Bogside, Loyalist mobs had rampaged through the Lower Falls. From the passenger seat of the car, a wide-eyed, nine-year-old Kevin saw the black hulks of burned-out cars and the smoking ruins of Catholic homes torched during the riots. He could not fathom why people would want to drive other people out of their houses and burn them down. He felt sorry for the people he saw carting away their furniture. He wondered where they would live now.

Seven years after they became Kevin's foster parents, Maeve and John welcomed a second child, Therese, in 1970. By the end of that year, John had moved the family out of Whitehouse to a house at 2 Lenamore Park in Jordanstown, Newtownabbey, an upper-middle-class suburb 20 miles northeast of Belfast, about a mile and a half away from Whitehouse. At age eleven, Kevin started attending St. Patrick's Secondary School, a private school on the Antrim Road. Barbed wire ringed the perimeter fence. In the mornings, police searched Catholic students leaving their neighborhoods on their way to school.

Each morning, Maeve dressed Kevin for school in a suit and cap and equipped him with a briefcase, before one of John Artt's employees picked him up to transport him to school. Kevin's natty appearance stood out at a school where many students wore jeans and carried their books in rucksacks. Some kids bullied him. It hurt Kevin, but it also toughened him up.

Kevin's introduction to sectarian violence directed at him came when he was twelve, near the Artt home on Lenamore Park in Jordanstown.

Like many residents of the neighborhood, Vivian Cairnes, a teenage girl who lived nearby, was Protestant. She had a boyfriend. She told him that Kevin was Catholic and needed a beating. The boyfriend and a companion readily obliged. They approached Kevin without a word and beat him up, blackening his eye and leaving him bloody.

Kevin went home. On seeing him, Maeve asked what had happened. Kevin told her Vivian Cairnes' boyfriend had beaten him up because he was Catholic.

Showing some of the same fire she had shown to Tony Thompson, Maeve took the matter into her own hands. She got Kevin cleaned up and bandaged. Then she got into her car and drove to a hotel on the Shore Road. She knew Vivian Cairnes worked there as a waitress in the hotel restaurant.

Maeve parked, entered the restaurant, approached the bar, sat down, and ordered a drink. After spying Vivian Cairnes, Maeve got up, approached her, and, without a word, started hitting her. Someone called the police, who arrived within minutes. Maeve resisted the constables' efforts to get her to calm down, knocking their hats off. It was a scene. Constables escorted her out to a patrol car and placed her in the back seat. Instead of taking her to the police station, they telephoned John Artt. John arrived soon afterward and escorted his wife home. Such was his rapport with the RUC.

In 2019, when asked about the episode, Maeve vaguely demurred.

"I would have been defending him," she said.

FIFTEEN

Keep Looking Behind You

On "Bloody Friday," July 21, 1972, the IRA detonated at least twenty bombs during an eighty-minute span in Belfast, killing nine people, seven of them civilians, and injuring one hundred and thirty, over half of whom were women and children. A pall of black smoke hung over the city, as though it had taken several rounds of artillery.

A destructive game of tit-for-tat, played by paramilitary groups on the opposite sides of the divide, had begun.

The RUC suspected John's brother, Fergus, of having knowingly lent his car to an IRA man who used it to bomb a pub, the Merville Inn, in Whitehouse. Constables arrested Fergus and interrogated him for two days concerning the episode. Afterward, they released him without any charges. Ever after, however, and given the family's unusual surname, John believed that police associated his family with Republican violence.

The IRA had started bombing police barracks, banks, hotels, bus stations, rail depots. In retaliation, Loyalist paramilitaries started bombing Catholic-owned businesses. One of these targeted the one thriving Catholic business situated in a Protestant area in Belfast—John Artt's garage.

On New Year's Eve of 1972, persons unknown tossed a pipe bomb in an area to the rear of the garage. The ensuing explosion blew asbestos tiling into the workshop area. John believed that either the UVF or UFF was responsible. Afterward, no one was charged in the incident.

John rebuilt the garage and went back to work.

The Artt house began receiving twice-weekly anonymous telephone calls. The calls usually came in the hour between 4:00 and 5:00 a.m. The script never varied.

Fucking Fenians—we want people like you out. Keep looking behind you. We're coming to kill you. Catholic Fenians out.

The callers never identified themselves.

In 2019, Kevin still vividly remembered being jarred awake by the sound of the telephone ringing in the dark in the early morning hours.

John Artt reported the threats to the RUC. Constables told him to change his telephone number and remove it from the telephone directory. John suspected the only way the callers could have gotten his new telephone numbers was directly from the authorities. The calls were still coming in 1975, when Kevin left home.

A second bombing followed, on February 7, 1973. Beforehand, the UDA had circulated warnings that all businesses in the area should be closed, in observance of a strike called by the Vanguard Party (a political affiliate of several Loyalist paramilitary groups). John feared retaliation if he failed to play along. He closed the place that day. It was a Wednesday.

Three miles away, John Artt heard the boom. The photograph in the *Belfast Telegraph* the following day showed the collapsed roof and walls and shards of shattered furniture and fixtures. The bombers had planted a bomb in the trunk of a car and left it in the forecourt of the service station, just across from the front door.

After John rebuilt, the bombers still weren't finished.

In late September 1973, John's friend Jimmy McGee warned John that "something was planned" for the garage.

"You should watch out," McGee said.

McGee was then a member of the Official IRA. He was privy to information learned from Loyalist informers about planned Loyalist paramilitary operations.

John reported the warning to the local RUC station. The constables seemed indifferent. They said that they would "check," but added that there was nothing they could really do. John, afraid of identifying McGee to them as an Official IRA man, said nothing about the source of the warning.

At about 10 a.m. on Thursday, October 4, 1973, John Artt sat in his restaurant at the Whitehouse Service Station, drinking a cup of coffee. A wide-eyed RUC constable rushed in. He was a friend of John's and one of the few Catholics employed by the RUC.

"John, get this place cleared. There's a large bomb here," the constable said. He explained that a "Captain Black" had telephoned the *Belfast News Letter* newspaper with a warning minutes earlier.

John immediately cleared the place. When satisfied everyone was out, he got away too. Police hurriedly cleared the area outside.

About a half hour later, a car bomb made with two hundred pounds of plastic explosive detonated with a shattering boom. The blast destroyed the gas pumps, the cover overhead, and the interior of the building, and started a fire. The explosion injured a British Army soldier who had been standing across the street. The bomb had been planted in the car of someone who had come in, asked for a clutch repair, and left it behind.

The *Belfast Telegraph* published a photo of the ruins. The premises were completely destroyed.

Shortly afterward, the UFF, via telephone call to the RUC, took responsibility for the blast, using the Captain Black pseudonym. The same night, the BBC reported the same. Afterward, the RUC's investigation was lackadaisical. No one was ever tried or charged for the bombings.

In October 1973, John Artt had had enough. He had rebuilt twice, only to see his business bombed to pieces. Guessing that only another bombing awaited, he felt it was futile to try again. He sold what was left and got out. He started doing automotive repairs out of a friend's auto repair shop, concentrating on the area a short distance from the old Whitehouse service station. Maeve became the breadwinner, working as a receptionist at Guardian Royal Exchange, an insurance company in Belfast.

In the Artt home, the anonymous phone calls didn't stop until 1982, after nearly a decade of harassment by parties unknown.

SIXTEEN

Lorraine

In 1975, Kevin met a pretty seventeen-year-old girl, Lorraine Keenan, at the Stardust Disco in Belfast. Lorraine was from the Catholic enclave of New Lodge in west Belfast. Kevin was fifteen. He quickly fell in love with Lorraine.

One night, Kevin and Lorraine babysat Kevin's younger sister, Therese, while his parents were out for dinner. Kevin was already aware of the simmering unease his parents felt over his relationship with his girlfriend, who came from a working-class family. Maeve drank. Sometimes when drunk, she was insulting and abrasive, as she was on this night.

As in many homes occupied by teenagers, other tensions had been festering too. Maeve and John objected to Kevin staying out late at night. It was a time when a Catholic who found himself alone on the streets at night could wind up dead at the hands of Loyalist thugs.

After Maeve and John had returned home from their evening out, they retired to bed at about 11:30 p.m. Like many Catholic mothers of the time, Maeve Artt objected to her son spending the night with his girlfriend, especially under her roof. Kevin called a taxi for Lorraine. By 1 a.m., it had still not arrived. To his horror, Kevin heard Maeve shout down the hall, "Hasn't that whore gone home yet?"

"The falling out was over his spending the night with Lorraine," Maeve recalled in 2019. "I wouldn't let him."

Full of teenage fury, Kevin ushered Lorraine outside without bothering to put on a coat. He took her down to the end of the street to wait for the taxi there. Kevin sat there fuming as rain fell on the young couple.

Kevin was proud and angry. Like many an indignant male teenager, he thought he knew everything. He dropped out of St. Patrick's a few months before turning 16. He had completed his O Level Standard, a secondary school-leaving credential roughly equivalent to an American GED. Kevin spent a week or so crashing at his grandmother's home in Andytown. He soon drove Theresa to distraction with his nocturnal habits. Kevin stayed out late every night, walking to and from the Keenans' house in New Lodge, a Catholic ghetto just north of the city center. Often, he came home after 2 a.m. The house lacked a telephone. Theresa lay awake worrying about where her grandson was. Her husband, John, had died suddenly the year before, and so she suffered from anxiety and depression in the first place.

Theresa's house lay in a location that made safe transit difficult for a lovelorn teenage boy who wanted to travel to the New Lodge, in that the most direct route there passed through the murder triangle. The murder triangle was in the rough shape of a scalene triangle. Its short base began just southwest of the jail and courthouse at the bottom of the Crumlin Road, at the intersection of that road and the Antrim Road, and ran north up the Antrim Road for a distance of about eight blocks. The first long leg of the triangle began at the intersection of the Antrim Road and Cliftonville Road, about three blocks short of the waterworks. A left turn there took one northwest. At the northernmost tip of the triangle, the Cliftonville Road converged with Oldpark Road. A forty-five-degree left turn there took one back in a southeasterly direction, down the second long leg of the triangle, past a fortress-like RUC station and its cluster of surveillance masts and aerials, to the end of Oldpark Road at its intersection with the Crumlin Road, just west of the jail and courthouse again.

The Shankill Butchers operated in and around the murder triangle from late 1975 to mid-1977. They were a small gang of UVF men based on the Shankill Road. Their leader was Lenny Murphy, a diminutive Loyalist fanatic and psychopath. In all, the group committed nineteen gruesome late-night murders of Catholic civilians. The Butchers did not hunt for IRA men or discriminate among the Catholics they chose for mutilation and killing. Any Catholic civilian would do, especially in the murder triangle.

One of the Butchers' victims was a neighbor of the Keenans', a father of young children. The Butchers killed and mutilated him. Then, in a kind of gruesome re-enactment of the last scene of the gangster film "The Public Enemy," they delivered the body in a sealed coffin to his family.

But none of that deterred Kevin from his late-night passages from Andytown, through the murder triangle, on his way to and from the Keenan house in New Lodge.

"In hindsight, it was insane," recalled Kevin in 2019. "Three or four nights a week. What was I thinking?"

Soon Kevin moved in with Lorraine's family, in a small, single-story flat at 11 Sheridan Street in New Lodge. Lorraine's parents, Brian and Gladys Keenan, welcomed him, as did Lorraine's brother, Stevie, who was one year younger than Kevin. The place had three bedrooms and one bathroom. Lorraine slept in one bedroom. Kevin and Stevie shared the double bed in another bedroom. Other times, Kevin slept on the sofa.

It was not long before Stevie Keenan began to regard Kevin as an older brother.

"He was part of the family for years," remembered Stevie in 1995. Kevin frequently took his meals in the Keenan home. Lorraine worked as a clerk for a sports bookie.

New Lodge was a small area, home to some five to six thousand inhabitants, all Catholics. Everybody knew everybody else. Compared to Jordanstown, it was a different planet. Unemployment in the district hovered around 40%, a percentage typical of other Catholic wards. Kevin had grown up among Protestants, in a middle-class area, with nice clothes, private schooling, and other trappings of a sheltered and privileged youth, about as far away as a boy could grow up from the Troubles and still live within twenty miles of Belfast's city center. Except for being beaten up that day at age twelve, he had never been exposed personally to bigotry or hatred. He had always seen the good in people.

But it was hard to see the good in the British troops whose patrols passed through Sheridan Street every four to eight hours. The soldiers, clad in helmets and full camouflage and armed with long rifles, did not treat the local residents kindly. The army considered Sheridan Street to be a hard-core Republican street. The troops were young, on edge, angry, crude, blunt, violent. They all seemed on a hair trigger, not hesitating to beat or arrest anyone who stood in their way.

Officially, the army was there to keep the peace and protect Catholic neighborhoods from Loyalist mobs. But they kicked down doors, ransacked houses, pulled out walls, tore up furniture, and heaped verbal abuse on the people they were supposed to be protecting. The furniture, appliances, and other property destroyed by the soldiers during their raids often were just the bare essentials, what the working-class occupants could afford to have in their homes. Kevin felt sympathy for them. They were down-to-earth people being treated like animals.

Suspecting him of IRA involvement, British soldiers arrested Stevie Keenan and took him to Castlereagh at least seven times during the late seventies. There he endured severe beatings and torture at the hands of RUC detectives. Three times they broke Stevie's nose. Once, Stevie so despaired of his state in Castlereagh that he tried to hang himself in his cell. Authorities never charged him with any offense.

"You felt dirty in there," Stevie recalled later. "They took your dignity."

One night on Donegall Street, just outside the New Lodge area, near the center of Belfast, Kevin and Lorraine were standing together in a doorway a few doors down from a Catholic church. Kevin had not yet turned sixteen years old. It was 1975.

A foot patrol of British soldiers neared. Their insignia identified them as members of the Royal Scots. The patrol passed in single file. The last soldier, walking backwards as he passed Kevin and Lorraine, raised his rifle and struck Kevin with the butt of it. Kevin had said nothing to provoke the blow. The soldier said nothing either. Kevin started to react, but Lorraine told him not to say anything, and he contained himself.

Brian Keenan had no connections to the IRA or any other illegal organization. But, like everyone else in the neighborhood, he was an IRA sympathizer. By the early 1980s, soldiers had kicked down the front door and searched the Keenan home at least sixteen times. At least once, they roused Kevin and Stevie from their bed with rifle butts. Not once did the soldiers ever turn up a single piece of contraband. They did manage to destroy Brian and Gladys Keenan's print of the Last Supper (torn in two), a cabinet, and other property. During the raids, the sneering and menacing soldiers practically burst with belligerence and insolence.

The feelings this treatment engendered in thousands of people in New Lodge and other Catholic areas were predictable.

"They hated me because I was born Catholic," said Stevie Keenan. "I hated them because of what they did to my family."

Not wanting to wait until he turned the minimum legal age of seventeen to get his driver's license, Kevin pressed John to give him driving lessons. When he felt confident enough to pass a driving test, Kevin falsified the date of his birth to 1958. He got his license just after turning sixteen, in September 1975.

Promptly, Kevin bought his first vehicle: a 250 cc motorcycle. Soon afterward, he upgraded to a larger bike, a Suzuki. Then he bought a used Morris Minor two-door sedan, purchased for thirty pounds. He fixed it up and re-sold it, then repeated the cycle several more times until he had saved up enough to buy a Ford Cortina—a two-door sedan which was the British version of the Ford Taurus sold in the U.S. John Artt co-signed the promissory note on the loan from the Bank of Ireland.

Except for a few nights spent at his grandmother's in Andersontown in west Belfast, Kevin lived in the Keenans' flat on Sheridan Street for about a year, before getting his own place at 148 Antrim Road, on the outskirts of New Lodge, in 1976.

By then, Kevin and Lorraine were engaged. Kevin had asked Brian Keenan for his blessing. Brian was glad to give it. Kevin bought Lorraine an engagement ring at the H. Samuel store, spending £189 on it.

The couple spent time together every day and evening. The two were virgins, and they stayed that way for the rest of their engagement.

SEVENTEEN

Ace

A person trying to understand the segregation that prevailed in the Belfast of the nineteen-seventies might start with a street map.

From the city center, a spaghetti network of streets sprawls outward in every direction. The layout recalls other northern European port cities whose histories of settlement go back to the Bronze Age. There is a web of discontinuous streets, with few right angles. The River Lagan bisects the labyrinth. It snakes its way from southwest to northeast into Belfast Lough, an intertidal sea inlet. Beyond lies the Irish Sea.

Superimposing a color-coded layer showing the concentration of Catholics and Protestants by electoral ward reveals more. A garish, multi-colored jigsaw puzzle emerges.

The puzzle pieces are irregular in shape, jagged, asymmetrical. Their colors are dark green, bilious yellow, bright red. The dark green pieces denote Catholic residency ranging from 81 to 100%, yellow from 41 to 60%, and red from 0 to 20%.

East of the pale blue ribbon of the Lagan lies a broad red swath. Punctuating it here and there is the odd, isolated yellow chunk: Botanic, Ballymacarrett (the Short Strand area), Rosetta, Stormont.

All the green pieces lie west of the Lagan. One can run a finger from southwest to northeast over an uninterrupted, verdant patchwork: Andersontown, Glen Road, Falls Park, Whiterock, Beechmount, Falls, Clonard. In north Belfast, some bright red pieces start to interrupt the jagged green field –Highfield, Woodvale, Shankill, Crumlin. The latter two, Shankill and Crumlin, separate a lone green shard, Ardoyne to the west, from other green shards, Waterworks and New Lodge, to the east, and Clonard and Falls, to the south.

Between the green and red shards, there was no mingling. A Catholic who found himself in a Protestant area was a drop of green in a small sea of red. Like a black person daring to cross a white neighborhood on his way to school in Selma, Alabama, during the 1960s, he could expect trouble.

Beginning in 1969, barricades sprang up in the "interface areas" separating Catholic from Protestant. They were put up to block Loyalist mobs from entering. By 1973, Catholics burned or driven out of their homes had relocated to exclusively Catholic districts, where they felt safer. Afterward, they avoided passing through Protestant enclaves. Those intrepid enough to work at firms dominated by Loyalists were intimidated into quitting.

Belfast became an urban war zone. The din of the Troubles interrupted the ordinary sounds of urban life with no warning. The sudden blast of a bomb, the staccato report of an Armalite or L1A1 self-loading rifle, the banging of trash bin lids on concrete by Catholic women warning their neighbors of approaching soldiers or police, the engine of a British Army Saracen roaring up a narrow residential street, the crash of one's front door as police kicked it in and raided your house and rousted your family from bed in the middle of the night, the deep thudding of the rotors of army helicopters as they hovered overhead day and night—the sounds were frightening, maddening, endless.

As a newcomer to New Lodge, Kevin started experiencing at firsthand what the Troubles were for ordinary Catholics.

Even after his falling out with Maeve, Kevin stayed on good terms with John Artt. In 1975, after he turned sixteen, Kevin resumed working for John at the garage, showing up when things got busy, deepening his knowledge of automotive mechanics and love of cars. He did repairs and became a skilled mechanic. He did paint and body work and welding, applied Bondo filler to dents, fixed clutches. There were Hillman Hunters, Morris Minors and Marinas, Leylands, Austins, Land Rovers, Jaguars—every type of vehicle that was available in the north at the time.

Kevin worked a series of other jobs—mopping out McLaughlin's Bar on New Lodge Road around the corner from the Keenans', making deliveries for a dental supplier just across the street from John's garage, selling carpet, doing construction labor, stocking shelves at a cut-rate retail store called Crazy Prices.

Kevin's social life was low-key. Kevin was "odd," a "quiet fellow" who "kept to himself." Some people thought Kevin a snob, because of the way he spoke. He was really just quiet, an introvert. His musical tastes ran to Led Zeppelin, Pink Floyd, and Van Morrison, a Belfast native.

Kevin moved to a slightly bigger flat, at 371 Antrim Road, where he would live until May 1979.

In late 1976, Kevin became a taxicab driver for Ace Taxi. Kevin drove for Ace at night, including Friday and Saturday nights. He would drive for Ace for nearly three years, from 1976 through late 1978 or early 1979, earning about $200 a week. He considered the pay excellent. He drove the murder triangle and other areas dangerous to Catholics.

The job changed his life permanently.

"That's when the problems started," remembered Stevie Keenan. "When he started driving."

Ace had its genesis in Catholic fear.

Ace's founders had started it for the benefit of New Lodge residents who could not find transportation into or out of their neighborhood, particularly at night, without the risk of harassment or worse.

Ace vehicles bore no signs, meters, or other indicia of a legitimate taxi service. Ace drivers drove their own personal vehicles, depositing "depot rent" each week and driving as much as they wanted. The company was unlicensed, paid no taxes, and did not comply with other regulations governing taxicabs. The cars lacked radios to hide the reality from police and soldiers.

During encounters with security forces, Ace drivers and their occupants denied they were driving or riding in a taxicab or that any money had changed hands, the better to avoid prosecution for driving an unlicensed taxi.

There were other taxi services in Belfast. But, as everything else was in Northern Ireland, rigid segregation prevailed. Protestant drivers served Protestant areas. Catholic drivers served Catholic areas and feared venturing outside them. The Catholic cab driver who operated outside a Catholic area risked being shot to death. Catholic passengers were scared to get into the wrong taxicab. If a cab driven by a Protestant even picked them up, there would be trouble afterward. With Ace, the Catholic in need of a ride through a Protestant area, say from Ardoyne to New Lodge and through the lower Shankill area, had some peace of mind.

Ace dispatchers worked out of modest depots on the Antrim Road, next to the Phoenix Bar, near the top of the New Lodge Road, on the very eastern edge of the murder triangle. After the location became too dangerous, Ace began operating out of a new depot on Hallidays Road, further east, just behind McLaughlin's Bar.

Kevin drove his fares primarily from the New Lodge Road area when they were on their way to Ardoyne to visit friends or go to clubs. He was one of ten to fifteen Ace drivers. Most of their runs were to and from New Lodge and Andersontown. They departed from the depots, picked up their passengers, and took them to their destinations.

The RUC and army viewed Ace as an organ of the IRA. They reserved especially harsh treatment for any Ace driver from New Lodge during the late '70s and early '80s.

"Any taxi driver who came from New Lodge, they abused," recalled Stevie Keenan. "Just being from New Lodge made you a target. You didn't have to be anybody for them to stop you. It was like a police state. You didn't walk without being stopped, searched, asked for all your particulars, called a Fenian bastard. That was the run of the mill in New Lodge."

Kevin's friend, Kieran Maxwell, drove for Ace in Andersontown.

"If they knew you drove for Ace, you were thought to be an IRA man," Maxwell remembers. "It was just the norm to get stopped. Everyone from west Belfast, New Lodge, was painted as IRA."

"They thought everyone [at Ace] was a member of the IRA," remembered Aidan Gorman, an Ace driver who befriended Kevin. Kevin related to Gorman several incidents in which police or soldiers had threatened to shoot Kevin. He viewed the threats as a source of amusement to his tormentors.

Some taxi drivers, weary of the constant harassment, quit.

Despite the tens of thousands of stops, officers never discovered any contraband. The reason was grounded in common sense. What IRA man in his right mind would use an Ace car to move contraband? The car was a red light to security forces in the first place.

During one traffic stop after another, police and soldiers told Kevin that Ace was an IRA operation and asked him if he was a member. They questioned him and the occupants of his car. They arrested him from time to time, at least once offering him cash if he would agree to work as an informant. Kevin said no.

Loyalist paramilitary groups hated Ace at least as much as the security forces did. They shot at one Ace driver, Dennis O'Hagan, three times while he was driving. They impersonated Republican civilians while calling for the taxi, then stabbed the driver to death once he arrived. Others detonated a bomb in a pub adjacent to an Ace depot.

Starting in 1977, Kevin started driving a dump truck during daylight hours for a construction company, Lake Glen Construction, to augment his income. His routes took him around Belfast. He delivered bricks to bricklayers. When not driving the truck, he mixed plaster. A short, dour, dark-haired man also worked there. Kevin didn't know him. His name was Charles McKiernan.

EIGHTEEN

Carmen

During the summer of 1978, Kevin, then nineteen, met a second pretty, petite, seventeen-year-old girl, Carmen Myers. Carmen worked for the civil service, in the government stationery office. She used Ace to get around. It was the only safe way for her kind to pass through Loyalist areas, especially at night. Carmen lived with her parents on Newington Avenue in north Belfast. The Myers were Republican in their politics and sympathies, like everyone else in their neighborhood. Before meeting Kevin, Carmen had been the girlfriend of Gerard (Jonah) McClafferty, who was doing life in the H-Blocks for murdering a prison officer and his wife. Before going inside, McClafferty had been Carmen's boyfriend for about a year. Carmen had met him when she was only sixteen, while McClafferty was married. McClafferty, in turn, was good friends with Maurice Gilvarry, a swarthy, short guy from Ardoyne, who was always dressed in fashionable clothes.

Carmen grew fond of riding with Kevin. Several times, Kevin picked up Carmen when she was leaving a club, tipsy. Kevin started asking her out. Carmen declined, telling him she knew he was engaged.

Kevin persisted. One day he drove Carmen to McClafferty's mother's house, on Herbert Street in Ardoyne.

It was a working-class Catholic neighborhood. Carmen was dressed nicely. Kevin kidded her, telling her she was all dressed up with no place to go.

As a passenger of Kevin's, Carmen began to experience the multiple stops of Kevin's car by police and soldiers. Though they arrested him only rarely, they stopped him constantly. Often, they wrote citations, for things like a cracked taillight or a supposedly bald tire. During one ride, on Chester Drive, police stopped the car, arrested Kevin, and took him to the police station. Carmen had no driver's license, so the police impounded the car and took it to the station too. Carmen had to call a friend to get a lift home.

Constables who stopped Kevin's car were unfazed by the presence of the pretty young lady in the passenger seat.

We're out to get ye, one officer told Kevin during a stop, *and we're going to get ye.*

To Carmen, Kevin seemed cocky in the face of such threats.

"The police were like a clique," she remembers. "A pack of wicked bastards."

Unable to take it anymore, Carmen eventually stopped accompanying Kevin on his shifts.

After a few months, Kevin falsely told Carmen he had broken off his engagement. Carmen relented. Kevin took her for a drink at the Lake Glen Hotel in west Belfast. There was a live band there, and they played good music.

The two started a casual relationship, consisting mostly of Kevin picking up a tipsy Carmen as she left a club and driving her home. Once, Kevin drove her to his flat on Clifonpark Avenue in north Belfast instead. The two had sex. By June 1979, Carmen was pregnant.

NINETEEN

Driving the Murder Triangle

Unaware of her condition, Carmen went on vacation to Spain with some friends. She was still trying to get over McClafferty. While still in Spain, she discovered her pregnancy. She broke the news to Kevin after returning home.

For a young man acutely conscious of the circumstances of his own birth, there was only one thing to do. On the spot Kevin told Carmen he would marry her.

Kevin was on good terms with Charlie McNutt, his biological father. But he lacked a normal father-son relationship with him. He had a good rapport with John Artt. But there was something artificial about it. Kevin did not want his own child to have the same experience. No one was going to call his child *bastard*. Like many adopted children, Kevin felt resentment at being separated from his true parents. He was not going to pass it on to the next generation.

Kevin was not in love with Carmen, but it was irrelevant. There was no proper option to matrimony and a nuclear family. Abortion was unthinkable. The families were Catholic. This was Ireland. The upright thing was to get married.

He broke off his engagement with Lorraine, his girlfriend of four years, leaving her bitterly disappointed, angry, and hating him.

Kevin appointed himself to break the news of Carmen's pregnancy to her father, Steven Myers.

"I know it really destroyed him," Kevin remembered in 2019. "Carmen was the youngest daughter. The rest had all been married, you know, properly. There was no pregnant before marriage type thing."

Steven Myers told Kevin he didn't have to marry his daughter. Kevin said he wanted to anyway.

"My mummy didn't want me to marry him," remembered Carmen in 2019. "She was very Catholic. She was annoyed at him. She felt he had taken advantage of her daughter. But she made us dinner and all and was very good to him."

The Keenans felt insulted and betrayed. That Kevin had stepped out on Lorraine with Carmen was bad enough. That he had done it while living under their roof added insult to injury.

In the meantime, Kevin was still driving for Ace. By now it felt like every man in the UDR, RUC, and British Army knew him by name and on sight. The RUC and the army were the worst. They stopped him every shift, several times a shift. Often, they addressed him by name without even first having checked his identification. In his off hours, Kevin heard of threats made against him by soldiers and policemen, from friends.

Tell Barry we're asking for him, RUC detectives told Aidan Gorman.

Ace dispatchers logged security forces' stops of their drivers. By far, Kevin was the one stopped most often.

The RUC and army thought Kevin was an IRA man and told him so. The stops lasted from five minutes to forty-five. Sometimes they happened several times a night. One day, the RUC stopped Kevin three times within twenty minutes, after he had left a pub where he had been watching

ABOVE THE GROUND | 125

a pool match. The soldiers or police would demand Kevin's driver's license, then order him out of the car and search him, sometimes roughly. They would ask the name, address, date of birth, destination, and relationship to Kevin of every occupant of the car. They would search the car, open the trunk, force Kevin to take off his jacket and shoes. Their manner of addressing Kevin rarely varied.

Fenian bastard. Taig.

The RUC did not confine its harassment of Kevin to traffic stops. On several occasions, they kicked in the front door of Kevin's flat on Antrim Road, entered, and made Kevin lie face down on the floor. After asking a few perfunctory questions, punctuated by the usual verbal abuse, they would depart, leaving the shaken Kevin angry and bewildered. As the hassles persisted, Kevin started mouthing off. Sometimes he asked British soldiers when they were going to get out of his country.

This is our country, you Fenian piece of shit, came the answer.

On the sidewalk, if things got physical, Kevin pushed back, and there would be a scuffle. When they acted cocky and aggressive with him, he responded in kind. He started treating the police and soldiers as they treated him.

Norman Cromie, an RUC detective who kept tabs on the stops, heard reports back from the constables. The term he used to describe Kevin's attitude with them was *cheeky.*

One night in 1978, unknown gunmen fired several rounds at the Antrim Road flat which Kevin sometimes shared with Fergie Ferguson, pockmarking the front door with bullet holes. The next day, police pulled Kevin over, ordered him and his passenger out of the car, and put them through the usual drill before bidding Kevin farewell with these words, whispered into his ear:

We missed ye last night. We'll get ye next time. We're not finished with ye yet.

SECTION IV

CASTLEREAGH 1978

TWENTY

I Am Not a Provo

On the morning of December 12, 1978, at Castlereagh, the detectives knew the identities of Kevin Barry Artt's friends, co-workers, and associates, the shebeens2 where he liked to go and have a pint, where the Keenans lived. They had done their homework. To Kevin, they left no doubt they saw him as an IRA man based strictly on his associations.

At length, the detectives got around to the Miles murder. Kevin spoke openly. He denied knowing anything about it. The name Albert Miles meant nothing to him. He had no involvement in it. He had never murdered anybody in his life, he said, nor would he even consider it. He was not an IRA man and knew no one who was. When asked where he had been on the night of November 26, Kevin said he had been at the Keenans', drinking tea and watching television, before meeting Stevie Keenan for a couple of pints at the Felons Club at 10 p.m. He had returned to the Keenans' at about 11 or 11:15 p.m. and gotten in a row with Lorraine about having gone out without her, he said.

On the night of December 12, detectives grilled Kevin from 8 p.m. until 11:20, returning to the Miles murder.

---

2. Shebeens were illicit drinking clubs where excisable alcoholic beverages were sold without license or payment of taxes.

Kevin remained adamant: he had had no involvement, nor would he even have known what to do with a gun if someone handed him one.

"Subject stated I would not take a life, I have no time for terrorists as I don't believe in what they are doing," wrote Constable Walker. "Put to subject that he was definitely involved, subject denied it emphatically. Subject asked if he ever was trained in firearms, stated he never saw a gun or never used one. Subject stated the only people he saw with guns was the police and army. Subject asked to account for movements, stated he went to girlfriends and stayed there to 10 PM. He stated he left his girlfriend's house and went to the Felons Club for a pint. Subject met Stephen Keen . . .

"Put to subject that he was the gun man on 26 November 1978 again he denied it stated 'I murdered nobody' I wouldn't murder anybody and never will no matter what pressure is put on me. I will never involve myself in terrorism. I am not aggressive enough to kill anybody."

The interrogation sessions continued, punctuated by trips to Kevin's holding cell, where a uniformed constable would lock him in until summoning him for the next go-round.

Day three was December 14, 1978. The two-man teams rotated in and out. They were relentless. They kept insisting Kevin had murdered Albert Miles. Kevin kept protesting his innocence.

Using a bluff they would renew three years later, detectives told him the case against him was strong:

> Put it to subject that there was a very strong case against him. Subject stated that he found it very hard to believe. He stated that he had told us everything he knew, and he had nothing to do with it.

Day four was December 15, 1978.

"Denied all knowledge of the murder," wrote Detective Armstrong. "Says he was at his girlfriend's house Lorraine

Keenan on the night of the murder. Denies being involved in the PIRA . . . very smooth-talking gent."

The officers kept after the IRA angle, probing Kevin's associations and workmates. Both were problems, they said. The RUC suspected Lake Glen Construction was a front for the IRA. All his associates appeared to be IRA men.

"Although he works with IRA men," wrote Detective Boyd, "he says that they don't trust him and tend to shun him during working hours especially if he walks in when they are having a conversation together. They stop talking when subject appears on the scene."

"Subject replied that he didn't know these people were involved until he came in here," wrote Boyle.

The interrogation continued on the fifth day, December 16. During one of the interviews, Detective George grabbed him and pulled him over the table, popping the buttons off of his shirt, telling Kevin that he had to shake him up to get to the truth.

The interview notes of detective George neglect to mention this incident.

In another interview, Kevin encountered Detective Inspector G.L. (Leslie) Fyfe.

Fyfe's written statement summarizing this interview was prosaic:

> At 10.30 am on 16 December 1978, accompanied by D/Constable Mackin I saw John Barry Artt [sic] in an interview room at the Police Office, Castlereagh. . . We spoke to Artt about his family background and any involvement in the PIRA and he denied having anything to do with the organisation. The interview terminated at 11.20 a.m.

Day six was December 17.

Kevin remained steadfast: he had been at the Keenans' until about 10 p.m. He did not know any Provisionals, he said. Detectives told him that Bobby Campbell was "the top Provie in the Lodge." Kevin said he knew nothing about it.

"He appeared calm, intelligent and adamant that he was in no way involved in PIRA activity," wrote another detective. "Was consistent in his answers to questions in respect of terrorist and ordinary life."

By that morning, the seven-day limit for detaining Kevin without charge under the emergency laws was approaching.

In a last-ditch effort, the peelers brought in a large, well-built man dressed in civilian clothes. They introduced him as an officer of the British Army's elite Special Air Service, the SAS.

You were observed that night standing outside the Shamrock Club, said the man in a plummy English accent. *It was a few minutes before ye and the others drove to Evelyn Gardens.*

The man stood over him. He was big and imposing, with a military bearing.

"I don't know what ye're talking about," Kevin said.

I think you do know what I'm talking about, the man said. *And I know you think you're walking out of here soon*, said the man. *I'll be waiting outside. As soon as you walk out the gate, I'll shoot you right there on the street.*

Then he stalked out.

For the first time, the detectives seemed unsure of themselves. They told Kevin he had been the gunman, then the supplier of the weapons, then the driver, then "something else." It seemed like they were fishing, grab-bagging.

Kevin remained adamant. He had not been involved, he said.

"Denied all knowledge of the murder and insisted that he was with . . . girlfriend Lorraine Keenan that day," wrote Boyd. "He said that he went to her house at 11 Sheridan St at approx. 2 p.m. & stayed there all day until approx. 10 pm when he went to Felons Club with Steven—Lorraine's brother."

Seven days of nonstop effort by twenty-one detectives to get Kevin Barry Artt to confess to the Miles murder had yielded nothing. There was no evidence to connect Kevin to the killing—zero.

The stories about Castlereagh had led Kevin to fear torture. But no torture had come.

At about 2:30 p.m., Kevin walked out into the chill of a December afternoon in Belfast, blinking his eyes in the natural light he had not seen in a week.

Charlie McNutt had come to pick him up.

To Kevin's deep surprise, Leslie Fyfe now escorted Kevin out to the parking lot, which lay inside the ten-foot-high brick wall which enclosed the compound. Charlie had parked there, which was out of the ordinary for a civilian coming to pick up a freshly released prisoner. For an RUC constable to walk a suspect out of Castlereagh to the parking lot was unusual too.

Later Kevin learned how this odd occurrence had come about.

Lorraine Keenan had called McNutt, who had called Fyfe. As schoolboys, the two had been friends, and maintained their friendship for years afterward. Fyfe had arranged the special parking privilege as a courtesy to his friend.

In the parking lot, Charlie McNutt and Leslie Fyfe greeted one another warmly, like old friends.

"I was walked out, Charlie McNutt had parked his car, had been allowed to bring this car in the police station at Castlereagh," Kevin recalled. "Mr. Fyfe walked me out. We sat in the car for a few minutes, then Charlie McNutt drove me to his sister's house off the Lisburn Road, where I showered and changed and spent some time with Charlie."

The same evening, or the following evening, Kevin met McNutt, Fyfe, and detective George at a pub, the Crows Nest Lounge in Skipper Street, just off High Street.

Fyfe tried to break the tension, joking about Kevin having lost the buttons of his shirt during interrogation.

"We have to do that sort of thing," Fyfe said. "I'll get ye a new shirt."

Kevin had the same questions any other person would after an arduous week of grilling and insomnia in Castlereagh. *Why am I being questioned about a murder? Why was I arrested in the first place?*

Charlie McNutt had the same questions. He was highly upset.

Fyfe replied that the problem was not the murder. He knew Kevin was innocent.

"I know you have nothing to do with any terrorist crimes of any description," said Fyfe.

It was Kevin's associations with Ace and Lake Glen Construction and some of his taxi passengers, Fyfe said, that were the problem. Security forces arrested people right and left based on nothing more than their associations and everyone knew it. They had done it to Kevin.

Kevin's name was coming up constantly in the computer printouts, in the mix with suspected terrorists, said Fyfe. His passengers were all from the New Lodge and Ardoyne areas. Everybody knew those were hotbeds of militant Republicanism. Some were suspect characters, and some were friends of Kevin's, as the records duly noted. They were undesirables. When security forces pulled Kevin over and asked him if he was taxiing, he always said no, he was just giving friends a lift, to avoid getting prosecuted for illegal hire. But the police and soldiers knew he was lying, Fyfe said. It was common knowledge that Ace drivers did the same thing whenever stopped and questioned. The RUC and Army believed the IRA used Ace to transport men, guns, explosives, and that Lake Glen Construction (for whom Kevin had driven a dump truck) was a front for the Provisionals. Kevin's employment by both implicated him in IRA paramilitary activity.

The security forces had not nailed him yet, Fyfe told Kevin. But they were relentless, and the day would come.

Kevin's question remained. Why had they arrested him for killing Albert Miles?

"Yer name appeared during their inquiries," Fyfe replied. "With all these details on file, they arrested ye as a suspect."

Kevin pressed him for more information. There were thousands of names and other details in police files.

"What made them focus on me?" Kevin asked.

"An informer," said Fyfe. "He's a high-grade informer. But they didn't do their homework properly."

The answers were vague, unsatisfying.

Fyfe's advice was blunt. It came in the form of a little lecture.

"Get the hell out of the New Lodge, Barry," said Fyfe. "Stay out of the Felons Club, all those other shebeens and pubs ye go to. Everybody knows they're IRA hangouts. Ye need to disassociate yourself from Lorraine Keenan–"

Kevin rolled his eyes.

Fyfe continued.

"–Stevie Keenan, Chubby White, John Campbell, all that crowd. No more driving for Ace. Quit Lake Glen Construction too. Otherwise ye can expect just more of the same as ye've been getting."

Kevin returned to his apartment at 371 Antrim Road. There he found the place trashed. RUC men had ransacked it, left drawers open or tossed upside-down on the floor, furniture turned over, the front door left open, the lock broken. The only thing missing was a dress sword. It had belonged to Charlie McNutt's grandfather when he was an admiral in the Royal Navy. Charlie had given the heirloom to Kevin as a gift.

Kevin filed a claim with the RUC over the theft of the sword. No one ever responded to it.

SECTION V

BECOMING THE HUNTED

TWENTY-ONE

They Seen Me, They Stopped Me

Kevin quit drinking in the Felons and in the New Lodge area. He stopped doing a lot of things. He quit Lake Glen Construction. He saw less of Stevie Keenan.

But he still drove for Ace.

On the shifts, things seemed worse.

In January 1979, a stop of Kevin's car was unfolding as usual—constables addressing him by name before seeing his license, a search of the car and all its occupants, the customary questions about everyone's dates of birth, destinations, relationships with Kevin. Before sending Kevin on his way, one of the constables had these parting words.

Ye're a marked man, Artt.

Yer days are numbered, Barry.

We're going to get ye.

Kevin had heard the words before, had shrugged them off. But there was something different about this time. It seemed real, not just bluster.

On a Wednesday night in January 1979, Kevin was headed home to his flat at 371 Antrim Road. A passing patrol of Royal Military Police of C company of the Green Howards (a British Army line infantry regiment) found him on the street just outside the little flat at 11 Sheridan Street and accosted him. It was the usual drill, being made to stand spread-eagled against the wall, asked for information the Army knew well from scores of prior stops, *Fenian scum.*

In 2019, Kevin could not distinguish the conversation clearly from so many others which he had with British soldiers during the late seventies.

What is clear is that at least one soldier slapped Kevin on the right side of his face, punched him in the kidney, and kicked him in the chest, likely after he collapsed to the sidewalk from the kidney punch.

The troops arrested him just before 11:00 p.m.

After transporting Kevin to the Army barracks at the Grand Central Hotel, a corporal filled out the arrest report form. It duly recited the phrase that made the arrest possible under the emergency laws:

> I arrest you under Northern Ireland (Emergency Provisions) Act 1973 Section 11 because I suspect you of being a terrorist.

A military physician, Dr. Ashworth, gave Kevin a cursory examination. His one-page written report noted redness on Kevin's right cheek that began below his right eye and extended to his lower jaw, as well as a bruise over the kidney area that was tender when palpated. Another form noted Kevin's complaint about a soldier having slapped him on the right side of the head.

The soldiers transported Kevin to Castlereagh, where they handed him over to a Sergeant Buchanan before midnight. There officers booked Kevin in, fingerprinted him, strip-searched him, photographed him naked, and arranged a medical examination by the medical officer on duty that night, Dennis Johnston, just after midnight.

Johnston's one-page form noted bruising on the left side of Kevin's chest, which Johnston attributed to Kevin's having been kicked before arriving. Officers escorted Kevin to holding cell G9. Thus began a new three-day stay at Castlereagh, punctuated by ten interviews conducted by rotating two-man teams of detectives. After learning nothing new, they released him, at 2:15 p.m. on January 13.

Kevin wasn't a spoiled kid from Jordanstown anymore. Like many young Catholic men who had experienced abuse at the hands of police in Belfast, he was angry, wanted to do something. He hated seeing the RUC and British Army manhandling his people day and night. Kevin had developed the same secret romantic desire that many other young Catholic men in the north had: to join the IRA.

His rationale was straightforward, patriotic, logical. The British were killing his people. The Army, police, courts, and every other institution except the church were biased against Catholics. The authorities never did anything about it because they were all for it in the first place. Police and helmeted soldiers with blackened faces and big guns stopped and searched you on the street for no reason. They taunted your kid sister every day on her way to school until she wanted to quit school. They arrested you, broke down your door in the middle of the night, came in yelling and brandishing guns, pushed everyone up against the wall, tore up the floorboards, smashed the walls, upended the furniture, called your mother *slut* to her face, called everyone else *Fenian bastards* and *Taigs*, laughed while they did it, told your dad to *shut the fuck up and mind yeur own fucking business, we're doing our jobs*, then got up in your face and sneered at you before leaving, *we'll get ye soon, ye Provie cunt, we'll get ye when ye're seventeen*, and left you to pick up the pieces afterward.

In 1979, Kevin approached a trusted friend and asked his opinion of Kevin's joining the IRA. As a young teen, Kevin's friend had been a part of the Fianna Éireann, marching on the Falls Road in parades commemorating the Easter Rising. Now the friend, like Gerry Kelly and hundreds of others like him, had joined the IRA.

The answer, said Kevin's friend, was no. Kevin was a red light. After years of stops and interrogations, his every detail was known to the police and army. The peelers pulled him over and searched his car every day. They recognized him on sight, had all his particulars, and knew everything about him.

To boot, Kevin was an outsider. He had not grown up in the New Lodge or any other neighborhood like it. He was from a fancy area, Jordanstown, which might as well have been five thousand miles from New Lodge or Ardoyne. The Provisionals had reorganized into small cells intended to minimize British infiltration and damage done by informants. Strangers needed not apply.

To Kevin's friend, the notion that Kevin could be considered a good candidate to join the ranks of the Provisionals was almost ridiculous.

Kevin dropped it. He never raised it again. It was the closest he ever came to joining the IRA.

Jim "Jaz" McCann was an IRA man. In September 1995, he gave a private interview concerning Kevin.

"Kevin was not in the IRA," said McCann.

Notes taken by Kevin's solicitors at Nurse & Jones during a confidential interview of their client in 1979 recorded this: "He is not a member of any illegal organisation . . ."

Nonetheless, as time passed, the RUC and army seemed determined to make Kevin's life more miserable and frightening.

In 1978, the RUC's records reflected 34 stops of Kevin. The number was a small fraction of the true total. In 1979, the number nearly doubled, to 54. Twenty of the stops were in March alone.

RUC logs recorded some of the constables' observations:

> *At 9.00 p.m., a Ford Cortina was stopped at Crumlin Road/Agnes Street. The driver was Artt and the passengers were Emmanuel Burns, John McGreevy, Gerald Small and Edward Taylor.*

At 1.15 a.m. a Ford Cortina, GIA 3587, was stopped on the Antrim Road. The driver was Artt and the passenger was Kieran Mulgrew.
On 31/10/78 Artt was taken in for screening by the military. At 2.15 p.m. Artt was seen driving along North Queen Street in a Ford Cortina, GIA 3587.
Artt was stopped driving a Blu Honda Motorbike, FOI 5360 at New Lodge Road/North Queen Street. His passenger was Stephen Keenan.
Observed outside Ace Taxis Antrim Road in BIL 848 a brown Ford Cortina.
Stopped at Antrim Road in GIA 3587.
Stopped at Cliftonville Road in GIA 387 with Anthony Curley and Thomas Henry.
Seen talking to Lawrence Dowie.
Seen in Donegal Street at 12.50 p.m.

Thinking it would throw them off the trail for a while, Kevin tried selling his car and replacing it with a new one. In what became a serial game of cat-and-mouse, Kevin sold his car and bought a new one, or traded it for a new one, again and again. From January 1979 until November 1981, Kevin owned and drove at least six different vehicles—a Vauxhall Saloon, an Austin 1800, a Honda motorcycle, an N.S.U. Ro 80, a Vauxhall Cavalier, and a Ford Cortina Mark III.

But, after a short spell following each switch, security forces caught up to him and the stops began anew.

In 1979, the Troubles were in their eleventh year, and the end seemed no closer than in 1972. In south Armagh, British Army troops no longer traveled the roads in Jeeps or armored personnel carriers. To avoid IRA land mines and snipers, helicopters ferried them to and from their barracks.

Kevin Barry Artt was not at war. But now it felt like those who sought to bring the war to him were closing in on him.

A UVF newsletter distributed in the staunchly Loyalist Sandy Row area in 1979 displayed a photograph of Kevin, along with photographs of other undesirables. All were police mugshots. Underneath each photograph was the name of the subject. "Watch for these men in your area," read a warning printed below the photographs. "They are known, active Republicans."

How police mugshots had wound up in the hands of the UVF was not explained.

TWENTY-TWO

You Shot the Wrong Man

One day in March 1979, a taxi fare told Kevin that a friend, Peter Heathwood, had just bought a house in the Cliftonville area of north Belfast. Heathwood, said the fare, was looking for a tenant to help defray the mortgage payments.

Peter Heathwood was a 26-year-old insurance salesman who had previously worked as a history teacher. He and his wife, Anne, had three young children. The house was their first. Their family had never had anything to do with the IRA, and the RUC had never set foot inside.

Kevin approached Heathwood about renting a room. The house was located at 187 Cliftonpark Avenue in north Belfast. The Heathwoods had remodeled it to house two or three tenants. There were locks on the doors and a second-floor kitchen meant for a renter. The neighborhood was a mixed area, with both Catholic and Protestant families. It lay in the heart of the murder triangle, just northwest of the jail and courthouse on Crumlin Road, where Kevin often drove his shifts for Ace. Peter's father had warned Peter not to buy a house in the murder triangle. Peter had reassured him, telling him that he had visited with a parish priest who told Peter that things had "quietened down" in the wake of the recent arrests of the Shankill Butchers.

The Heathwoods interviewed Kevin. He told them he was a taxi driver. There was no discussion of politics. Kevin assumed that the Heathwoods were Catholic. They were. Peter did not tell Kevin what he did for a living and Kevin did not ask. The parties agreed quickly on terms.

Kevin signed a lease, then moved in early during the month of September 1979.

"He was quiet," Anne Heathwood later remembered. "A taxi man."

The house was a three-story, red brick, side-by-side duplex. There were large bay windows on the first and second floors. A low brick wall topped by a wrought iron railing separated a tiny garden from the asphalt sidewalk in front. A dormer window with a gabled roof protruded from a pitched slate roof on the third floor. The Heathwoods occupied the ground floor and part of the second floor—half of the house. The other half, rented to Kevin, consisted of a second-floor kitchen and bathroom and third-floor bedroom. The dormer window afforded him a view of the street.

September 27, 1979 was a Thursday. The country was abuzz with news of the impending visit of Pope John Paul II, who was scheduled to arrive in Ireland on Saturday. Peter was planning on taking his mother and dad down to Drogheda to try to catch a glimpse of the pontiff.

At around 6:00 p.m., Kevin arrived home from a taxi shift. He parked his car, a brown Ford Cortina, in the street, just in front of the house, half on the sidewalk. It was starting to get dark, but there was still light outside. Kevin entered through the front door, then through the half-glass, half-wood vestibule door just inside. He went straight upstairs to the second floor. There he went into the bathroom and shut the door, then sat down on the toilet.

Peter's plan had been to work late at his office in Lisburn, just over nine miles away, that evening. But Anne called him and said she had made one of his favorite dishes, shepherd's pie, a meat pie made with mashed potato. Peter changed his plans and came home early. He figured he would return to the office after dinner and finish his work.

The doorbell rang.

"I'll get it," said Anne.

Anne opened the door. There stood two young men in "snorkel" coats, waterproof coats with hoods and fur on the collars. One carried a pistol in his hand.

"Gunmen, gunmen!" Anne screamed. "There's a Provie in here!"

Anne tried to shut the front door. The two men muscled it open and forced their way inside. Anne scrambled backward, toward the living room. She opened the door to it, to warn Peter, who was inside. One of the men declared, "There's a wee Provie bastard in here and we want him!"

Fear shot through Kevin. Instinctively, he knew the gunmen had come for him.

With his pants still down, he sprang out of the bathroom and looked down the stairs to see if anyone was coming up the stairs. His mind raced a step ahead. If the gunmen came up the stairs, he thought, he would go straight out the bathroom window, jump down into the front garden, and run.

Downstairs, the first man through the door had grabbed Anne. He had her by the hair. Peter did not hesitate.

"It was the 1970s," Peter recalled later. "You knew nobody was messing."

Peter was big and powerful, an athlete, proficient at his favorite sport, handball. Like a linebacker at a ballcarrier, he launched himself at the man manhandling Anne, managed to free her, and pushed the man back out through the door while Peter's son, Patrick, age six, gamely kicked the man in the shins. Peter's five-year-old daughter, Anne-Marie, was nearby. However terrifying the scene must have been, she did not try to flee.

Peter saw a second armed man. He scooped up Anne-Marie and retreated into the living room, then slammed its door shut behind him, to separate himself from the man. The door had frosted glass panels.

Peter saw three muzzle flashes and an explosion of glass but heard no sound. The gunman had fired through the frosted glass panel in the door that separated the hallway from the living room, over Anne-Marie's head.

Everything went black.

Upstairs, Kevin had heard the slam of the living room door and the shots, which sounded like cracks. He heard Anne screaming. Kevin ran down the hall and up the stairs to the third floor, to the very top of the house, and into his bedroom. There he ran to the small window which looked out on the street. He saw two men in snorkel coats running away, with their backs to him.

They ran up Cliftonville Road toward Manor Street and out of sight.

Kevin rushed downstairs. There he found Anne hysterical. Peter lay on the floor, face down, wounded in the arm and shoulder, with foam coming from his mouth. Two rounds had ripped into Heathwood's upper body, splintering nine ribs, and shredding a lung. There were shards of glass, but no blood, on the floor. Peter's three-month-old baby daughter, Louise, was alongside him. Kevin thought of rolling Peter over but feared making Peter's condition even worse. Heathwood was breathing deeply, moaning that he was dying.

Kevin lunged for the phone. He dialed 999 and summoned police and an ambulance. Kevin feared Peter was dying in front of his family on the floor.

Kevin knelt over Peter, praying that he wouldn't die, telling him he was going to be all right and that he should hang on because the ambulance was on its way. Kevin asked Peter where he was hit. Peter was moaning, incoherent. He could not form an intelligible response. The bullet which had caused the shoulder wound had ricocheted off Heathwood's clavicle and severed his spinal cord.

Twenty-five minutes later, a gaggle of RUC men, some in uniform and some in plain clothes, arrived. British soldiers accompanied them. The constables had come from the North Queen Street station, which was less than a mile away, a five-minute drive. One of them was Norman Cromie.

Cromie and his colleagues walked in lackadaisical, nonchalant. Their ambling, casual manner irritated Kevin immediately. He wondered how they could be so blasé. Their body language did not suggest arrival at the scene of a shooting and medical emergency. Instead, it said, *ho hum.* To Anne Heathwood, it looked like the cops were just arriving at a party. They were laughing and joking. Not one of them made a move to radio for an ambulance.

One of the RUC men walked up to the spot where Peter lay. He placed a foot alongside the head, then looked down at Peter.

Who the fuck's he? the constable exclaimed.

On making eye contact with Kevin, the constables' eyes widened. They were shocked—not at the sight of a paralyzed and bleeding Peter Heathwood on the floor, but at the sight of an upright and uninjured Kevin Barry Artt.

"You shot the wrong man," said one of the RUC men. "Artt lives upstairs."

TWENTY-THREE

We'll Get Ye Next Time

Only after seeing Kevin did the police begin to act like there was a real emergency and radio for an ambulance. Instantly their body language transformed from cavalier indifference to urgent professionalism.

The ambulance got there five to ten minutes later. Peter Heathwood had been lying on the living room floor, grievously wounded, for over a half an hour. A priest arrived from the family's parish, Sacred Heart, and administered last rites.

The paramedics tried to muscle a gurney through the front door, but it was too narrow. They improvised a stretcher out of a body bag and loaded Peter onto it. Kevin, taking up the rear, helped three of them start carrying him out to the ambulance.

Once outside the front door, Kevin saw the paramedics stepping over something on the curb, just outside the little gate that separated the sidewalk from the house's front garden. As he neared the gate, he saw what it was: a pair of legs, horizontal, on the ground. Kevin stepped over the legs, noticing that whoever they belonged to had soiled his pants.

The legs belonged to Herbert Heathwood, Peter Heathwood's father, age 64. He had arrived minutes earlier from his home at Fitzroy Avenue off the Ormeau Road, two and a half miles away, summoned by Anne's frantic phone call from the house. Previously, he had suffered from angina. Tonight, just as he rushed through the little gate, just before Kevin and the paramedics had carried Peter out the front door, he had collapsed on the ground, stricken by a massive heart attack.

Kevin stepped over Herbert Heathwood's body while carrying the limp body of his son, Peter, to the ambulance. The ambulance crew tried to revive Herbert using CPR, but he was dead.

The ambulance sped off. Kevin went back inside. He found Anne, who was by now dazed and glassy-eyed. There were at least eight RUC men inside: two superintendents (Boyle and Hood), Cromie, and Constables Hamill, Jordan, Reid, Ritchie, and Wann. They had decided to forego interviewing Anne for the time being. They figured it was pointless given her state. Neither Peter nor Kevin knew it, but one of the constables, Cromie, was a member of the Special Branch's E4A unit, notorious for involvement in extrajudicial killings of Republican suspects.

Kevin escorted Anne and the children outside to his car. He loaded them in and started driving them to Anne's parents' home. He dropped them there, then turned around and returned after Anne remembered she had forgotten a cot (or baby's crib) and blankets. By now there was police tape out in front. Detectives allowed him in. Cromie asked Kevin if he had seen what happened. Kevin said no. He told Cromie what he had heard and seen. Cromie asked him to go to the RUC station at North Queen Street, to make a statement. Kevin promised he would do so after dropping off the cot and blankets to Anne and the children.

After dropping off the crib and blankets, a stunned Kevin headed back north, to the RUC's North Queen Street station, at the bottom of the New Lodge Road. As he drove, he could not believe what had just happened.

Why would anyone want to kill me?

He parked and went inside. A detective invited him into an interview room and shut the door. The man was heavy-set, with dark, greying hair, in his late forties. He did not identify himself. He sat on the desk, leaned forward, and put his face an inch away from Kevin's.

That was meant for ye, Artt, you bastard, and I'm fucking sorry they didn't get ye, the detective snarled.

By now Kevin was in no mood to give a statement. He had not yet even had time to sit down. He stormed out and left the station. He did not recognize the detective or know who he was.

Getting hassled by RUC men and soldiers during traffic stops was one thing. Getting shot at was a new one.

At the Mater Hospital, Peter Heathwood lay on a gurney as doctors tried to stabilize him. One of them inserted a chest tube into Peter's lungs, which had filled with fluid. As he drifted into unconsciousness, Peter hallucinated an image of his father at the foot of the gurney, looking upward and beseeching God to take him instead of Peter.

Kevin drove to the hospital. By the time he arrived, Peter was in the intensive care unit, unconscious. Kevin found Anne sitting at her husband's bedside. Anne told Kevin it was his fault that her husband was paralyzed. Police had told her the hit was meant for Kevin.

Norman Cromie arrived soon afterward. He seemed oblivious to Anne's presence. He greeted Kevin, then related the moment when the call had come in to North Queen Street that someone had been shot at 187 Cliftonville Road.

Let's have champagne, Cromie had said to his fellow constables. *We got Artt.*

His colleagues had greeted the news with cheers, Cromie said.

Cromie slapped Kevin on the shoulder and called him a bastard.

We'll get ye next time, he added.

"Fuck off," Kevin replied angrily.

Anne Heathwood, who was standing there, heard the exchange.

Afterward, the RUC assigned a detective to head up the investigation into the Heathwood shooting. It was Norman Cromie.

The *Belfast Telegraph* covered the incident in an article published the following day, September 28, 1979. The story noted the dreadful duty that awaited Anne when Peter woke up: breaking the news to him that he would never walk again, and his father was dead.

A few weeks later, a terse entry appeared in the classified ads of a bulletin published in Belfast. It identified the author as the Woodvale Defence Association, a Loyalist vigilante group who operated in the Woodvale area of Belfast, to the north of the Shankill Road. In the ad, the WDA claimed responsibility for the Heathwood shooting. There was an apology and an explanation. The shooting had been a case of mistaken identity, it said.

A Protestant friend of John Artt brought the newspaper to John's garage on the Ballysillan Road. Kevin was there. He read the ad. Though his name did not appear, it was plain who had been targeted: him. The gunmen had lain in wait, timing their attack for a few moments after Kevin arrived at home. They had missed him by a few seconds.

TWENTY-FOUR

We're Out to Get Ye

Kevin Barry Artt and Carmen Myers were to be married on November 3, 1979.

The night before the wedding, Kevin and his best man, Paul Fennell, went to pick up rented tuxedos. Fennell was the husband of Carmen's sister, Georgie Myers. The two planned to go directly to Kevin's bachelor party after picking up the suits. Well aware of the happy occasion, the British Army was waiting. Four soldiers accosted the two young men. One, grinning, addressed Kevin, in an English accent.

'ello, Barry. Section 14. Let's go.

After letting Fennell go, the soldiers hauled Kevin off in a Jeep to the Grand Central Hotel Army base on Royal Avenue, in the center of Belfast, where they arrived at 11:25 p.m. There was no interrogation nor any reason for the arrest given. The soldiers laughed and jeered at Kevin about his nuptials.

You're not gettin' married tomorrow, Kevin, said one. *We're going to keep you here.*

After two hours or so, the troops released Kevin, leaving him to walk to the bachelor party in the rain. By the time he arrived, the groomsmen had abandoned any pretense of awaiting the guest of honor before getting things started.

They were all pretty well inebriated and they gave Kevin a rousing welcome.

Kevin and Carmen married the next day, November 3, 1979, at the Myers family's parish church, Holy Family Church, on Limestone Road in north Belfast. The old stone church stood a few blocks northeast of the murder triangle. Beneath the joyous facade, there was tension. Kevin's family viewed him as having married beneath him and hanging out with the wrong people. Carmen was three months pregnant with the couple's son.

Kevin and Carmen moved to a three-room apartment at 18 Cliftonville Avenue in north Belfast. British Army foot patrols routinely passed through the neighborhood. Often, they entered the flat, where they would "shuffle about the place."

During the first or second quarter of 1980, Kevin employed a painter, Thomas O'Halloran, to do some painting and wallpapering in his flat on the Antrim Road, in exchange for free rides in Kevin's car. O'Halloran worked on the job for about two and a half days. After finishing, O'Halloran departed.

Shortly after he left the flat, uniformed RUC constables in a Land Rover stopped him. One of the constables asked O'Halloran why he had been at Kevin's flat.

"I've been doin' work there," O'Halloran replied.

It's silly for ye to be workin' there, said the constable. *Artt will be dead soon anyway.*

O'Halloran understood the comment to mean what had seemed obvious to Kevin for months: his details had found their way from the hands of police to Loyalist paramilitaries, who would use them to hunt down and assassinate him. O'Halloran made no reply. The RUC men drove off. Later, O'Halloran reported to Kevin what he had heard.

Carmen gave birth to the couple's son, Barry Paul, on April 18, 1980, naming him after Kevin and Pope Paul VI.

Later that month, constables told Kevin to report to the RUC's Tennent Street station, just off the Crumlin Road, adjacent to the upper Shankill Road. The neighborhood was a Loyalist enclave.

For a Catholic, it was a dodgy area, not safe to enter.

When Kevin arrived, an officer ushered him into a room. A detective inspector Irwin entered and introduced himself. He told Kevin the RUC had raided the home of a Loyalist paramilitary. The ensuing search had yielded a cache of handguns and ammunition. Among the material they seized, police had also found Kevin's "details"—his movements, his car, where he lived, places he frequented.

"Can I see what you found?" Kevin asked.

"No," said Irwin. "It's not allowed."

"What paramilitary organization did the man belong to?"

"The Woodvale Defence Association," Irwin replied.

The name rang a bell. Woodvale was a well-known Loyalist enclave at the top of the Shankill Road, just beyond Ardoyne. The WDA had taken responsibility for shooting Peter Heathwood a few months earlier and apologized for missing their intended target, Kevin Barry Artt.

Kevin wanted more details. Irwin refused to give them.

The RUC had tormented Kevin for three years. It now managed the single gesture of concern it ever showed him.

Irwin's memo followed on April 9, 1980. It read:

> During January of this year, I received information that a Loyalist paramilitary group intended to assassinate Barry Artt. The address, however, known to the organization was 371 Antrim Road, Belfast.
>
> Artt, who was informed of the matter for his own safety, was living at the time of my contact with him at 18 Cliftonville Avenue. His previous address was 371 Antrim Road.

A functionary at the Housing Executive had added a note on the bottom of the memo:

A1 status is approved in this case in view of the RUC report. Rehouse with urgency within area of choice.

Kevin thanked Irwin and left.

Later, a chief inspector Nesbitt signed a form agreeing with Irwin's recommendation.

Kevin quit Ace at last. The money was good. But with every passing day Kevin felt more like a marked man. Shortly before he quit, persons unknown had left a bomb on a window grill at the Ace depot. The manager summoned police. They managed to defuse the device. Kevin was on his shift, having just left on a taxi run.

Kevin was a married man with a wife and baby. He needed a lower profile. He picked up a series of jobs: driving a van for Table Ready Meats, driving a dump truck on a building site, working for a stone mason, Robert Hart.

To the RUC and Army, it mattered not. Their treatment of Kevin only escalated. Soldiers kept arresting him, taking him to one barracks or another, and cutting him loose after the last minute of the fourth hour, the maximum period allowed under the emergency laws. The barracks were all over Belfast: Girdwood, Flag Street, Royal Avenue, North Queen Street, Henry Taggart. Kevin became familiar with each one.

During one stop of Kevin's Ford Cortina, officers ripped the car apart while Kevin stood spread-eagled against it. His passenger, one-time roommate Fergie Ferguson, watched from the sidewalk as a constable pressed the muzzle of his weapon to the back of Kevin's head.

"You're going on a ten-year vacation, Barry," the constable whispered into Kevin's ear. "Better watch your back."

"'78 to '81 was a tough period," remembered Kevin's friend Al Sloan in 1996. "The cops were allowed to go wild."

TWENTY-FIVE

Run

Al Sloan and Kevin had known one another since about 1976, when they met at John Artt's garage, where Kevin was then working. Sloan had a few convictions—for stealing a car, for assault, for fighting. Except for one weekend, he had never been to jail.

It was December 29, 1980, a couple of nights before New Year's Eve. It had been eight months since detective inspector Irwin of the RUC had warned Kevin of a Loyalist paramilitary threat on his life.

In the little flat on Cliftonville Avenue, Kevin and Al were enjoying some drinks and company—Carmen, Al's brother George, Stephanie Myers (who was also Carmen's cousin), and a few of Carmen's friends, among them Bobby Thompson, his girlfriend, and Pat Thornton. It was a bit of a party. People were just hanging out, socializing.

Around 1:00 a.m., or maybe a little later, Sloan bid his friends good night. He had promised his brother he would babysit for him. He had not drunk any alcohol. Kevin offered to accompany him down to a nearby Chinese restaurant on the Antrim Road, where there was a phone. There the friends could have a late snack and Sloan could call a taxi after they finished. The place was about three blocks away.

Like many flats in Belfast at the time, Kevin's lacked its own telephone.

The two men walked down toward a T intersection, where Brookvale Avenue met Cliftonville Avenue. It was cold and dark. The streets were utterly deserted, "not a sinner around." The two men could see their breath as the water vapor in their exhalations came in contact with the frigid air.

As they reached the corner, a car passed them–a Morris Marina, a four-door sedan, painted red or orange, not uncommon colors for a car in Belfast at the time, with no police markings. After driving about fifty yards past them, the driver slammed on the brakes. The car came to a screeching halt. The driver shifted into reverse and hit the gas. The wheels spun, smoke rose from the pavement.

The car barreled back toward them, at high speed.

Both men spied the barrel of a machine gun poking out of the driver's side back window, which was all the way down, to their left. There were four men inside the car.

In Belfast, if someone pointed a gun at you, you ran.

Kevin, his eyes wide, turned to Sloan.

"Run," he said.

TWENTY-SIX

Discreditable Conduct

A man scrambled out of the car with a pistol in his right hand. He started chasing Kevin. Al bolted straight back toward the front door of 18 Cliftonville Avenue.

"We ran like fuck," remembered Al Sloan in 1996.

Kevin dashed in the opposite direction, sprinted away from the flat, down toward the alley that straddled Cliftonville Avenue and Brookhill Avenue. Before turning right at Brookhill, he glanced back and caught a glimpse of his pursuer. The man chasing him was wearing an Afghan coat –a piece of civilian attire, "kind of a hippie coat." It billowed out behind him as he chased Kevin.

Kevin reached Brookhill Avenue, then turned right, back in the direction of the flat, and kept on going, past a row of derelict houses. He reckoned on getting back into the flat through the back.

He ran as fast as he could.

"I got the speed of light," Kevin remembered. It was the sight of the gun that gave it to him. "Nothing like a guy with a gun chasing you to motivate your legs to move."

As Kevin passed the backs of the houses, he saw a vacant lot, where the house had been razed. Kevin ran across it.

Al had sprinted directly to the front door of the flat. The driver, still driving in reverse, chased him, trying to catch up and draw even with him. Al could hear the car's engine racing as it drew nearer.

The front door was ajar. Al feared being shot at any second. His fight-or-flight response had kicked in. The car drew parallel with him, then slowed down. Al glimpsed several long rifles inside.

Al burst through the front door, which swung inward. Ahead of him, the vestibule door was closed. Like many such doors in Belfast, its top half featured a see-through glass panel.

There was no time to fiddle with it. Al did not break stride. He heard the car's engine racing behind him.

He went horizontal and dove headfirst through the glass panel, shattering it. The glass was old-fashioned glass, not safety glass which cubed when broken. It was a quarter of an inch thick. The jagged edges lacerated Al's face from nose to forehead. Al's momentum carried him through the top half of the door and into a heap on the floor.

As Kevin sprinted, he felt like his heart was going into tachycardia. On the fly, he invented a plan to get back inside the flat, through the back. In the street, he had gotten a head start on the man in the Afghan coat. Maybe the man had not made the corner in time to see Kevin duck down the alley. He thought he might have a chance to slip inside unseen by his pursuer.

There was a wooden fence about six feet high separating the back of the house from the alley. The fence had a gate with a latch. Kevin decelerated, then flipped the latch up, opened the gate, stepped inside, and shut it behind him. He heard glass shattering inside the house, not knowing it was the sound of Al Sloan's head going through the vestibule door.

For a moment, Kevin listened for footsteps but heard nothing. He guessed he might have given the man in the Afghan coat the slip. Little jets of steam emanated from his mouth as he panted in the cold. Then he heard the orange Marina zoom through the alley.

Kevin peered through the slats of the gate. He spied the car as it passed. It slowed down, then stopped, where the alley met the street. The man in the Afghan coat walked up to the driver's side window and exchanged a few words with the driver.

Kevin crept up alongside the house in the dark, through the side garden toward the front of the house. There was a hedge parallel to the house. It provided some cover. Kevin heard the engine of the Morris Marina again, returning from a spin around the block. Now the car reappeared in the street in front of the house.

Kevin felt invisible to the men in the car. He did not have his keys on him. He kicked in the side door. It led to the main hallway. There Kevin saw shattered glass and blood on the floor. Al was there, bleeding from his face. He stumbled into the living room. Kevin went in after him. Everyone in there was oblivious, still having a drink, when the two entered.

Everybody's eyes widened as they looked up at the bloody Al and the out-of-breath Kevin.

"There is somebody out there trying to shoot us, me and Barry!" Sloan cried as blood streamed down his face.

Carmen and Kevin's friends jumped up and started streaming out into the street. They saw four or five men in the Marina. Everyone was nervous, confused, upset, wondering what the hell was going on. The Marina idled in the street. George Sloan's wife strode fearlessly up to it and opened one of its doors. Out fell a bottle onto the pavement. Other vehicles had gathered as well. Suddenly the street seemed full of cars. Someone had called the police. Some of Kevin's friends started arguing with the men in the car.

Kevin emerged in the driveway. There was a lot of commotion going on. He saw an RUC officer, half in civilian clothing and half in uniform, taking up a position on a nearby corner, as though he were a lookout.

A marked RUC Land Rover rolled up. Four RUC men in plain clothes piled out of it. Three went straight to the orange car and started questioning the men inside. One of them was the man in the Afghan coat. Carmen spied a bottle of booze in the car. The fourth RUC man approached Kevin and flashed a badge. He said the men in the orange car were cops. Kevin took down his badge number.

Kevin and Sloan kept looking at the occupants of the car. They had not gotten out or identified themselves. They wore civilian coats. Peering inside the car, Kevin and Sloan spied black boots and bottle-green pants. They were the uniform pants worn by RUC men.

Before and after their shifts, RUC officers sometimes wore civilian jackets or anoraks over their tunics while driving unmarked vehicles, to reduce the likelihood of being identified as police and possibly becoming targets for attack by the IRA.

One of the plain clothes RUC men from the Land Rover now approached Kevin.

"Who the fuck are those guys?" said Kevin.

I understand ye're upset, said the man, who appeared to be a sergeant. *They're part of an undercover group, looking for car thieves.*

"Car thieves, my ass," said Kevin, disgusted.

It was improvised bullshit. Kevin was angry and amped up. He walked up to the driver's side window of the Marina and leaned down to look at the driver.

"Excuse me, sir," Kevin said. "Can I see your identification, please?"

Fuck off, said the man.

Kevin started writing down the car's license plate number. Some of the men standing there warned Kevin they were going to arrest him for writing down the license plate number of a police vehicle.

The Land Rover officers went back to the Marina and huddled near the driver's side window. They had a few more words with the men inside. Then the Marina drove off into the night. Elapsed time from the arrival of the Land Rover and the departure of the orange car was about a minute.

When the police had finished questioning everyone, they told Al and Kevin they would have to come down to the station and give statements to police. They said what had happened was a "routine check" and that Kevin and Sloan had aroused suspicion by having run.

The officers got into the Land Rover, drove off, and disappeared.

Kevin took Sloan to the Mater Hospital. He was woozy from the blow to his head and bleeding heavily from the nose.

To Kevin, the episode reinforced what he already knew: he was a target, and his would-be assassins were police. It was well-known at the time that off-duty RUC men sometimes assassinated Catholic civilians. Now some of them had come after him. They'd been unable to get a clear shot at him before on-duty RUC men arrived. Then they'd invented a bullshit story for investigators, about looking for car thieves, having seen a couple of guys running, and giving chase.

Kevin figured his days were numbered.

The next day, December 30, 1980, at the urging of Paddy Devlin, a politician who was a friend of Carmen's father, Kevin went to the Old Park RUC police station, to file a complaint. The station was at the intersection of Cliftonville Road and Old Park Road, beside Ardoyne. Kevin turned in the complaint to an inspector, one T.A. Turkington.

It was two-and-a-half pages long. It named Norman Cromie as one of the officers who had been present.

"I'd like to file a complaint, please," Kevin said at the counter.

Turkington and the other constables laughed out loud.

Later, Turkington noted the nature of the complaint: "discreditable conduct."

Years later, the British produced a copy of the RUC's file concerning the incident. It was dated August 31, 1981. It noted the names of four officers: Montgomery (a constable), Verner (a constable), Houston (a sergeant), and Graham (a constable). The four men in the car may have been Loyalist paramilitaries when they were off duty. There was no question about their day jobs. They were RUC men.

The file recorded the disposition of Kevin's complaint of December 30, 1980. No action was taken. It noted that Kevin Artt, the complainant, had been duly informed of the outcome, on October 8, 1981. (He had not.)

No one ever told Kevin Artt why four officers of the RUC tried to chase him and kill him on the night of December 29, 1980.

On the night of April 3, 1981, Kevin left Carmen and Barry Paul at home and attended a charity dance at the Polio Fellowship Hall on the Antrim Road with his brother-in-law, Paul Fennell, alongside. Shortly after 1 a.m., Kevin and Paul decided to call it a night and started walking. Two RUC Land Rovers came alongside and slowed. One of the windows rolled down.

All right, Barry, where ye going tonight?

"Home," Kevin replied, looking straight ahead, not breaking stride.

I don't think so, Barry. Ye're coming with us.

"I'm busy," Kevin replied.

Out came five constables. They descended on Kevin, grabbing him roughly.

Inside Kevin, something snapped. He had had enough. This time, he was not going to go easily. This was bullshit. Kevin resisted.

Out came the batons. From behind, one of the constables hit Kevin in the head with his baton, causing Kevin to black out and fall.

He came to just as the officers were putting him into the back of a Jeep. In a daze, Kevin started struggling. Now the RUC men rained baton blows and fists on Kevin.

Kevin later compared the beating to what Rodney King had endured at the hands of the LAPD that night in Los Angeles.

Kevin fought. He was dizzy from the blow to his head, but his adrenaline was surging.

In the melee, he and a small cluster of constables wound up on the hood of one of the Land Rovers. Kevin tried to use their bodies to shield himself from more baton strikes. It was a full-on brawl, a cluster of men swinging and grabbing and shouting and cursing.

Kevin rolled off the hood. In the scrum on the ground, with constables all over him, Kevin bit one of them on the thigh.

The swarm of constables finally got control of Kevin. They stood him up, handcuffed him, and threw him in the back of the Land Rover, with his feet near the door. When they tried to come in after him, Kevin kicked at them, using his feet to try to keep them out. A constable managed to jump inside and on top of Kevin. Two or three more soon joined.

The constables put Paul Fennell in the other Land Rover, and the little motorcade headed for the RUC police station at Fort William.

They rode to the police station with Kevin lying on his back on the floorboard of the Land Rover and three or four constables on top of him. It felt like they were crushing him. Kevin's head was bleeding and throbbing with pain.

After moving him to York Road police station, the constables allowed him to see a doctor. The doctor found eighteen contusions inflicted by batons and a large laceration on Kevin's head.

On the form he used to record the results of his examination, the physician wrote: "obviously injured

. . . must not be <u>detained</u> he must go to <u>HOSPITAL</u>. . . This patient has extensive injuries. HE MUST GO TO HOSPITAL <u>NOW</u> to have his head X rayed and stitched."

Soon afterward, Kevin filed a complaint at the York Road RUC station.

In August 1982, officers' notes duly recorded the results of the ensuing investigation: nothing. In the box labeled "means by which complainant has been told of result," no marks appeared. None of the officers who beat him up ever faced any charges or discipline. In the meantime, police charged Kevin with disorderly behavior and assaulting constables Samuel McCann and William Woods.

While Kevin was still recovering from his injuries, and after a year and a half of waiting for secure housing, the little family moved out of the Cliftonville Avenue flat and into the last house they would ever inhabit as a family, at 12 Marsden Gardens, in the Fortwilliam district. The flat sat on the top level of a six-unit building at the back of a cul-de-sac off the Cavehill Road. The area was safe, low-profile, about a mile and a half northwest of the New Lodge. Most of the neighbors were older. The Northern Ireland Housing Executive, a government agency, owned the building. The front door was a security door. Kevin reinforced it in case gunmen should try to break it down.

Not everyone got notice of the move.

One evening soon after the move, there came a knock at the door of the Cliftonville Avenue flat.

The new tenant, a woman, opened the door. There stood a masked man wielding a pistol. Without a word, the man strode past her into the house. Other people were there—her husband, a few friends. At the sight of the man, they froze, sitting and standing in their places.

The gunman moved through the ground floor. His demeanor bespoke authority and casualness, as though he might be a police officer. He stalked around, from room to room, as though hunting for someone. Then he left without firing a shot or saying a word, as abruptly as he had appeared.

SECTION VI

CASTLEREAGH 1981

TWENTY-SEVEN

If I Help Youse, Will Youse Help Me?

In 1981, Christopher Black was a twenty-six-year-old IRA man from the Catholic ghetto of Ardoyne in north Belfast. He had left school in 1970, at age fifteen, and joined the Provisionals in 1975. Afterward he underwent training in the use of firearms at an IRA camp in Donegal. Later, he participated in a number of operations. He handled, moved, and used firearms in Belfast, took over homes from residents at gunpoint when his comrades needed a house from which to operate, and helped plant bombs.

Before 1981, Black had not fared well in his paramilitary ventures. In 1975, the same year in which he joined the IRA, police arrested him for armed robbery. He served five years in the Maze. One of his fellow IRA prisoners, Anthony McIntyre, recalled Black as a "bit of a bully" who "found his time very hard to do."

In November 1981, Black and a pair of brothers named Jimmy and Kevin Donnelly set up a roadblock in the Brompton Park neighborhood of Ardoyne. The roadblock was meant to show the IRA's intent to protect the neighborhood from Loyalist thugs who might retaliate against residents for the IRA's assassination of Unionist politician Robert Bradford days earlier. The men had three rifles and two handguns among them. Black had drunk most of a bottle of vodka the night before. He was hungover and feeling ill.

Black and the Donnellys spent perhaps twenty minutes operating their brazen Provie show of force before disappearing without security forces descending on them. A government truck belonging to the Department of the Environment was the last vehicle allowed through the roadblock before the men dispersed. Possibly its driver was the one who phoned in a report of the spectacle of masked men in broad daylight brandishing rifles, stopping vehicles, and asking drivers for their identification before letting them through.

Had they gone straight home or lain low elsewhere, Black and the Donnellys might have gotten away with it. Instead, they decided to hit the pubs in the Marrowbone neighborhood and spread the word about their exploits.

Police intercepted the three and escorted them straight to Castlereagh.

A mugshot taken at Castlereagh on November 14, 1981, shows a slight, dark-haired man with a broad mustache. A bushy hairstyle recalls Arnold Horshack of TV's "Welcome Back, Kotter." Black stares glumly at the camera, straight into the lens.

Detectives went to work on Black starting on the morning of November 22. After several more sessions which stretched from 11 a.m. until 8:30 p.m., detectives kept Black in interview room BF 2 for over ten uninterrupted hours overnight.

The conversation evolved as many such conversations do. Black went fishing for a deal.

"If I help youse, will youse help me?" he asked.

The detectives cocked their heads, listening.

"If I admit me part, will youse keep me right?"

Black needed some help.

He was married, with four young children at home, and a deadbeat, who owed money all over town. Of late, he had been reduced to borrowing cash from his mother. He nursed a drinking habit at watering holes in the Bone and Ardoyne neighborhoods. He was facing a slew of charges, including for the Julian Connolly murder, that could send him to the Maze for life.

Another session started at 8:30 p.m. on the evening of November 23. It went until nearly 8 a.m. the following morning. Time elapsed during the sessions now exceeded thirty-eight hours. Black felt exhausted, disoriented, desperate.

Black wanted two things from the detectives: all charges against him dropped, and a guarantee of security for his family.

The answer was yes.

By the end of the day on November 24, 1981, and before making any statement incriminating anyone other than himself, Black and the RUC had struck a pact which was unprecedented in both generosity and scale. The terms were lavish: full immunity from prosecution, guaranteed payments in cash, relocation of himself and his family overseas, and the British equivalent of placement in the U.S. federal witness protection program. For a suspect-turned-traitor, it was the informant's sweetheart deal of all time.

To earn it, all Black had to do was go Queen's Evidence and testify as the detectives wanted.[3]

Overnight, Black's debts vanished.

In the meantime, a small, innocuous-looking form gave a glimpse of the deal. A Sergeant Hamilton of the RUC signed the form, entitled "Release/Removal from Police Custody," at 9:10 p.m. on November 24, 1981.

"NO CHARGE," it read.

While Hamilton filled out the form, Black visited with his wife and mother-in-law. They must have been stunned to

---

3. The U.S. equivalent of going Queen's evidence was "turning state's evidence," choosing to reveal evidence to prosecutors in exchange for reduction or dismissal of charges.

hear the news of what had happened to the pale, disheveled man whose name and image would become infamous in the north for decades afterward.

To Black's captors, the problem which soon emerged was the volume of what he knew. It was slim. Black was able to relate a single instance of murder (Julian Connolly's), a wounding, and a handful of false imprisonments, in which IRA men had temporarily occupied local houses for the purpose of shooting at police or soldiers from inside.

It was no problem, the detectives decided. The DPP and RUC were desperate to smash the IRA in west and north Belfast. Black could prove an able and eager instrument in the venture. They could send him to school, immerse him in data—names, dates, places, and incidents, all meticulously recorded in the files that filled yards of shelf space inside Castlereagh. Black could be made to digest and regurgitate it convincingly in court when the time came. He could be made into a kind of ventriloquist's dummy or stage actor. If he remembered his lines and hit his marks, he would earn his keep.

Detectives started taking Black on a whirlwind tour of the interview rooms in Castlereagh. In each one sat a hapless suspect and a pair of detectives. Black was dressed in a pair of jeans, with his shirttail hanging out. He looked full of dope, sleepless, exhausted. One of the men who escorted Black on the tour was well-known to Kevin Barry Artt. It was Norman Cromie.

In each interview room, Black answered a series of perfunctory questions put to him in front of the supposed accomplice seated there.

Many of them had never met Black. It didn't matter.

Do ye recognize this suspect as Patrick Markey?
Yes.
Do ye recognize this man as an IRA member?
Yes.

And was this man involved in a shooting in the Oldpark area?
Yes.
Then detectives would lead Black out again. On and on it went.
Is this the man known as Gerard Loughlin?
Yes.
Is this the man that's a member of the IRA?
Yes.
Is this the man that planned the murder of the UDR man?
Yes.

On November 26 and 27, Black answered, "yes," at least twenty times, fingering Desmond Breslin, James Copeland, Samuel Graham, Paul Kane, Gerard Loughlin, Patrick Markey, Tommy Prendergast, Joseph Walsh, Anthony Barnes, Arthur Corbett, Jackie Donnelly, Patrick Fennell, Joseph Kelly, Peter Lagan, Anthony McIlkenny, Roger McKiernan, Paul Mulvenna, Paul O'Neill, and Patrick Teer. It was as if detectives had compiled a list of males from Ardoyne or New Lodge who had a record of conviction for a terrorism-related offense, fed the names to Black, and asked him to implicate each one. Black did so. When he expressed puzzlement at a given name, the detectives told him not to worry.

He could learn the facts later. There would be plenty of time for that.

In the early morning hours of the next day, the RUC raided dozens of homes, concentrating on the Ardoyne, Bone, and Newington areas of Catholic north Belfast, arresting thirty-eight suspects.

The RUC and NIO swiftly orchestrated a chorus of media accounts of the arrests. News outlets announced an upcoming trial which would feature a witness, Christopher Black, who had obtained a grant of complete immunity in advance of his testimony. British television breathlessly reported on Black's rounds of the interview rooms at Castlereagh. The RUC spirited Black's wife, four children, and mother-in-law away from their home in Belfast's Oldpark area and into a secret hiding place in England.

The IRA soon announced that it had added Black's name to its "death list." The Republican newspaper, *An Phoblacht*, printed Black's photograph on its front page alongside his name. The accompanying article denounced Black for betraying over twenty of "his people" and for "damaging Republican resistance to British rule."

The RUC was taking no chances of its star witness winding up dumped by the side of a road somewhere with a bullet hole in the back of the head. The IRA knew how to take care of informants. It had already executed four of them that year. Black soon vanished into protective custody in England, where he lived under heavy guard with his family. The hard men of the IRA's nutting squad would never lay hands on him.

TWENTY-EIGHT

McKiernan

One of the men swept up in the wave of arrests following Black's epiphany inside Castlereagh was Charles McKiernan.

McKiernan was twenty-two years old, slight in stature, unemployed, and illiterate. His friends viewed him as slow and dim-witted. He had never attended school. Other than drinking in pubs, his only known hobby was gambling on cards and horses. Nonetheless, in 1977, McKiernan was an IRA section leader, with a certain swagger to him. He had been imprisoned at Long Kesh, in Cage 10, at age 17. After his release, he had gone straight back to active service.

At 9:45 a.m. on November 24, 1981, RUC officers arrested McKiernan at his home in the massive Unity Flats apartment complex, a housing project occupied exclusively by Catholics, by the Loyalist stronghold along the Shankill Road in west Belfast. They took him to Crumlin Road Jail. Guards escorted him to a cell in the basement, where he would be held overnight.

In the morning, RUC men drove him to Castlereagh.

McKiernan did not enjoy a high reputation among his colleagues.

"A tool, a weak person," remembered Gerald Loughlin, one of McKiernan's co-defendants at the Black trial.

Carmen Artt, too, described McKiernan in less than charitable terms.

"He was a dirt ball," she remembered in 1996. "A gutter rat. I never liked the looks of him. He was messy, a man that needed a bath and a haircut, illiterate."

"As bad as [Christopher] Black," recalled another Black trial co-defendant, Kevin Mulgrew. "Always working a deal, always looking for immunity. That's why they put him in protective custody."

After they sat McKiernan down, detectives got to the point. Black had named McKiernan in one of the few crimes Black actually knew something about, the murder of Julian Connolly. Black had been an accomplice to the Julian Connolly killing at the Zoological Gardens.

A series of interrogation sessions began, at least a dozen. The sessions would wind up spanning six days: November 24, 25, 26, 27, 28, and 29, 1981. McKiernan feared a beating, but none came.

Having just flipped Black with an informant's deal of the century only a day earlier, detectives now dangled a glittering prize before McKiernan.

He could go supergrass and help them roll up the IRA in north Belfast, they said. Or he could spend decades in prison and see his young family ruined. A cascade of charges was about to rain down on him: two murders, attempted murder, false imprisonment, various firearms and ammunition possession offenses, hijacking, and membership of the I.R.A. The detectives had him convinced he was going in for life if he did not play ball and tell them what they wanted to hear. He had so much at stake, so much to lose. The peelers were threatening to bring in his wife, Nancy. She was twenty years old, and the couple had an eight-month-old son.

It was an easy call.

On day 3, November 26, Braithwaite confronted McKiernan about whether he had been involved in the Miles murder.

McKiernan agreed to confess to it. He signed a fourth confession late that morning, after just 18 minutes with the detectives, admitting involvement in the Miles murder. The language was stilted and vague. There was no mention of Kevin Barry Artt or the names of any accomplices.

The statement of Detective Sergeant Stewart varied from this confession in one big way. Stewart attributed to McKiernan the naming of two accomplices:

> He went on to say that the gunman was Barry
> Artt and the driver was Frankie Steele . . .

A third detective signed Stewart's statement, reflecting he had received it. He was Norman Cromie, the same detective who had known Kevin Barry Artt since childhood, pretended to investigate the Heathwood shooting, and escorted Christopher Black on his rounds in Castlereagh.

Over the course of an hour on the night of his third day in custody, November 26, McKiernan signed three more confessions, implicating himself in the false imprisonment of occupants of three houses to be used as snipers' nests for IRA gunmen. There was no mention of the Miles murder or Kevin Barry Artt.

During an interview over the noon hour on November 28, McKiernan orally repeated his confession to the Miles murder, naming Kevin Barry Artt, John Campbell, Maurice Gilvarry, and Frankie Steele as accomplices.

By the end of the fifth day, at the urging of detectives, McKiernan had named several men thought by the RUC to be prominent IRA men: Gerard Bradley, Sean Connolly, and Gerard McKee.

The detectives egged McKiernan on.

The statements kept coming.

Just after noon on November 29, McKiernan signed an eighth confession, at the end of another short session with

Stewart and Braithwaite. The document addressed the Miles murder in eleven lines of text.

Again, the language was stilted and easy on the details. There was nothing about Kevin Barry Artt, Frankie Steele, Maurice Gilvarry, or the Highfield Club:

> I have already made a statement about the murder of the Deputy Prison Governor, Mr. Myles. There's something else I want to say about it. I had a gun that night when I went to the door. I was given it when I got into the car. It was a 9 mm pistol. I was told there was only one round in it. When I was holding the woman against the wall I had the gun in my right hand. During the struggle the gun went off. I don't know where the bullet went but I think the gun was pointing up towards the ceiling. . .

At 8:21 p.m. on the night of November 29, Braithwaite began a session that would yield the tenth, final, and longest signed written confession of Charles McKiernan. The session lasted over three hours, until nearly 11:30 p.m. that night. The bulk of the ten-page confession which resulted was given over to episodes unrelated to the Miles shooting.

For the first and only time, a confession signed by McKiernan named Kevin Barry Artt as an accomplice:

> The first job I was involved in was the murder of Mr. Myles. I have already made two statements about that. I received my instructions from John Campbell from New Lodge Road. He is the brother of Bobby Campbell and works for Downtown Taxis. He told me to go to the Shamrock Club in Ardoyne and meet Barry Artt and Frankie Steele. I met them. Artt told me that we were going to shoot a Prison Officer. He gave me the gun and told me what to do. Steele was the driver of the car. When we came back and dumped the car at the bottom of Northwick

Drive we went to the Shamrock Club. We spoke to Maurice Gilvary, who is dead now, and Steele told him to get rid of the car. Artt left and went to the Highfield Club and gave the guns to John Campbell. I heard Campbell and Artt arranging this just before we left to do the job.

McKiernan's collapse in Castlereagh came as little surprise to other Republican prisoners. To them, he made excuses, saying the detectives had coerced him to a point of willingness to name anyone they said. They thought of McKiernan as susceptible to breaking under pressure. He had done just that.

One, Gerald Loughlin, recalled scornfully: "He broke as soon as Black came."

In 2018, former IRA man Anthony McIntyre remembered McKiernan, whom he had befriended during their time together in the H-Blocks, in a post on his weblog, *The Pensive Quill*. McIntyre had landed in the Maze after murdering a UVF man and served eighteen years there. Of McKiernan's confessions and recantation, he wrote:

> Charlie, when arrested—not long married and with a baby son —panicked and went into a tailspin. He quickly retrieved the lost ground but never forgave himself . . . [T]hose of us who know Charlie McKiernan and spent a long time in prison with him came to see human frailty rather than treachery as the root cause of his wobble.

In 1995, Kevin's former solicitor, Ted Jones, saw McKiernan's actions differently.

"McKiernan was a liar," Jones said. "He got in trouble. To make a deal, he named Artt. When his deal fell apart, then he became a defendant too."

TWENTY-NINE

Dublin

During the last week of August 1981, a marital row had split the Artt household.

"He was a womanizer," Carmen recalled in 2019. "I don't hold grudges. But he was."

She told him to get out.

Kevin, furious, stormed out.

"I'm leavin', and I'll not be coming back," he yelled before slamming the front door behind him.

He headed south, to Dublin.

Even before the blowup, Kevin had wanted to move the family there. Kevin had quit taxiing. He was staying off the streets, not even driving his own car, trying to minimize his interactions with security forces as much as possible. The RUC and Loyalist paramilitary groups saw him as an IRA man. Police and soldiers stopped him every time they saw him. Kevin viewed his premature death as inevitable and strictly a matter of time unless he made himself scarce in Belfast and got south.

The RUC had nothing for which to arrest him. But, under the emergency laws, no reason was needed. They were the lesser of his worries compared to the WDA and UVF. Their favorite method of executing those whom they disliked was shooting them in their bedrooms in the wee hours of the morning after sledgehammering their front doors off the hinges. Kevin feared waking up suddenly in the middle of the night to the sounds of his door being sledgehammered and glass breaking before being shot to death in front of Carmen. They had narrowly missed him at least twice. The odds of them missing again did not seem good.

One day, as Kevin walked down the street with his friend, Henry "Fergie" Ferguson, an unmarked car pulled up alongside. Two RUC men alighted, hailed Kevin, drew their pistols, and walked up to him. Fergie and Kevin put their hands in the air. The constables drew in close to Kevin, standing at right angles. They cocked their weapons, gripped them with both hands, and pointed them at Kevin's head.

I've got shaky fingers, said one of them, staring at Kevin.

Go to fuckin' Dublin, Barry, said the other.

The men holstered their weapons, got back in their car, and drove off.

To Fergie, who had experienced much abuse at the hands of the RUC himself, it seemed like the escalation in the security forces' torment of Kevin had brought him near a breaking point.

"Let's go," Kevin told Carmen afterward.

But, like many Catholic families in Belfast, Carmen's entire family –all of her sisters, all of her in-laws—lived within a square mile of one another. The sole exception was Carmen's brother, who lived in Switzerland.

Carmen did not trust Kevin enough to pick up everything, leave her family behind, and start a new life in Dublin.

Her answer was no.

To raise the cash to finance the trip, Kevin sold his motorcycle. He rode the train to Dublin. There he stayed with Maeve's sister, Eileen McMorrow, and her husband John.

Before much time passed, Kevin felt bereft. He longed for Carmen and Barry Paul. He knew he belonged with them. But pride and stubbornness prevailed. Kevin stayed in Dublin.

As the weeks passed, Kevin's sojourn there turned into a binge. He spent his free time drinking. For a time, he thought he might stay in Dublin and start a new life on his own. On weekends, he enjoyed the company of a small stream of visitors—Al Sloan, Charlie McNutt, Jr., and his sister, Therese, and Lorraine Keenan.

But Kevin continued to miss Carmen and Barry Paul. He sought out a Catholic priest and confided his plight to him in a confessional.

Afterward, he decided he would swallow his pride, summon his courage, go back to Belfast, and ask Carmen to take him back.

November 3, 1981 was the second anniversary of Kevin's and Carmen's wedding. Kevin chose that day to ride the train back home.

After he arrived at the flat, Carmen told him she would take him back on the condition that she would leave him for good if he "put a foot wrong."

He returned to work at Robert Hart Memorials in Newtownabbey, working as a truck driver and laborer, starting on November 16, 1981. Hart remembered Kevin from his work there in 1980. He saw Kevin as a friendly, outgoing person who did good work and created no problems.

One day, a demure, middle-aged widow visited, seeking a proper headstone for her late husband. Her name was Florence Miles. Her dead husband's name had been Albert.

After a salesman showed her some samples, she ordered a headstone and departed. A few weeks later, she returned to inspect the completed headstone. Robert Hart showed it to her. She liked it.

Off it went to Carnmoney Cemetery, in a truck driven by Kevin Barry Artt himself, to be erected over Albert Miles' grave.

After unloading the stones, Kevin arranged them over the grave. The headstone was big and heavy. After setting it in place, Kevin placed other stones around the grave in a rectangular shape, then scattered white stones over the sod on top.

Kevin stood back to look at his handiwork. The inscription read:

A Devoted Husband and Father
Albert (Bert) Miles,
Deputy Governor, H.J. Prison Service,
Died 26th November 1978.
A Brave Man May Fall, He Can Never Yield.

THIRTY

To The Shock of Everyone that Knew Me

In the last week of November 1981, Kevin was an anxious, young married man with a seventeen-month-old son. He had endured near assassination, constant harassment by security forces, a seven-day stay in Castlereagh, and the fear and anxiety which attended all those things. But he was alive, well, employed, ensconced in secure housing, and newly reunited with his wife and son after his self-imposed exile in Dublin.

Nevertheless, a pall of sadness hung over the little family. Steven Myers had died suddenly of a heart attack on November 20. The family buried him on Monday, November 23.

Kevin was guilt-stricken over the death. He suspected the heart attack resulted from Steven's stress over his daughter's marital troubles, exacerbated by worry over her marriage to a man who seemed at risk of imminent death or incarceration.

"I think the fact they'd been trying to kill me for friggin' years . . . had something to do with it," Kevin ruefully recalled in 1996.

November 27, 1981 was a Friday. Kevin talked Carmen into an outing to the Chester Park Hotel. The Chester Park was nearby on the Antrim Road. It had a pub. Carmen was sad, and Kevin was worried about her mental health. He wanted to help take her mind off of her father's death, if only for a couple of hours. Al Sloan was coming along, he said. Carmen agreed. Off they went, to have a pint or two.

While they were gone, the couple's babysitter, the fourteen-year-old Mary McManus, minded Barry Paul. By 10 p.m. she had put him to bed in the baby's room, at the rear of the flat, and gone to sleep there herself.

After returning home at around midnight, Carmen, Kevin, and Sloane smoked some hashish. After Carmen and Kevin went to bed, Sloan passed out on the sofa in the living room.

It was pitch black and bitterly cold outside Flat 12 of Marsden Gardens at 5:40 a.m. on the morning of Saturday, November 28, 1981.

All inside lay dead asleep in the dark.

A banging at the door ruptured the silence. Carmen got up, groggy, and heard officers outside. They were shouting at her to open up.

Carmen threw on a nightgown and got to the door, then opened it. It was better than them kicking it down.

About eight RUC officers stood there, some in uniform, some in plain clothes. Behind them, idling in the street, were Jeeps and Land Rovers. Carmen blinked as her eyes adjusted. The little cul-de-sac was aglow with the flashing lights of the police vehicles. The police had thrown up barricades and cordoned it off.

In the prior five years, the RUC and army had kicked down the front doors of several houses in which Kevin had lived. But, this time, they had only knocked, and waited for Carmen to open up. They did not draw any weapons. One officer offered condolences immediately upon greeting Carmen at the door. They knew of the recent death of Carmen's father. At least one of the officers was a woman, a rarity for the RUC at the time.

We're here to arrest Barry Artt, said one. *Saction twalve.*

The awful realization that she would be losing both a father and a husband in the same week hit Carmen.

She looked down and stood aside without a word.

Three officers piled into the front bedroom. Kevin awoke, still drunk, naked, blinded by the flashlights they beamed onto his face. They stood over him, surrounding the bed. One was the female officer.

Barry Artt, ye're under arrest. Saction twalve. Gat up.

Kevin asked them to leave the room so he could get dressed in private. They said no. Kevin hurriedly dressed. The constables handcuffed him and walked him out to the street.

One, Detective Constable Thomas Patton, recorded the arrest on a form: "John Kevin Barry ARTT, DOB 19.9.1959, labourer of that address, by virtue of Section 12, Prevention of Terrorism Act 1976." Noted as present in the RUC's record of the search were "Barry John Artt [sic]," Carmen, Barry Paul (then only seventeen months old), Kevin's friend Al Sloan and the babysitter, Mary McManus, aged fourteen.

"Call Ted Jones," Kevin called to a stricken Carmen before they bundled him into a Land Rover. "Tell him I need to speak with him at Castlereagh, as soon as he can get there."

Off went the column of vehicles in a cloud of exhaust, bound for Castlereagh. Three officers, including the woman constable, rode with Kevin in the Land Rover. The five other officers stayed behind. They rousted Al Sloan.

Then, as Al and Carmen watched, they tossed the place, looking for contraband they did not identify.

Despite their thoroughness, they missed the hashish the occupants had been smoking only a few hours before. It sat out in the open, by the fireplace, in plain view of anyone who might have cared to look there.

Kevin arrived at Castlereagh about forty minutes later, at 6:32 a.m. It was just over three years after Albert Miles had died on the floor of his house in north Belfast.

Carmen had called Ted Jones and asked him to go to Castlereagh and demand admittance to see her husband.

Jones rushed down there. The detectives refused to let him in.

THIRTY-ONE

Lying, Murdering Bastard

To Kevin, after three years since his last stay there, Castlereagh looked much the same.

So did the routine. Things got started just after 11 a.m., with the usual drill. A uniformed guard escorted him from his cell to an eight-by-eight-foot interview room. No windows or clocks were visible. Only four hours removed from drinking at the Chester Park and smoking hashish, Kevin felt hungover, if not still drunk. He felt upside-down, like he did not know whether he was coming or going.

As he shuffled to the interview room for his first round of questioning, Kevin recalled his first spell in the Romper Room in 1978. The detectives had kept him there seven days. Near the end, they seemed to be fishing, unsure of themselves, in the dark, bluffing that they knew something and hoping they could get Kevin to knuckle under.

This time would be different.

Sergeant John Hewitt was a big man with blonde hair. He introduced himself to Kevin during the first session. It began at 11:20 a.m. on November 28. With him was Constable James Whitehead.

Hewitt was sitting on the table. Kevin sat in a chair. Hewitt loomed above Kevin, almost on top of him.

Hewitt started showing Kevin photos of a dead man lying naked on a slab.

That's Albert Miles, he said.

Hewitt had something in his right hand—a piece of metal. He held it between his thumb and forefinger. He started hitting Kevin on the side of the head with it.

It was a lead bullet.

Ye shot him through here, Hewitt cried, suddenly raising his voice.

Ye murdered him. Bastard. We've got ye by the balls. Ye're going down the tubes.

Kevin recalled the moment years later.

THIS IS A BULLET, YE BASTARD, Hewitt continued. *THIS IS WHERE YE SHOT HIM, YE MURDERING CUNT!*

He struck Kevin's skull over and over with the bullet. Hewitt did not tap the bullet against Kevin's head. He rapped it, snapping Kevin's head back with each blow.

Kevin felt terrified. If his stress level at being pulled across a table in 1978 had been ten on a scale of zero to twenty, his stress level now felt like eighteen to twenty.

"I didn't shoot anyone," said Kevin. "I don't know what you're talking about."

Lying, murdering bastard!

Hewitt kept hitting Kevin in the head with the bullet. He was red, huffing and puffing in a rage.

Ye shot him through here, ye bastard!

"I didn't shoot anyone," Kevin said. "I need to speak to my solicitor. His name is Ted Jones."

Hewitt laughed scornfully. Whitehead stood by, impassive.

Notes taken by Kevin's solicitor, Ted Jones, during an interview of Kevin in the Crum a few days later reflected what Kevin told his lawyer about his introduction to Hewitt:

1st interview . . . sat on edge of a desk banged me on the forehead with a bullet & said that's where you shot him. . .

Over the course of four grueling sessions on November 28, Hewitt and detectives Brian Connolly, Michael Rutledge, and James Whitehead grilled Kevin.

Kevin started answering questions right away.

His inquisitors wasted no time getting to the point: the Miles murder.

There are eyewitnesses to the murder, said detective Brian Connolly. *Are ye willing to participate in an identification parade?*

"It's no problem," said Kevin.

There were at least two eyewitnesses to the shooting: Florence Miles and Alan Miles. They had seen and heard the killing of Albert Miles from a few feet away on that night in 1978. The RUC's own written notice to persons in their custody, likely shown to Kevin at the time of his booking into Castlereagh, expressly described the procedure for a lineup.

But no lineup would be done. No one called Alan or Florence Miles and asked them to come down to the station and identify Kevin or anyone else.

"I've been questioned about this murder before," Kevin told his captors. "In 1978. They had me in here for a week. I told them everything they wanted to know. I was released without charge."

So bloody what? said Connolly.

"I'll tell you the same thing I told them," said Kevin. "I was at the Keenans', in 11 Sheridan Street until 10 p.m. that night. Then I went drinking with Stevie Keenan at the Felons' Club on New Lodge Road.

"I've never been in the IRA, never shot anyone, never had a gun in me hand."

Detective Constable Michael Rutledge interjected.

We know ye shot him, ye murdering bastard, he said.

"Who said I did?" Kevin asked.

Rutledge said nothing.

"Whoever said it is a liar, and if I knew who it was, I would tell them to their face," Kevin said.

A uniformed constable escorted Kevin back to his cell and locked him in.

Kevin quickly lost track of time. He was still hungover. He was also exhausted, dehydrated, disoriented, and afraid—every sensation which Castlereagh was designed to produce in a suspect.

The probing resumed in a fifth session, at 10:30 a.m. the following morning, November 29—day two. It was the first of four sessions which would consume over nine hours that day.

Three new detectives now quizzed Kevin for over two hours: Armour Hill, John McCollum, and Robert Turner. Hill had been one of the detectives who had interrogated Kevin in 1978.

We'd like ye to describe your role in the Miles murder, said one.

"I know nothing about it. I had nothing to do with it," he said. "I was at the Keenans' that night. I went to the Felons' Club with Stevie Keenan around 10 p.m. I told you all this three years ago. I have never had anything to do with guns. I wouldn't know how to shoot one if you put it in me hand. I would like to see my solicitor, Ted Jones."

Hill, McCollum, and Turner laughed at him.

Ye can see your lawyer when we say ye can see him, said Hill.

During a two-and-a-half-hour session in room B.F. 9, the burly Hewitt returned to the interview room. He glowered at Kevin.

Charlie McKiernan will be here in twenty minutes. Then we'll have you sorted out.

Charlie McKiernan?

The name McKiernan meant nothing to Kevin. He looked at Hewitt quizzically.

Ye are fucked, Barry, said Hewitt. *We are going to bring in Charles McKiernan to point ye out. There's nothing ye can do. He's going to point ye out and ye will be going down the tubes.*

In came Charles McKiernan, led into the room by detective inspector Raymond Caskey and another detective, and followed by a third. Visible just outside the door was a cluster of more detectives. It was a regular crowd, an audience. Kevin assumed the door was left ajar so they could listen to whatever it was that was going to happen now.

Caskey wore a facial expression of sneering triumph.

McKiernan looked familiar to Kevin. He wore a poker-faced demeanor. He was smoking a cigarette and also seemed to be chewing gum. He looked like he was trying hard to appear relaxed.

"Well, Barry, . . . I told them the heap about the Miles job," McKiernan said. His tone was strangely cocky. "You might as well make a statement, too."

Kevin went crazy. He started yelling at McKiernan.

"What the *fuck* are ye talking about? Are ye crazy? Ye bloody know I had nothing to do with this. What have I ever done on ye that ye are trying to implicate me in this fucking thing?"

Shut the fuck up, Hewitt snapped.

McKiernan shrugged his shoulders, then looked at Caskey. It looked like he was trying to read Caskey's face for cues about what McKiernan should say next. McKiernan hardly took his eyes off Caskey for the duration of the time he spent in the interview room.

Caskey handed McKiernan off to a couple of other detectives. They hustled McKiernan off to his next confrontation. It was with IRA man Gerard Bradley, who sat waiting in an interview room down the hall.

"I had no involvement in the Miles murder," Kevin said to the detectives. "I don't know what he is talking about. I want to see my solicitor. His name is Ted Jones."

Ye'll see your solicitor when we decide ye can see him, Caskey said.

Then Caskey came up, put his face right up in front of Kevin's, and bared his teeth. They were clenched. His face was red, his features contorted in anger and hate.

I am going to see that ye rot in hell for this, ye murdering bastard, Caskey hissed. *We don't need any of yer fucking statements. Ye are fucked. Mark me words.*

Kevin felt scared stiff.

Caskey and two detectives then departed, leaving Kevin with Hewitt and Whitehead. The little audience of detectives outside the door remained, watching.

Ye are fucked, Artt, said Hewitt. *Do ye know McKiernan now?*

"His face is familiar," Kevin replied. "But the name doesn't ring any bells. Maybe he was a fare one night when I was driving for Ace."

He sure as hell knows ye, replied Hewitt.

"There's something wrong with that guy's head," Kevin said. "I have never had anything to do with any shooting and I never will have."

The detectives gave Kevin a rundown, the narrative of what he had supposedly done on the night of November 26, 1978.

Ye went to the Shamrock Club on Flax Street in Ardoyne, west Belfast. There ye met other people. Someone handed ye a .38 revolver and gave McKiernan a .45. Then ye and McKiernan got into a car. Ye sat in the front, McKiernan in the back. Ye rode to Evelyn Gardens. Ye followed McKiernan up to the front door of the house at the end of the street. Someone opened the door. A woman screamed. McKiernan grabbed the woman. Ye shot Albert Miles, then ran back to the car. Ye returned to Ardoyne. Ye took the guns to the Highfield Club.

Kevin listened.

"I'm telling ye again," he said. "I had nothing to do with it."

Rutledge put his notepad on the table. He started drawing a little diagram of a courtroom.

See this little box here, Barry?

Rutledge pointed at a square he had drawn on the diagram.

That's the dock. That's where ye'll sit during the trial. This rectangle up here is the bench. That's where the judge will be sitting, looking at ye. Over here, to his right, to your laft, is the witness box. McKiernan and Frankie Steele will sit there when they give their testimony against ye.

Ye can sit there in the dock and deny it all ye want. Here's three people who are going to say this. We're going to say this. Ye're going to say otherwise. Who the hell is the judge going to believe? Ye? Or McKiernan, Steele, and the RUC?

Steele was doing twelve years as it was, for kidnapping.

He'll probably draw another twelve years on this thing, said Rutledge. *But the judge will let him serve the time concurrently with his existing sentence. So Steele will have nothing to lose by naming ye.*

Brian Connolly chimed in.

Ye do have something to lose, Barry. Ye're gonna be goin' down for thirty years, and all of it. Thirty stipulated.

A thirty-year "stipulated sentence," in the parlance of Diplock justice, meant just that—thirty years in prison, with no remission or parole, thirty years to the last day of the thirtieth year. Carmen and Barry Paul would be long gone. Connolly and Rutledge would see to it, they said.

By the time ye get out yer wee lad will be thirty, said Rutledge. *Can ye imagine yer son thirty? Ye're not even thirty yersalf.*

All of that was what Kevin was looking at if he kept stonewalling, said the two men. Was that what he wanted?

Kevin's eyes were pinned on Rutledge's little drawing. He stared at it, imagining the trial to come.

There's a better way, the two detectives told Kevin.

If he cooperated, they said, they would stand up in court for him. He would be adjudged guilty of murder and sentenced to life. But the actual time he would serve would be much less than that. Kevin would be eligible for furloughs during the summertime and at Christmastime. There would be remission and parole if he behaved well in prison. What it boiled down to was a seven-year stretch in the Maze.

On the third day, Connolly and Rutledge began again, in an eighty-minute session that began at 9:55 a.m.

"I'd like to see my solicitor, Ted Jones," Kevin said immediately after sitting down.

Ye don't have a right to see him, said Rutledge. *Once ye see him, it will be too late to make a statement to us. Then our hands will be tied, and we won't be able to help ye. If that happens ye'll be going away for a long time.*

Kevin had lost track of the number of times he asked detectives to see Ted Jones.

Rutledge held something cupped in his hand. He bent toward Kevin and stretched out his arm. Kevin asked him what it was.

Rosary beads, the detective replied.

"Well, what do I need rosary beads for?" Kevin asked.

To pray to God, to ask forgiveness for killing Albert Miles.

"I don't need rosary beads to pray for forgiveness, and I don't need rosary beads to pray to God," Kevin countered. "I can pray to Him anytime I want."

It must have been the wrong thing to say.

Rutledge jumped up out of his seat and came at Kevin like a boxer going for a knockout. Kevin ducked down in his chair. Rutledge started landing blows on the back of Kevin's head. Seeing Rutledge's fists coming, Kevin put his hands up to protect himself. The punches came in a flurry, four or five of them. As Kevin tried to parry the blows, Rutledge went low, burying a left hook into Kevin's ribcage, just below his left armpit.

During the barrage, Rutledge yelled at Kevin. Rutledge was loud, incomprehensible. His words sounded like gibberish. To Kevin it seemed like Rutledge had gone insane.

The blows ceased.

In his chair, Kevin sat doubled over, with his arms up around his head. His nerves were shattered. His head and ribs were throbbing. Kevin was afraid to look up even though the punches had stopped.

He thought it important to be as nice as possible to Rutledge to avoid being torn apart by him.

Rutledge seemed flustered, nervous. He was breathing hard, red in the face. No one said anything. Several silent minutes passed.

Rutledge began pacing the floor, opened the door, looked down the hall.

No one was coming.

"You didn't have to hit me," said Kevin.

I just lost my cool, replied Rutledge. *We're trying to help ye. Ye're in serious trouble. Ye were rejecting us.*

"What does that mean?" asked Kevin.

If ye don't make a statement, our hands will be tied, and we won't be allowed to help you. Ye'll be going away for a long time.

"Yes, for something I didn't do."

Ye done it and we know ye done it.

"That's impossible," Kevin said. "I didn't have anything to do with it."

Again, Kevin asked to see Ted Jones. Again, they ignored him. A uniformed constable took Kevin back to his cell and locked him inside.

Bathed in sweat, Kevin tossed and turned, trying to sleep. The fluorescent light overhead shone down all day and night. No one ever shut it off.

THIRTY-TWO

The Bear

Day three was November 30. Just before 1:45 p.m. that day, a guard escorted Kevin from his cell to interview room B.F. 7. A new pair of detectives now appeared: Detective Robert Turner and a sergeant, Norman McLaughlin.

"I had nothing to do with it," Kevin told McLaughlin and Turner.

Was it the twentieth time he had said it? The fiftieth?

McLaughlin and Turner now introduced another new tactic in the person of William Hylands, the detective chief superintendent in charge of the investigation.

In 1981, Hylands' nickname was well-known among Republican prisoners as well as among his own subordinates. The big mustachioed man in the duffle coat was known as the Bear.

Kevin had never seen him before.

The Bear was a big man. He stood over six feet tall. He had a big head, big neck, big shoulders, massive hands. The confines of the cramped interview rooms of Castlereagh seemed to magnify his size. He had threatened prisoners with physical harm for resisting the signing of confessions before. He was vulgar, crude, coarse, well-known to lawyers and prisoners alike as a thug with a badge.

The Bear barged into the interview room at 2:45 p.m., about an hour into the session.

Turner asked, "Should we log you in?"

Hylands said no.

Hylands came in close, took off his glasses, bent down, and got up in Kevin's face.

He repeated the same litany the detectives had battered Kevin with for the last three days.

McKiernan has fingered ye as the shooter. All the facts point toward ye as the murderer of Albert Miles. There's no doubt about it.

To this, Hylands added a new twist.

Albert Miles was a personal friend of mine, he growled. *I'm going to see to it personally that ye rot in prison for the rest of your life. It's going to be a thirty-year stipulated sentence for you. Ye haven't a hope in hell of getting out of this. I don't need a statement from ye. I'll make sure ye get thirty stipulated. Do ye know what thirty stipulated is?*

Kevin did not. Hylands explained it to him. It meant doing all thirty years. No remission, no parole, no furloughs, no coming home early.

Kevin felt terrified.

Having told his prisoner emphatically he knew him to be a murderer, Hylands now had some questions.

How did he do it? How many shots did he fire?

"I don't know," Kevin replied. "I didn't do it."

I'll ensure you get thirty stipulated. Mark me fucking words, said Hylands. Then he turned on his heel and left the interview room.

Kevin felt the Bear had sucked the life out of him. He felt he could not take any more.

Yeah, he's the Bear, said McLaughlin. *When he says something, he means every word of it. If anyone can ensure ye get thirty years stipulated, he's the one man that can. He's my boss's boss, a very important man in the RUC.*

Are ye ready to make a statement? McLaughlin asked.

Kevin looked at him.

Ye can make a statement, or sacrifice Carmen and Barry Paul instead. Up to ye, McLaughlin said.

Kevin shook his head no.

"I had nothing whatsoever to do with this. You have got me all wrong," Kevin told McLaughlin. "I was never involved in anything like this. I am not a killer. I couldn't kill anyone."

Ye need to make a remorseful statement, replied McLaughlin. *We're only trying to help ye. It's an easy thing to get involved with an organization and be sent out to commit murder.*

The glow of his reunion with Carmen and Barry Paul following his ten-week sojourn in Dublin was still fresh. While separated from them, Kevin had realized he could not live without them. He was more emotional about his relationship with them than he had ever been. Now he faced indefinite separation from them.

Continuing to protest his innocence was pointless. It was that simple.

McLaughlin and Turner kept grinding.

Ye went to the Shamrock Club. Ye met Charlie McKiernan. Ye got two guns. Ye got a .38, he got a .45. Ye got in a car with Frankie Steele. Ye drove down to Evelyn Gardens. Ye walked up to 8 Evelyn Gardens, rapped the door. Mrs. Miles opened the door. McKiernan grabbed the woman. Mr. Miles came into the hallway. Ye shot him. Ye ran back to the car. Ye took the guns, went to the Highfield Club, gave the guns to John Campbell, and that was it.

It was as though they were teaching him by rote.

Turner left the room, leaving Kevin alone with McLaughlin. The detective put an arm around Kevin's shoulder.

I've got a son around your age, McLaughlin said, now using a soothing, fatherly tone. *He's a pretty good lad. Thank God, he's doing well for himself education wise. I know you're a good lad too and you've just been caught up in this.*

God forbid if it were my son who ever found himself in this position. If he did, I would tell him to make a remorseful statement, to enable the police to help him out when his case got to trial.

Kevin started to cry. Turner returned and brought him a handkerchief.

Kevin was exhausted, not sleeping at night, unaware of whether he was up or down or sideways. Maintaining his innocence would have been like talking to a wall for all the good it did. But the detectives were not a wall. A wall is inert and silent. These cops were angry, full of poison, tireless, relentless. They just kept on coming. Every denial only provoked them into angry interruptions and tirades.

"I couldn't get through," Kevin recalled in 1996. "They did not want to recognize the fact."

THIRTY-THREE

I Would Have Signed Anything

At 7:30 p.m. on the night of November 30, McLaughlin and Turner opened the eleventh interrogation session of Kevin Barry Artt.

Again, they led Kevin through the rundown. It was the same litany, about the Shamrock Club, driving to Evelyn Gardens, walking up to the front door, shooting Albert Miles, driving away.

For three days, Kevin had used his energy trying to convince the detectives he had nothing to do with the Miles murder. It had been futile. Kevin was exhausted and in despair. The ship was sinking, and he just wanted to get it over with.

He started repeating the rundown back to McLaughlin and Turner.

"I just went flop," he recalled later. "They'd sucked all the energy out of me."

McLaughlin started writing up a statement by hand. He needed some details. What did the gun look like, for example?

Kevin had never held or even seen a handgun in his life. He had no idea how to describe one or say how it was fired. All he had to go on was what he had seen on television and in magazines.

"A barrel that spun, silver colour," was the best description Kevin could muster.

"I pictured those cowboy guns you owned as a child and that's where this description came from," Kevin wrote years later.

McLaughlin's finished product was choppy, sloppy, richly detailed on some things, light on details or wrong about others, but not so wrong as to seem unbelievable on its face.

McLaughlin's document regurgitated the rundown:

> I . . . was told I had to go to the Shamrock Club and meet people there. I was told that I would be told more about it there. I personally thought that I would have to move guns or something like that. I had no idea what was in store. When I got to the Shamrock Club two guns were supplied. A car was also supplied. I don't know from where. Three of us left the Shamrock Club after being told to go to Evelyn Gardens and we were to shoot a jail warden. I was the front seat passenger in the car and I had a small gun with me. It was one with a barrell [sic] that spun, silver colour. We arrived at Evelyn Gardens and the back seat passenger and I went up to the front door of a house. We had been given the number of the house before leaving. The other person knocked the door or rung the bell, I stayed back a bit. The next thing I remember was the door opening and I heard a woman scream. She was pushed to the side by the other man. I think I heard a shot then and there was a lot of noise. I moved behind the other man and fired through the door at a man who appeared in the hallway. There was nothing said. It was so quick and the two of us ran back to the car which was parked just outside. I was the first back at the car. . .

Kevin signed. It was 9:10 p.m. on November 30.

At that point, what they wanted him to sign no longer mattered. Kevin would have signed anything they put in front of him.

The hard work done, McLaughlin and Turner exited at 9:35 p.m.

Kevin's confession to the shooting of Albert Miles would become the largest factor of his life for the next thirty years.

"It sure ruined my life," Kevin wrote in 1995.

THIRTY-FOUR

Going to the High Jump

Five more sessions followed on December 1 and 2, 1981. The detectives wanted details about the guns, the car, who had hijacked it, other things. They pressed Kevin for them. *What was the caliber of the guns? What did they look like? What about the car—what was the make and model?*

Kevin was unable to tell them anything.

The detectives left well enough alone.

On Wednesday, December 2, Kevin had been under interrogation for nearly thirty-three hours over the course of five days.

For at least the fifth time, he asked to see his solicitor, Ted Jones.

Letting Kevin see Jones was now a pointless formality, so the detectives allowed it at last.

Kevin had made at least four prior requests to see Jones. Detectives recorded none of them in their notes, but they carefully noted this request, as though to make it seem it had never occurred to Kevin to ask for his lawyer several times before confessing.

Officers ushered Ted Jones in to see his client at 11:53 a.m. They had kept the lawyer separated from his client until the moment after it was too late for the lawyer to do anything, a neat trick they had perfected over years of practice.

"What's happened?" Jones asked.

"I confessed to killing Albert Miles."

"Ye did *what*? Oh, Jesus."

Kevin sat slumped at the table, his face in his hands.

"What am I going to do? What can we do here?"

"Don't say anything else," Jones replied.

Jones summoned officers to let them know he and Kevin were through and then left. He had spent seventeen minutes in the room with Kevin.

A constable took Kevin back to his cell.

Kevin was frightened, drained, and disoriented. He felt claustrophobic in his cell. He knew he was going to prison, but he was not sure what came next. The one solace he had was knowing he was getting out of Castlereagh at last. It was cold comfort.

A seventeenth and final session ensued about two hours later, with Connolly and Rutledge.

Now, Barry– said Connolly.

Kevin interrupted him.

"My solicitor has told me to say nothing more," he said.

With the confession in the bag, Connolly and Rutledge laughed out loud.

Kevin's time at Castlereagh was over at last.

Police transported him to the RUC station at Townhall Street, where Kevin arrived at 8:55 p.m. on the evening of December 2, 1981.

There Detective Sergeant Michael Braithwaite formally charged Kevin with the murder of Albert Miles and membership of the IRA.

Brusquely, an officer relieved him of his clothing and personal effects: a £5 note, fifteen pence in pocket change, cigarettes, a watch, his shoelaces, a betting slip, a cigarette lighter.

Officers escorted Kevin to a cell. There was a plastic mattress and pillow. The floor of the cell was below street level. The street was at eye level. There was a small window of translucent thick glass blocks which sat behind steel bars. A little light glowed through.

At 9:20 p.m., a guard opened the cell door and brought in tea and biscuits.

Five minutes later, before he could finish the spartan meal, Kevin heard the thud of the guard's boots approaching his cell again.

Artt, said the man as he unlocked the cell. *Yer wife's here.*

The man escorted Kevin to the visiting area.

As an officer escorted Carmen to meet her husband, an RUC constable recognized her.

He's going to go to the High Jump! he shouted, grinning. *What are ye going to do now?*

Carmen did not know what the taunt meant.

Carmen was "utterly destroyed." She spent ten minutes with Kevin and left some clothing for him with the guards before departing at 9:35 p.m.

As a guard walked Kevin back to his cell, Kevin felt like he was asphyxiating with despair. The prospect of never seeing Carmen, Barry Paul, Maeve, and John again except in the visiting room at the Maze prison was suffocating. He was sick over the shame that would descend on them once news of the charges and his confession got out.

The guard bid Kevin goodnight.

Just wait 'til they get yeu in the fucking Kesh, he growled. Then he slammed the cell door shut.

THIRTY-FIVE

To the Crum

The next morning, after breakfast and a cursory medical examination, officers whisked Kevin off to the Crumlin Road Jail in north Belfast.

Kevin had driven past the Crum hundreds of times, ferrying passengers up and down the Crumlin Road. But now inside it, he felt as if he had traveled back in time to the nineteenth century. As Kevin entered the intake area, he heard a din—guards shouting, steel doors slamming, boots clacking on the polished red tile floor. Keys jangled from one side of the guards' belts. Batons hung menacingly from the other.

Guards hustled Kevin into a small holding cell no bigger than a telephone booth. The tile floor featured a black-and-white checkerboard pattern. Steel mesh overhead was the ceiling. Kevin was told to take off his clothes and put them in a bag. The guards strip-searched him, then locked him in a cell.

Not long afterward, the RUC visited Carmen.

They arrived in the middle of the night, entering the little flat in Marsden Gardens after kicking the front door clean off the hinges. There were four or five of them, in uniform, all drunk, all armed with rifles and side arms. The men piled into the bedroom. The smells of booze and body odor filled the room. The constables reeked of it. Carmen pulled the blanket up, shielding Barry Paul, who lay next to her in bed, screaming.

We'll give ye what your husband can't, one said, and they all laughed.

Carmen feared they might rape her.

One of them started urinating in the hallway just outside the bedroom.

After a few minutes, the men departed.

Presently, one of the constables returned, to retrieve his rifle. It was on the floor, leaning against the wall. The man had drunkenly forgotten the weapon and nearly left it behind.

News of Kevin's arrest spread quickly. Kevin's employer, Robert Hart, the man who had carved Albert Miles' headstone, heard it on the six o'clock news on the evening of November 28. Soon afterward, he visited Marsden Gardens. As Carmen started to weep, Hart handed Kevin's final paycheck to her.

SECTION VII

THE IRISH TRIAL OF THE CENTURY

THIRTY-SIX

I Have to Get Out of Here

The Crum was a Victorian pile of black basalt quarried from the Belfast hills and finished with sandstone imported from Scotland during the 1840s. Its designer was Sir Charles Lanyon, one of Victorian Belfast's principal architects.

Lanyon's hulking creation sat on ten acres at the bottom of the Crumlin Road in north Belfast, across the street from the courthouse. A pentagonal wall enclosed the grounds. Five feet below lay a ninety-yard-long tunnel, completed in 1852. It ran underneath the Crumlin Road, connecting the jail to the courthouse. The subterranean passage spared the public from the indecorous view of haggard prisoners in chains crossing the street on their way to their hearings and trials. To the prisoner tramping through it, the dank brick passageway felt medieval.

Cells measured seven feet by twelve. Their furnishings were spartan: a bunk bed, a couple of chairs and a table, a narrow wooden wardrobe, no sink or toilet. A pane of thick frosted glass in a small arched window near the ten-foot-high ceiling offered some natural light.

A list of those jailed at the Crum during the Troubles reads like a Who's Who of Irish Republicanism: Éamonn de Valera, Martin McGuinness, Bobby Sands. During the nineteenth century, others confined within its walls included suffragettes and children from poor families who had committed "unruly behavior" or stolen food or clothing in order to survive. Their names have been forgotten.

To his fellow Republican prisoners, Kevin remained an outsider, with no political affiliations. Some ridiculed him. How could a man *not* be political, especially one who had undergone the persecution and harassment he had? In the meantime, the IRA was anxious to protect McKiernan from any retaliation from Kevin.

One day, a fellow prisoner entered Kevin's cell.

"McKiernan's coming out into the general population," he told Kevin. "Don't lay a finger on him. If you do, ye're fucked. Understand?"

Kevin understood.

McKiernan soon moved back into the general population. The IRA tolerated men who confessed in Castlereagh and implicated others, so long as they recanted and got IRA men off the hook.

McKiernan sought out Kevin. He explained that he had put Kevin "in the loop" in Castlereagh only because he knew Kevin had no involvement in the Miles murder.

What?

It sounded like a non sequitur, until one considered the clear connotation. McKiernan was under orders to protect IRA men. Those orders included an instruction to *not* recant his confession to the Miles murder. That way, at least one guilty man could remain at large while Kevin, who was a nobody to the Provisionals, took the fall for what he did. Withdrawing his naming of Kevin would mean a valuable IRA man who had gone uncharged in the murder would be at risk of prosecution.

To the Provisionals, truth took a back seat to expediency. The identity of McKiernan's accomplice, whoever he had been, would stay secret.

Kevin now inhabited the very prison where Albert Miles had worked among his colleagues. He would spend the next two to three months there. The guards wasted no time in starting to menace him. *Bastard. We're going to get you. Ye're the bastard in for Albert. Provie cunt. Fenian bastard. Once ye get to the Kesh, ye'll be dead.* Another guard told Kevin they would take care of him. He smelled of alcohol.

The guards abused Kevin without cease or mercy. During cell searches, the guards destroyed Kevin's personal effects, whatever they might happen to be that day—a religious medal, prayer cards, reading materials. When Loyalist prisoners were allowed out of their cells, guards made sure to unlock Kevin's cell door, inviting any Loyalist prisoner with nothing to lose to have at him.

The verbal abuse from the guards was continual. *Murdering bastard. Scumbag. Provie bastard.* The guards insulted Carmen too. When Kevin had visitors, guards made sure to keep them waiting for hours and subjected them to petty harassment at the front gate while Kevin, expecting the visit, was kept waiting in his cell. Letters from Carmen that did not vanish took two weeks to make it the 150 yards from the censor's office to Kevin's cell. Maeve tried sending in a Bible and rosary. The guards confiscated them. Kevin complained to the jail chaplain about the thefts. It did no good.

After lights-out, guards passing by Kevin's cell flicked the lights on, then off again. They repeated the cycle every ten to fifteen minutes afterward, and shouted through the door, just in case sleep had momentarily overtaken Kevin. The petty torments had their intended effect from time to time when Kevin broke down weeping.

Kevin's health worsened. He started vomiting. The vomiting went on for six weeks. After losing nearly a hundred pounds, his body weight dropped to 110, nearly half what it had been the night he was arrested. Kevin's waist shrank from thirty-six inches to thirty inches. Kevin's visitors noticed his weight loss and skinnier frame. His skin turned yellow. Guards ignored his requests for medical treatment. When a prison doctor did examine him, he misdiagnosed Kevin's condition.

The OC of Republican prisoners in the Maze, Bobby Storey, heard about the situation. Big Bob threatened action unless Kevin received proper treatment. Kevin eventually found himself in the prison hospital, with a case of jaundice.

Maeve learned of his condition and tried to get in to see him. The guards refused to let her in. When she lashed out at them, they sneeringly threatened to arrest her.

What humor existed among Republican prisoners at the Crum could be cruel, if cleverly designed. Upon his entry into the Crum, a fresh Republican prisoner would receive a briefing from the OC (Officer Commanding). The briefing included an announcement of the impending arrival of "the Sinn Féin priest," who was expected there shortly, to hear confessions and pray with the men.

Unknown to the rookie, the priest was an impostor—a fellow Republican prisoner, dressed as a clergyman, complete with a Roman collar. He displayed a solemn, compassionate bearing. The fake father would greet the greenhorn warmly, invite him to kneel, then take him through the paces of the sacrament, gently encouraging him to admit his sins—the more personal, salacious, and sexually-oriented the better.

After milking the last embarrassing revelation from the newcomer, the counterfeit reverend would ask the penitent to bow his head and close his eyes to receive his penance and absolution. When the victim complied, his tormentor silently donned a large boxing glove. Then, in a theatrical move played to the balcony, he wound up and delivered a roundhouse punch to the head of the kneeling man. The blow carried enough force to floor the helpless confessant, who stared up in shocked bewilderment at the black-clad thespian. The "priest" returned his victim's bewildered stare with a quizzical deadpan gaze as the audience, which had been watching from a distance, exploded in raucous laughter.

As though that were not humiliation enough, the bogus cleric then broadcast to his comrades the more scandalous secrets he had learned from the new man, to the amusement of all.

An alternate torment also employed an impostor, the "Sinn Féin doctor," whose visit was explained as part of an agreement with prison authorities whereby prisoners received medical care from outside physicians who were both sympathetic and independent of the prison service.

This character, too, was thoughtfully costumed and outfitted. He wore a white jacket and a stethoscope around his neck. Kevin's co-defendant Terry Kirby once played the role himself.

A thorough medical examination conducted in an area visible to the others would ensue, with the patient being asked to strip naked after being asked a few perfunctory questions about his health. The pretend sawbones listened to the prisoner's heartbeat with the stethoscope and inspected his eyes, ears, and mouth. With the victim thus distracted, an accomplice stealthily gathered up the patient's clothing and slipped away, then hurled the clothes onto the corrugated tin roof of a shack in the courtyard. When it dawned on the naked newcomer that he was being had, he would frantically search for his clothes, again while the others watched, hooting and cackling. How he might manage to retrieve his clothes from the roof was his problem.

THIRTY-SEVEN

The Sacrificial Rite

The Belfast Crown Court, a grand, columned building designed in the Neo-Palladian Classical style during the reign of Victoria, sat on the south side of the Crumlin Road, across the street from the Crumlin Road Jail. On December 6, 1982, dozens of defendants, lawyers, police, and prison guards packed the long, rectangular courtroom known as the Number One Court.

It was the first day of the Christopher Black trial, the first-ever supergrass trial in Northern Ireland.

"The Court stands open!" cried the clerk. "God save the Queen!"

All there assembled rose in unison.

Lord Justice Basil Kelly, sixty-two years old, the former Attorney General of Northern Ireland, one-time Unionist member of the Stormont Parliament, and ardent member of the Orange Order, appeared from behind a red curtain and strode onto the bench. In the high-ceilinged, wainscoted courtroom, Kelly, draped in his scarlet robe, appeared majestic. Atop his head sat a white wig of mysterious provenance. The judge peered out at the packed courtroom over gold-rimmed glasses.

On the wall above the bench was a plaster coat of arms representing the British crown. *Dieu et mon droit*, read the inscription, *God and my right*, the motto of the British crown. A Masonic ring adorned Kelly's ring finger. As Kelly settled into his chair, he seemed to embody the Orange State and its control of the court and the law itself. Among Irish Republicans, Kelly had a reputation as a bigot.

The few known photographs of Sir John William Basil Kelly, Q.C., reveal a stolid, implacable face one might think well-suited to the role of judge. Thinning, combed-over gray hair covers a half-bald head. On the bench, he was a formidable, imposing presence who could intimidate the most experienced of defense lawyers.

The courtroom was imposing, majestic in design. "It seemed to be a place where great things were meant to happen," remembered former IRA man Anthony McIntyre. "Where judicial ritual could express itself. It was a very grandiose setting. This was a place where you'd imagine dukes and queens and kings could sit in their own sort of surroundings and be pompous. There were no great paintings or artwork in it, but there was a sense of gravitas."

In each corner of the long rectangular courtroom stood an RUC constable armed with an M1 automatic rifle and holstered pistol. The four men were Kelly's bodyguards. They gripped their rifles with the barrels level at all times, as though pointing them at all there assembled. Beneath his robe, Kelly wore a bulletproof vest.

Outside the building, police clustered in strategic positions, awaiting an IRA attack. British Army helicopters sometimes hovered above the courthouse during proceedings. The racket of their rotors and engines penetrated the courtroom, making it hard to hear what was being said. The display of weapons and muscle was profuse, theatrical, like something out of a Hollywood movie.

The heavy security related to a rumored IRA assassination attempt against Kelly. Police had apprehended an IRA man, Eamonn Collins, who had driven a milk truck near Kelly's residence with two other IRA men trailing him. In the truck bed, concealed amid the milk crates, lay explosives and a sniper rifle. The plot had called for installing the explosives inside a parked vehicle and affixing a pressure plate, such as the IRA commonly used to trigger land mines, on the exterior. At the moment Kelly's vehicle passed by, an IRA sniper would fire a round at the pressure plate, triggering a blast which would kill Kelly.

Such an attack on Kelly would not have been out of the question for the Provisionals. Five weeks after the trial began, the IRA shot dead one of Kelly's colleagues, William Doyle, as he walked home from Mass with his family in south Belfast.

Heavy media coverage attended each day's proceedings. Newspapers published daily stories about it on their front pages. The tone of the coverage was breathless, sensational. It was one of the darkest and deadliest times of the Troubles. The atmosphere was electric, heavy, unbelievable.

In London, the Christopher Black trial was important, a public proving ground for the criminalization policy introduced in 1976. The hope that criminalization would lead to a gradual elimination of terrorist activity had proven wrong. The state of emergency was into its ninth year, with no end in sight. The Maze hunger strikes of 1981 had catalyzed support for Sinn Féin. The Republican movement had credibility and legitimacy in the eyes of the world, to the largest degree since partition in 1922. The IRA had proven durable and deadly. It was nowhere stronger than in north Belfast. Convictions of the defendants could deliver a sledgehammer blow to the Provisionals there. So long as Kelly conducted a fair trial, it would showcase British justice to a world skeptical of London's way of dealing with Northern Ireland.

The Christopher Black trial would consume 121 trial days, including statements and arguments by the attorneys and Kelly's reading of the judgment and sentences. It would be the longest trial in Irish history. The expense to the taxpayer was in the millions of pounds. The public tab included the fees of barristers for all the defendants, Kevin Barry Artt included. The transcripts and records of proceedings would exceed 70,000 pages, whose volume would fill over thirty boxes. All thirty-eight of the defendants would sit through every court session of the trial in its entirety and listen to the testimony of all 550 witnesses.

Nearly all the accused had a few things in common. They were from New Lodge and Ardoyne. Most were males whose ages ranged between seventeen and twenty-four. The charged offenses had mostly occurred in north Belfast during the summer of 1981, during the chaos that had followed the deaths of Bobby Sands and nine other hunger strikers at the Maze. The period had been one of the bloodiest of the Troubles, claiming 61 lives. It had made for a busy time for the detectives at Castlereagh.

The charges covered sixty-two single-spaced pages of typewritten text. There were scores of them.

Attempted murder of RUC officers.

Possession of firearms and ammunition with intent.
Conspiracy to murder RUC officers in a Land Rover in or about Oldpark Road.

Conspiracy to murder such member or members of the Royal Ulster Constabulary as might enter or leave Oldpark Royal Ulster Constabulary Station.

Carrying a firearm with intent to hijack a motor vehicle, or to resist arrest or to prevent the arrest of another.

Conspiracy to cause an explosion of a nature likely to endanger life or cause serious injury to property in the United Kingdom.

Assisting an offender by rendering medical aid to him and accompanying him in a vehicle to the Republic of Ireland.

Failing to give information within a reasonable time to a constable. Assisting offenders by disposing of a post office worker's coat belonging to Francis Xavier Joseph Murphy.

Hijacking a Ford Cortina.

Possessing 500 grams or thereabouts of commercial blasting explosive, an electric detonator and an improvised power source and switch assembly.

Conspiring to rob from Thomas Dickson & Company of Belfast firearms or imitation firearms.

False imprisonment of a Josephine Ann Glackin in a flat at 2 Cliftonville Avenue in Belfast.

There were no charges against any Loyalist paramilitary, RUC constable, or British Army soldier who had killed unarmed Catholic civilians.

Buried amid the mass of charges were the ninetieth and ninety-first, lodged against Kevin Barry Artt and Charles McKiernan: murdering Albert Miles, and possessing "two firearms and a quantity of ammunition, with intent by means thereof to endanger life . . ." The 166th count charged Kevin with membership in the IRA.

Apart from Kelly's four bodyguards, at least thirty other uniformed RUC men flooded the courtroom every day, creating a roughly 1:1 ratio of police to defendants. On some days, more than *seventy* policemen crowded into the packed courtroom, making the ratio nearly 2:1. The color of their dark green uniforms mixed with the dark blue of prison service officers who sat at the ends of each of the benches, arrayed on each side of the courtroom, where most of the defendants sat. The lead prosecutor, Ronnie Appleton, also had an around-the-clock security detail for the duration of the trial. His mode of travel to and from the courthouse each day was a bulletproof armored car.

To Carmen, the sight of armed police crowding the courtroom was frightening but understandable.

"They were afraid of a riot," she recalled in 2019.

The atmosphere in court was oppressive and tense. By the end of each court day, the air in the packed chamber was warm and stale, redolent with body odor, some of it of prisoners allowed to shower only every other day in the Crum.

The gallery was too small to hold all of the family members of the accused who wished to attend the trial. The court limited the number of relatives who could sit there to one per defendant.

As the trial opened, defense lawyers felt a sense of grim resignation. They had done their homework, interviewed hundreds of witnesses, and crammed with their clients in the last few weeks before Kelly strode out onto the bench. But the game was rigged.

Ted Jones saw the writing on the wall.

Carmen Artt had no illusions about what lay in store in the Number One Court.

"You knew what was gonna happen," she remembered. "You just didn't want to say it."

THIRTY-EIGHT

A Stranger in a Strange Land

In December 1982, ascending each morning from the dank tunnel underneath the Crumlin Road into the dock in the brightly lit courtroom, a 23-year-old Kevin Barry Artt felt like a character in a surrealist 3-D movie, or Kafka's Joseph K., charged with something he hadn't done and secretly accused of it by somebody he didn't know. There were all the barristers in their white and pearl-gray wigs and black robes. Dozens of RUC men lined the walls, scowling. Basil Kelly, on the bench, bedecked in his own wig and a scarlet robe, glowered down at the men in the dock and on the benches. The judge seemed to radiate bitterness. He was grumpy, imposing, formidable, angry. Kevin had never been in such an environment. He felt like he had fallen onto another planet.

During a trial which turned into a nine-month marathon, Kevin would be one of only four of the defendants who was made to sit in the elevated goldfish bowl of the dock.

The other three were Charles McKiernan, Kevin Mulgrew, and Patrick Teer. Kevin guessed that prosecutors had singled them out as ornaments for display, as the worst of all the defendants. Mulgrew was facing eighty-two charges, Teer sixty-nine. McKiernan and Mulgrew were the only other defendants also charged with murder. Kevin did not want to be seen associating with the other three in the courtroom. In the dock, Kevin tried to keep himself as far away from them as possible. He avoided talking to them during the proceedings.

The personal politics were complicated. Kevin resented McKiernan for having falsely named him in the Miles murder. Mulgrew saw McKiernan as a traitor and rat, no better than Christopher Black, willing to betray anyone the peelers wanted to charge if there was something in it for him.

In appearance, the men made for an odd foursome. Mulgrew sported long hair and a mustache. He wore a jacket and tie to court each day. To his right sat a bearded Patrick Teer. Often the two leaned forward in the dock and rested their folded arms on it. Beside them sat McKiernan, in a burgundy-colored pullover and matching tee shirt. Kevin wore a suit every day. His courtroom demeanor was unfailingly formal. He sat bolt upright, cocking his head occasionally to one side, sometimes loosening his tie when it got warm and sticky in the jam-packed courtroom near the end of the day.

The other male defendants sat packed on benches on either side of the courtroom. The five women defendants sat in one of the front benches, guarded by female prison officers.

In front of Kelly's perch on the bench sat two senior Crown counsels, the fifty-four-year-old Ronnie Appleton and his more senior colleague, the thirty-eight-year-old Malachy Higgins, and four senior defense lawyers, at tables divided in the middle by a lectern. Behind them sat junior lawyers, scribbling on legal pads.

On the bench, Kelly had a spotter chart, like a football play-by-play man would use during a broadcast to keep track of names and numbers of the players on the field. It showed the photograph of each defendant and his or her seat in the courtroom. Kelly needed it to keep track of who was who.

One day, a defendant, Patrick Markey, sat in a different seat than usual. A prison officer scolded him and told him to go back to his customary seat so that Kelly would know who he was.

On December 6, 1982, Ronnie Appleton rose to deliver the Crown's opening statement.

Appleton was fifty-four years old. He had a florid complexion, a cherubic countenance, and deep blue eyes set below a pair of big black eyebrows. Appleton was a rarity in the Belfast bar in the early 1980s: a Jewish barrister, in a city whose Jewish population was small. On his own time, he was a passionate player of bridge, at which he excelled. Politics did not matter to him. It was said he would do anything to win. He was known to every Republican defendant as the Crown's most formidable prosecutor.

"May it please your lordship," Appleton began. "The indictment in this case contains some 184 counts and it involves thirty-eight defendants. The charges include murders, attempted murders, conspiracies to murder, conspiracy to cause explosions, the possession of firearms and explosives, robbery, hijacking and intimidation. The main witness for the prosecution is Christopher Peter Black. He will tell your lordship that he joined the Provisional I.R.A. in 1975 and was sworn into the organisation in the month of September of that year."

Appleton's references to Christopher Black in his opening speech numbered one hundred sixty-eight.

The entirety of Appleton's opening statement devoted to the Miles murder spanned forty-nine lines of transcript— some 1% of Appleton's entire opening statement, in a trial involving only two murders (Miles' and Connolly's) charged along with a host of lesser offenses.

"The Crown say that these two defendants were the two men who carried out the murder," said Appleton. It sounded stilted and restrained for a prosecutor charging two men with a cold-blooded murder. Appleton accused Kevin of having fired "a number of shots through" the vestibule door, "at least one of which struck Mr. Miles."

The trial crawled by at a snail's pace. On the bench, Kelly took notes in longhand, as he would for all 121 days. The fraction of trial time which would be devoted to Kevin's case would occupy about a week.

Each day, Maeve and John Artt took turns sitting in the gallery. It seemed no secret that they were the nearest to affluent of any of the parents of the other defendants at the trial. Carmen attended many days of the trial, along with her sister, Isabelle.

As the trial dragged on into the spring of 1983, Carmen found herself unable to drive anywhere in Belfast without being stopped and searched by the RUC.

"I couldn't even go into town," Carmen recalled in 1996. "I was stopped and bodily searched like a dog in the city center."

Aidan Gorman was friends both with Kevin and several other defendants. He managed to attend several days of the trial. One day, an RUC sergeant approached him during a recess. The man spoke with a South African accent.

I don't believe the hassle they're giving Barry Artt, the officer said. *It's a shame what they're doing to him.*

Christopher Peter Black, the Crown's star witness, took the stand on January 12, 1983.

By any fair assessment, Black was the sort of government witness that would make any honest prosecutor cringe. He was a weasel, a scumbag, a murderer. He was also a perjurer. In 1975, he had lied in open court before Kelly himself, something he had neglected to tell either Appleton or the detectives.

Black gave testimony over the course of three weeks. Each morning he entered the courtroom from a side door to Kelly's right, accompanied by a small phalanx of RUC men. Then he walked the five yards to the witness box.

Black had spent over a full year with his minders. They had spent it grooming and rehearsing Black in a secret location, under heavy guard, with breaks to visit his wife and children.

On the witness stand, Black was soft-spoken, well-rehearsed, robotic. His sentences came out as though he were a humanoid automaton who had been programmed to give testimony. He testified in a low monotone, without emotion, with utterly flat affect. It struck observers as unusual given the nature of the things Black claimed to have seen and heard. Black seemed to be testifying from a script that he had committed to memory.

As the days spent listening to Black drone on turned into weeks, the defendants and their lawyers guessed that Black was rehearsing with detectives each night before the next day's performance. He was.

Before the trial, Black had sported a mustache and had a few gray hairs. He had looked pale-faced, drawn, haggard, unkempt. Now the mustache and gray hairs were gone. His hair was jet black, cut short, and neatly groomed, his face clean-shaven. He wore a crisp gray jacket, black tie, white shirt, and black trousers to court every day. Black looked healthy and fit, like a dashing young actor dolled up for an audition, nothing like the bedraggled, doped-up mess who had made the rounds at Castlereagh the year before.

Even his diction had improved. Before November 21, 1981, Black had spoken with a lisp and stuttered when excited. Now the lisp and stutter were gone. People who knew Black said he had never talked like that in his whole life. The RUC had arranged private elocution lessons for him.

Up in the dock, Kevin had a better view of Black than practically everyone. He could see over the cohort of RUC minders, some uniformed, some in plain clothes, that surrounded Black in the witness box. They were like a pack of sentinels or bodyguards. Black sat amid them with his chair turned to his left so he could face Kelly directly. From it he addressed an audience of one. The little coterie of policemen dwarfed Black, preventing defense lawyers from seeing his face even as they tried to cross-examine him. Muted by their bodies, Black's low voice was often inaudible to all but Kelly, who sat only three feet away. The Crown's star witness almost never turned to one side to look at his questioner or at any of the defendants. Sometimes, when being cross-examined by defense lawyers, the minders offered reassuring touches on the shoulder to Black, in case he might be feeling anxious. Kelly sat on his perch, taking notes nonstop. Sometimes Black paused so that Kelly could catch up.

Those who caught a fleeting glance at Black while he testified also noticed an unusual rapport between the witness and the judge hearing his testimony. While hundreds of eyes strained for a glimpse of him from the benches, tables, and gallery, Black's gaze seldom left Kelly. As though to encourage the witness, Kelly often complimented Black from the bench.

Kevin recognized one of the minders. It was Norman Cromie, who had arrested and interrogated several of the defendants himself and also been present when Black named names in Castlereagh. Before and after each court day, in and around the holding cells beneath the courthouse and in the tunnel, Kevin found himself excluded from the huddles of his co-defendants. Kevin only heard secondhand bits and pieces afterward. Mostly, his co-defendants were talking about Black, and how remarkable were his daily performances for Basil Kelly.

Back at the Crum, during hours when Loyalist prisoners were allowed out of their own cells for association or for meals in the dining hall, the guards often unlocked Kevin's cell door. Kevin expected to be attacked by Loyalist prisoners in his cell at any time.

There were other torments. Each day, Kevin set up prayer cards and prayed in front of them in his cell. The guards tore them up and left the pieces on the floor. On Sundays, during hours when Republican prisoners were let out to attend Mass in the jail chapel, guards locked Kevin inside his cell, preventing him from attending. Kevin took to fasting and praying in private.

In the tunnel and the holding cells, the guards addressed Kevin menacingly.

Fenian scum. Taig. When ye get to the Kesh, ye're dead.

"No, I'm not," Kevin replied. "I'm goin' home."

He was sure of it.

THIRTY-NINE

That Concludes the Evidence in Relation to Mr. Miles

The widow of Albert Miles took the stand on December 16, 1982.

The transcript does not reveal Florence Miles' demeanor, the tone of her voice, any tears which fell from her eyes.

Appleton gently guided her through the events of the evening of November 26, 1978, beginning at about 8:20 p.m. Florence had been in the breakfast room, Albert in the kitchen.

Florence described the knock at the door.

"My husband called that there was a knock at the door, and I said, 'Who would it be at this time,' and he thought it was a neighbor, Miss Brown, who always gave a rat-a-tat at the door," she said.

"I went out to answer the door. I shouted, 'Who is there?' and a voice said, 'Butler.' I thought it was from across the road. I didn't quite catch the name."

Where was your son at the time? Appleton asked.

"He was on the telephone in the hall speaking to someone in Bangor."

To come to the door did you have to pass him?

"Yes."

So what did you do?

"I opened the vestibule door and I asked, 'Who is there?' and the voice said, 'Butler.'"

Was the outer door closed at that time?

"It was closed."

Then what did you do?

"Then I opened the outside door and as soon as I opened the door a man kicked the door open."

That was the outside door.

"The outside door."

You were then between the two doors . . . Then what happened?

"When that happened, I realized what was going on or what was happening. I screamed, thinking my husband and my son might realize what was happening and go out or get out by the back door, but that didn't happen."

Then what happened?

"When I screamed, the person put his hand over my mouth and shot through the vestibule door."

Did you see or hear the shooting?

"Oh yes."

Which was it? Did you see or hear it?

"Heard."

And when the shooting started what happened?

"When the shooting started there were further shots came from, I presume, the gate. I couldn't see, but I saw flashes going past my eyes and the door shattered."

And when the shooting stopped, what happened? What did you see?

"I didn't see anything other than the flashes going past my eyes and hearing the sound of the gunfire."

And when that finished?

"As soon as that finished all I could think of was closing the outside door, which I did, and then when I tried to get back into the house the vestibule door wouldn't move. It was shattered."

Why would it not move?

"Because my husband was lying behind it."

Mrs. Miles described where Albert, grievously wounded, lay on the floor. She recounted shouting to Alan to call police and an ambulance and seeing her neighbor, James Townsley, give mouth-to-mouth resuscitation to her stricken husband.

There were some questions which went unasked.

Did you see two shooters or one?

Can you describe the face, or faces, of whomever you saw?

Did you tell detectives on the night of the murder that you saw a gunman with black curly hair and a knitted cap on his head? How could you tell he had black curly hair if he had a knitted cap on his head?

Did either door obscure your view of the gunmen? Was the space well-lit, dimly-lit, or lit in some other way?

Can you describe the clothes the gunmen were wearing? Do you wear eyeglasses? Were you wearing them at the moment of the shooting?

Do you see the men who killed your husband in the courtroom today?

Florence Miles left the witness stand without being cross-examined.

McKiernan's and Kevin's lawyers, Richard Ferguson and Michael Nicholson, felt they could leave well enough alone. Florence Miles had not pointed out either one of their clients as someone she had seen at 8 Evelyn Gardens. It was impossible to know what she might say if asked in open court if she recognized either man.

Two RUC officers who had examined the crime scene, bullets, and casing found outside the front door of 8 Evelyn Gardens testified briefly about their findings. Neither implicated Kevin.

With that—three witnesses, whose testimony consumed less than a single day—Appleton announced: "That concludes the evidence in relation to Mr. Miles . . ."

He had not called Alan Miles, who had seen the two men who shot his father from a few feet away, to the stand.

In a tactical decision which foreclosed any possibility of disputing the circumstances of his confession to Kelly in person, Charles McKiernan elected not to testify. His lawyer, Richard Ferguson, did not bother to challenge the admissibility of his confessions or call any witnesses in his defense.

FORTY

These Are Not Little Plots, My Lord

On February 7, 1983 Kevin's barrister, Michael Nicholson, called his client to testify. It was the thirty-third day of the trial.

Kevin climbed down from the dock and walked to the witness stand. It was on the left-hand side of the bench, slightly below it. The clerk told Kevin to place his hand on the thin, dog-eared Bible that sat there, and swore him in. Kelly stared haughtily down at Kevin.

Kevin took his seat. In front of him was a card that read, "Call the judge 'My Lord.'"

Before Kevin had even settled into the witness chair, he spied Kelly's body language. It telegraphed open hostility. Kelly glowered at Kevin over his gold-rimmed glasses. Kevin guessed that the judge preferred he not testify at all.

Among the three defendants charged with murder (himself, McKiernan, and Kevin Mulgrew), Kevin was the only one who would take the stand in his own defense.

At fifty years of age, Nicholson was an experienced trial lawyer, a Queen's Counsel, as able a defense lawyer as one could want in Belfast in 1983. Tall and distinguished in appearance, he looked the part. Within three years, he would ascend to the bench himself.

Nicholson opened by asking Kevin to describe day one of his interrogation at Castlereagh on November 28, 1981.

"Well, I explained to them that I was arrested before in 1978," Kevin said, "and that as far as I was concerned I took it that the police were satisfied after I was released from Castlereagh in 1978 that I had nothing whatsoever to do with this, my lord."

"Was there any question of an identification parade or an identity parade?" Nicholson asked.

"Yes, I was asked would I go on an identity parade, and I said that I would."

The detectives who rotated in and out of the interrogations—Caskey, Clements, Connolly, Hewitt, Hill, Hylands, Johnston, McCollum, McLaughlin, Rutledge, Turner, and Whitehead—had seemed utterly disinterested in Kevin's responses to their questions, Kevin said.

"They did not want or did not seem to want to give me a chance to explain myself," Kevin said. "They said to me 'Are you trying to tell us that you are innocent?' And I told them that I was innocent and that I had nothing to do with this. But they would not believe a word of what I was telling them at any time."

Nicholson brought Kevin to the day on which he had crumbled: day three, November 30, 1981.

Kevin described the choice detectives had given him: continuing to assert his innocence and drawing a thirty-year stipulated sentence that would cost him Carmen and Barry Paul, or cooperating and receiving a lighter sentence that would give him a chance of keeping them in his life.

"It scared me, my lord. I mean I was crying. I just could not cope with the thought of losing my wife and child, and that is what it was and they had left me with the impression that I had no other choice . . . but to make a statement otherwise I was going to lose my wife and child because they said that otherwise I would get a thirty years stipulated sentence. . .

"I felt just totally shattered . . . I just could not comprehend it, I just could not believe that all of this was happening to me."

Nicholson led Kevin through the rundown with which detectives had hammered him for three days. For the first time, Kevin had begun repeating it back to them. Nicholson asked Kevin why he had played along.

Kevin said he felt he had had no choice.

"It was what the detectives had been telling me, my lord, that if I did not make a statement I was going to get thirty years, the chief superintendent saying that he was going to go out of his way to see to it that I got thirty years but that if I made a statement admitting to this that I would be out after seven years therefore I would not lose my wife and child. There was a good possibility that I would not lose them whereas if I got a sentence of thirty years I would lose them, my lord. . .

"My lord, my whole life revolved around my wife and son, and I knew that I just could not cope with losing them. It was just as simple as that. That is the only reason why I made that statement. I was told that I had no other choice but to do so. I had nothing to do with this at all. . . I was completely shattered, my lord."

Nicholson sat down.

Kelly adjourned for the day.

"I will rise now and sit again at 10:30 in the morning," he said grandly. He vanished through the red curtain behind the bench.

Court resumed the following morning, February 8, with Kevin back in the witness box.

Ronnie Appleton rose and began a lengthy cross-examination.

He opened with the obvious: *why had Kevin confessed?*

Kevin did not vary from what he had said the day before. He had felt he had no choice but to confess, he said, so as to avoid a lengthy prison term, have a chance of keeping

Carmen and Barry Paul, and induce detectives to speak on his behalf at the trial.

Appleton's cross-examination soon descended into an argument with the witness.

Hadn't Kevin known that his confession would result in a life sentence no matter what detectives had promised him?

Didn't Kevin expect to lose Carmen and Barry Paul even if he did leave prison after only seven years?

Had Kevin made up the tale of Rutledge beating him in the interview room on November 30?

Hadn't it been Kevin's ungracious refusal of Rutledge's offer of a rosary which had provoked the detective to punch him in the head and ribs?

Why hadn't Kevin complained to the doctor on duty about the beating or being insulted by the detectives?

Hadn't the doctor who saw Kevin on the night he was charged viewed Kevin as "composed"?

Didn't Kevin agree that Rutledge's apology was genuine?

How could Kevin remember the events of his interrogations in such detail if he had been "utterly shattered" at the time?

When asked if he thought the beating by Rutledge had constituted torture, Kevin said no.

Appleton accused Kevin of fabricating his account of the interrogation sessions, calling Kevin's account "little plots that you have made up."

"These are not little plots, my lord," Kevin said. "I have told you the truth."

Throughout what turned into a full day's grilling, the prosecutor seemed to radiate contempt and condescension. Kevin maintained a polite and respectful demeanor toward Appleton, never failing to append "my lord" to each of his answers.

Appleton, a proud and accomplished prosecutor, might have felt some irritation. He had engaged Kevin in a protracted argument which produced only answers which were exculpatory and often redundant of things Kevin had already said. Perhaps Appleton thought he could wear Kevin down by sheer persistence, as the detectives had at Castlereagh.

He kept on.

"Why did you not say to the police 'I am going to take my chance rather than lose my wife and child?'" he asked.

"Because they were telling me that I had no chance, my lord," Kevin said.

"And you accepted that from them?"

"I had no choice but to accept it."

Now Kelly jumped in.

"But why accept that?" he boomed from the bench. "It was your word against theirs, was it not?"

Kevin, startled, looked up to his left at the judge.

"For a start, my lord, Mr. Hylands came in and he had told me that he was going to see to it personally," he said. "He said that Mr. Miles was a friend of his and that he was taking this personally and he was going to see to it that I was going to get thirty years prison."

Kelly raised his eyebrows in disbelief.

As the court day neared its end, Appleton concluded by thrusting Kevin's confession, trial exhibit 105, at him.

He asked Kevin to agree that his signature appeared at the bottom of each page.

Kevin agreed it was true.

"And did you not make this statement of your own free will?" Appleton said, his voice rising.

"No, my lord, not really," Kevin replied. "I made the statement, and the police went through the statement with me. But I am telling you the reasons why I made this statement. This statement is not true, my lord."

Kelly adjourned the trial for the day, vanishing behind the curtain.

Kevin returned to his cell at the Crum exhausted. He felt like he had run a marathon or gone eight rounds in a boxing ring.

The next morning, Appleton pivoted to the topic of the handguns used to shoot Albert Miles.

His questioning Kevin seemed only to expose Kevin's ignorance about firearms.

"Did they ask you to describe the guns that you had used?" Appleton asked.

"Yes, my lord," Kevin replied.

"And did you say that the one you had was one with a round barrel and silver colour and the other one was a bigger one, ugly looking?"

"Yes."

"Why didn't you say a .38 and a .45?"

"Because they asked me to describe them. They asked me what type of guns they were. I told them what they had already told me. They asked me what sort of guns they were, and they asked me to describe them, and I described them. Well, what I thought they would be like."

"Where did you get the 'round barrel and silver colour' from?"

"That's what a revolver is like, isn't it, my lord?"

"You invented it?"

"That's what I took it a revolver is like, my lord."

Kelly and the defense lawyers did not know it, but the RUC had the murder weapons. Constables had recovered them seven weeks after Albert Miles was killed, on January 5, 1979, at Northwick Drive, by coincidence, while investigating an unrelated IRA operation in which two Provisionals had blown themselves up with their own bomb. The cache of weapons which the RUC men found nearby went into an RUC evidence room miles from the courthouse. Forensic examination of one of them, a .45 caliber pistol, matched it to the bullet which had killed Albert Miles. The other, a .38 caliber revolver, was deemed very likely to have been used to fire the other rounds at 8 Evelyn Gardens.

The idea of trying a murder case without putting the murder weapons into evidence or tying them to the defendants accused of firing them would strike many prosecutors as odd. But the .38, the weapon supposedly fired at Albert Miles on the night of November 26, 1978, would never see the inside of the Number One Court.

FORTY-ONE

You Were Brought Up in the New Lodge Area?

In March 1983 the trial dragged on into its fourth month.

No more witnesses would testify about the case of Kevin Barry Artt until April 12, 1983, when Lorraine Keenan took the stand.

She had just arrived at the courthouse from the airport in a taxicab.

By now Lorraine was twenty-four years old. Dozens of surly armed police surrounded her in the Number One Court. From the bench, Kelly scowled down at her.

Lorraine was still bitter over Kevin's having jilted her and married Carmen. But she had taken time off from work and traveled from London in order to testify for him.

Years later, Kevin remembered her demeanor.

"The only reason she was there was she knew I was with her the night [Miles] was killed," he said. "She was scared to death."

Nicholson turned to the Sunday night that had changed the lives of the Artt and Miles families forever.

It had been "just the usual Sunday," Lorraine testified, "messing about watching TV." After dinner with the family, she and Kevin had gone into Lorraine's room to listen to records before coming into the living room to watch television. Kevin had come over the night before at around

2 a.m. after catching a late movie and spent the entire day there.

Nicholson turned to the critical period of time between 8 and 10 p.m.

"Well, we had watched television," Lorraine said. "He would have went into the room where we were playing records and we went back into the living room watching TV again and then Barry left to go to the Felons for a drink."

Nicholson asked her what time Kevin had departed the house.

"It must have been ten o'clock, a quarter to ten or ten o'clock," said Lorraine. "It was for last orders[4] that he went 'round there."

Kelly interrupted again.

"Does that mean that he was in your house all Sunday until about ten o'clock?"

"Yes," replied Lorraine.

Nicholson focused on the news bulletin. Had it been a part of the ten o'clock news, or had the station interrupted other programming to air the bulletin at an earlier time?

"There was a news flash about a murder," said Lorraine. "It was not on the main news."

"And who was present in the house when you heard that news flash?"

"Both my parents and Barry and Stephen, my brother," Lorraine answered.

Nicholson yielded the witness. Now it would be Appleton's turn to cross-examine the frightened young woman from New Lodge.

He asked Lorraine how she knew Kevin was innocent.

"Because he was with me when the murder happened," she answered evenly.

---

4. Northern Ireland's equivalent of what Americans would describe as last call.

If that was so, said Appleton, why had she not gone to the police as soon as they arrested Kevin and told them so?

Lorraine offered a view probably shared by everyone in New Lodge.

"People get arrested in Northern Ireland all the time for things that they did not do," Lorraine said.

Appleton clownishly arched his big black eyebrows, feigning indignation and incredulity.

"You say that people get arrested in Northern Ireland all the time for things they did not do?"

Lorraine nodded, adding, "And my going to the police station would not have done anything to help him."

Appleton sensed an opening.

"What is your attitude to the police and the Army?"

"I do not have any."

Appleton asked whether Lorraine thought the police would have listened had she only gone to the station and spoken to them.

"No," she said.

"Why not?"

"It is what we are led to believe, that they do not listen."

"You were brought up in the New Lodge area?"

"That is right."

"And were you led to believe there that the police brutalized people and would not listen to reason?"

Lorraine did not hesitate.

"I *seen* the police brutalize people," she said.

"And you believe that they would not listen to reason?"

"Yes."

Appleton now tried to make the most of what Lorraine had given him to work with.

"You feel strongly about the police?"

"I do not think anything about them at all," said Lorraine.

"Even although they brutalize people and do not listen to people, you do not think anything of them?"

"No," replied the young woman. "I moved out of Northern Ireland to get away from the Troubles and all of this."

"But you are back now," said Appleton.

"I am back because Barry is up for a murder he did not do," Lorraine replied.

Testily, Appleton brushed the answer aside and kept on. Perhaps he could bait Lorraine into disparaging the security forces, revealing a bias he could use to discredit her credibility with Kelly.

"And there are forces of law and order here whom you believe brutalize people and will not listen to reason?"

Theatrically, Appleton swung his arm wide, sweeping in the clusters of RUC men in their dark green uniforms and the prison officers gathered at the ends of the rows of defendants seated in the benches.

It seemed like there were fifty of them. Many now stared straight at the young woman on the witness stand.

"Yes, that is right," said Lorraine.

"If that was your view you would be opposed to those forces that acted in that way, would you not?"

"Yes, I am opposed to them."

"You are opposed to them?"

"Yes."

Appleton now put as fine a point on it as he could.

"You are opposed to the forces of law and order in Northern Ireland?"

"Yes, I am."

Appleton asked Lorraine how long she had felt this way about the police and British Army.

"Since I seen the way they get on in the streets," Lorraine replied.

"Well, is that from when you were very young?"

"About ten or twelve," she said.

Appleton pressed on, trying to tempt Lorraine into expressing support for terrorism.

"You do not condemn the IRA?" the prosecutor asked.

"I don't condemn them, no," Lorraine replied.

"You think that it is not to be condemned that they kill policemen and soldiers?"

"I did not say that. I did say I do not condemn them."

"But they kill policemen and soldiers. Do they not?"

"Yes."

"And you do not condemn them for it?"

"I do not condemn anybody."

"Except the police for brutalizing people, is that so? If you do not condemn the IRA for shooting police and soldiers, would you support people who are members of the IRA?"

"I did not say that either."

"No, but I am asking you that, Ms. Keenan."

Lorraine paused.

"No," she said.

"There was a long pause before you answered that," said Appleton.

"I was taking in the meaning of the question."

Appleton now turned to seeing if he could poke any holes in Lorraine's timeline or memory. Perhaps he could induce Lorraine to confuse the events of the night of Sunday, November 26, 1978, with some other Sunday night.

Lorraine mentioned probably having had an argument with Kevin over his having gone out to the Felons Club that night. Appleton sought clarification.

"Why do you say that you had an argument that night?"

"I did not say we had. I said we probably had."

"I am sorry, that is absolutely right. That is my mistake. Why do you say that you probably had an argument that night?"

"I did not like Barry drinking in the clubs. When he said he was going out to meet Stephen in the Felons . . . more than likely I had an argument with him about it."

Appleton bore down, showing his chops as a cross-examiner. If he could cause Lorraine Keenan to vacillate on what had happened that Sunday night, he could discredit Kevin's alibi as the product of faulty and wishful recollection.

"This sort of thing happened on a number of Sundays, did it?"

"No, not every Sunday. Most Sundays he stayed at my home."

"But it happened on other Sundays that he went off?"

"It had happened, yes."

"Could you have got some of these confused which nights he went off and which he did not?"

"No."

"Did he stay at your house every Sunday?"

"Not every Sunday."

Appleton now turned to Kevin's account of the day. He reckoned Lorraine, who had arrived only that morning from London, had not heard what it had been. Perhaps he could draw out a contradiction between their two accounts, even invite Lorraine to call Kevin a liar and see if she took the bait.

She did.

"He told the police when he was arrested in December of 1978 that he did not come to your house until two in the afternoon. Would that be a lie?"

"Yes."

"It would be?"

"Yes."

"Would it?"

"Yes."

"Pardon?"

"Yes."

"You are absolutely certain that he was there?"

"He stayed. He came on Saturday night about two o'clock."

"About what time?"

"It was after midnight, and I think it was about two o'clock."

"About two o'clock on Sunday morning?"

"Yes."

"You have no doubt about that?"

"No."

"You remember that?"

"He came Saturday night after the film. He stayed on the settee. We stayed talking to about four or five and then I went to bed. The next day we got up and had lunch and he was there all day."

Appleton, feeling the lawyerly sensation of scoring points, kept pouring it on, trying to confuse the young, frightened witness.

Now he turned to the time of the news bulletin broadcasting the Miles murder.

"It was not the ten o'clock news?"

"I don't think so. I think it was a news flash."

"Well, could it have been the ten o'clock news?"

"I suppose it could have been."

"It could have been?" The big eyebrows arched again.

"Yes."

"Miss Keenan, you have no recollection of that at all, have you? There is a big difference, is there not, between hearing something on a news flash interrupting a programme and hearing it on the ten o'clock news?"

"Not when you are not taking any interest in it."

"You think that it was a news flash?"

"Yes."

"But it could have been the ten o'clock news, and this was just before he left to go to the Felons Club?"

"It was not just before it."

"It was not just before it?"

"No."

"Well, how long was it before he left to go to the Felons Club?"

"I don't know. Stephen was there. When he heard the news, he left and then Barry left after him. It could not have been the ten o'clock news."

"It could not have been the ten o'clock news because Stephen was still there?"

"Yes."

"And how long before Barry left did Stephen leave?"

"I don't know."

"It was very important, this news flash, because it fixes the alibi, is that not right?"

"I don't remember."

"You don't remember?"

"No."

"Do you really remember that day, Miss Keenan?"

"Just vaguely."

"Just vaguely?"

"Yes."

"And all that you really want to say is that Kevin Barry John Artt did not do the murder?"

"Well, he was with me when the murder happened, so he could not have done it."

Appleton now descended into bullying.

"You see, I suggest to you that your evidence is quite untrue. What do you say to that?"

"It is the truth."

Appleton now observed the last cardinal rule of cross-examination. He sat down.

"She was honest," said defense barrister Arthur Harvey in 1996. "That's probably what Kelly didn't like about her. She had enough intelligence to present herself as she chose.

"If she had wanted, she could have fudged her testimony regarding her opinions of the RUC. Instead, she was truthful."

Following several days of closing arguments, Kevin's solicitor, Ted Jones, thought Nicholson had done a good job. He called Kevin's parents and told them Kevin was going to be coming home.

Basil Kelly decamped to a secure location in London. There he holed up, under heavy guard provided by SAS men, to write his judgment, after having listened to 119 days of testimony spanning nine months.

FORTY-TWO

Incantation

On the morning of August 2, 1983, Kelly emerged through the red curtain behind the bench for the biggest performance of his judicial career. An air of suspense and gloom hung over the defendants, their lawyers, and their relatives in the jam-packed gallery.

Kelly's reading of his judgments and sentences would consume the next four days.

Kelly addressed the matter of what weight to give to the testimony of Christopher Black, on which so many convictions solely depended.

"In deciding whether Black's evidence is credible," said Kelly, "I must not only examine its content but . . . also look at his record and character, the circumstances and motivation which led him to give information to the police and to give evidence at this trial."

Black had murdered three people, including Julian Connolly, the zoo groundskeeper and part-time UDR man. He was a convicted bank robber. Then, of course, there was "active and wholehearted" involvement "up to his neck in terrorist activity throughout 1981." To refine his skills in handling firearms, Black had attended an IRA training camp in Donegal. He had shot to kill. He had falsely imprisoned people in their homes at gunpoint to facilitate murder. He had planted bombs meant to kill.

There was no way to avoid saying it, so Kelly said it. Black was a "dangerous and ruthless terrorist."

Then there was the awkward matter of Black's lies from the witness stand *in the Black trial itself.*

It was no problem, said the judge.

The discrepancies, misstatements, and omissions had been "very few indeed in the context of the whole case," he said. Poor Christopher Black had had a lot to remember. He had been "tired, confused, frightened and mixed up" when talking to the Bear inside Castlereagh. He had felt marital pressures. What married man in his position wouldn't?

Black "genuinely did forget" some things, Kelly said. He remembered crimes committed by the defendants only "at the last moment" before trial, after having not told police about them. But the crimes, Kelly said, were "comparatively trivial," easy to forget until just before testifying.

Kelly turned to one of the bigger elephants in the room. It was Black's prior perjury in his own courtroom in November 1975 in a double murder case, *R. v. Robert John Martin Crawford.* The perjury, said Kelly, had concerned whether Black kept a rifle in a house and whether Black had been with the defendant, Crawford, on the night of the murder. It was peripheral, a trifle, hardly warranting the "amount or proportion of adverse criticism" poured on Black by defense attorneys.

Black was not perfect. But, Kelly asked, where was the perfect witness?

So it went. Kelly ruled out any possibility that Black could be falsely accusing any of the defendants. It was practically unthinkable, something Kelly now explained in a series of rhetorical questions.

Why should he do this?

Why should he name innocent men as terrorists who are not?

He may be making an honest mistake in identity but is he making an honest mistake then in respect of twenty-three of them or in respect of some of them?

If he is naming innocent men falsely as members of the IRA what are his motives in doing this?

To everyone in the courtroom but Kelly, some common-sense answers suggested themselves. No one said them out loud.

Black had all the motivation in the world: cash, immunity, a new identity, unification with his wife and four children abroad, and paid bodyguards to protect him from enemies who were known to torture and murder turncoats like him. The motivation was not to tell the truth, but to please the government agents who controlled the benefits, even if it meant lying in court.

If any of that troubled Basil Kelly, he left it unmentioned.

Whatever the holes in Black's testimony, Kelly said, they mattered much less than Black's demeanor while under cross-examination. And it had been "confident, calm, deliberate and measured . . . rarely hesitant . . . at times thoughtful in recall."

Kelly pronounced Black's testimony believable and convincing.

"He was, as various counsel have described, a terrorist, a person involved in murder and a perjurer," Kelly said, correctly. "He was all of these things and more. But at the end of the day, at the end of his evidence after the fifteenth day before me, my conclusion was that in his account of the incidents and their participants he was one of the best witnesses I had ever heard.

"By that I mean that he was one of the most convincing witnesses I had heard in my experience of criminal trials and other trials. I am confident that any tribunal of fact sitting by who had heard him would have reached the same conclusion and the same degree of conclusion. . .

"Very, very many situations, conversations and comments he described in language and manner which suggested only truth."

The hard work now complete, Kelly got busy with the rest, going case by case.

Kelly resolved each conflict in testimony between Black and the defendants in Black's favor. Black had been the sole witness against twenty-one of the defendants who had not confessed, and the sole witness against fifteen more who had.

Kelly's words sounded like incantations, repeated again and again, like a churchman's prayers read aloud from a missal in a big echoey stone church.

I am satisfied beyond reasonable doubt that on Black's evidence the accused is guilty of the offence charged.

I warn myself of the danger of convicting on the uncorroborated evidence of an accomplice, but it is so convincing that I am satisfied beyond reasonable doubt . . .

It seems to me quite unlikely that Black would falsely name such a person . . .

I am quite satisfied that this was an innocent omission by Black.

I can see no rational explanation for Black making up an incident of this kind.

I have no hesitation in reaching the conclusion on the weight of Black's evidence alone.

For defendants and their witnesses, Kelly had a different litany.

I did not believe a word of his defence of mistaken identity.

There is no substance in the allegations against the police.

The confessions were freely and voluntarily given, and I can give them full weight.

I have no difficulty in rejecting the alibi.

I do not believe him.

I simply do not believe this.
I just do not believe it.
I do not believe this.

Such phrases recur over and over whilst one turns the pages of Kelly's judgment. After a while they produce a numbing effect in the reader, like the droning echoey monotone of Learned Hand's old man in a long nightgown making muffled noises at people who might be no worse than he.

Kelly embarked on his second day of reading out the judgments the next day, August 3.

"He cleaned up north Belfast all right," said Carmen Artt. "It was just another form of internment, a way to get them off the streets."

FORTY-THREE

I Am Satisfied

On August 4, 1983, Kelly at last turned to Kevin's case.

It was the 120th day of the trial. Kevin had waited for this day for over twenty months.

"Charles McKiernan and John Kevin [sic] Barry Artt are charged with the murder of Mr. Albert Miles, aged 49 years, late of 8 Evelyn Gardens, Belfast, former deputy governor of the Maze Prison."

Kelly started with McKiernan's confessions.

Kelly noted that McKiernan had named Kevin as the other gunman, as well as the one who had given him both a gun and instructions about whom they were going to shoot, during a meeting at the Shamrock Club in Ardoyne.

Kelly described how he believed Albert Miles had died on the floor of his home that night in November 1978.

"McKiernan and Artt were armed respectively with a .45 pistol and a .38 revolver," he said. "They went to the door of the house, McKiernan held Mrs. Miles, and both fired shots at Mr. Miles who had come to the door, a number of which entered his body and one of which caused his death.

"Professor Marshall's *post mortem* showed that Mr. Miles had been hit by four bullets. One bullet struck the back of his right forearm probably while his arm was drawn up defensively in front of his head and lodged in the skin above the elbow. A second bullet struck his right temple but while it perforated the skin it did not enter the skull. A third bullet struck the back of the head, entered one and a half inches of scalp and then exited. It probably would have caused immediate unconsciousness but not death. The fourth bullet was the fatal one. It entered the back between the shoulder blades and lodged in the pelvis where it was recovered. It led to massive haemorrhage and it was fired after he collapsed face down to the floor. . .

"I am quite satisfied that two guns were fired at Mr. Miles, a .38 revolver and a .45 pistol and that the strike mark on top of the left-hand column was caused by one of these guns."

Here, Kelly's finding was in harmony with the findings of the inquest and the forensic evidence taken at the scene and the morgue.

Kelly found McKiernan's confessions to be "admissible and . . . made under such circumstances that full weight can be given to them."

Kelly hardly could have found otherwise. Richard Ferguson, McKiernan's barrister, had put on no semblance of a defense. McKiernan had sat there, in the dock, impassive and inert, for eight months.

What ably represented man accused of murder, but not guilty of it, sits through a nine-month trial without putting on a defense?

Kelly found that it was McKiernan who had fired the fatal bullet and therefore that he was "guilty of murder as charged."

Kelly now turned to Kevin's case, noting immediately that the case against him depended "solely on his own admissions to the police. There is no other evidence in the case against him and anything said about him by McKiernan in McKiernan's statements or confrontation is not of course evidence against [Kevin]."[5]

Kelly found that Kevin had made verbal admissions of guilt on November 30, December 1, and December 2, and that he had "dictated and signed a written confession (Exhibit 105, page 821) between 7:43 p.m. and 9:10 p.m. to Detective Sergeant McLaughlin and Detective Constable Turner."

Kelly summarized Kevin's confession, "as noted by the interviewers."

"[H]e was told to go to the Shamrock Club one night and meet other people . . . He said when he went there he met two others and they were given two guns . . . they drove to Evelyn Gardens where they were told they had to shoot a jail warden. . . He did not know that it was the deputy governor. When they got to the house . . . him and one of the other men got out and went up to the front door . . . a woman came out and the other man held her . . . just fired at the man in the hallway. I can remember seeing that man's face but I killed him."

If some rough stuff had gone on inside Castlereagh, Kelly said, it was just good police work.

"Courts do not always hear all that goes on in an interview room from detective witnesses. Even a full and honest account in the witness box of an interview cannot give the full flavor or atmosphere of an interview. Detectives use all their skills, their differing techniques, and their

5. In making this ruling, Kelly was relying on the principle of British law disallowing use of the confession of one defendant for the purpose of incriminating another defendant. Theoretically, this made McKiernan's confession, to the degree it incriminated Kevin, inadmissible for the purpose of determining Kevin's guilt.
On a human level, however, the possibility that Kelly could banish it from his mind seems far-fetched. Kelly was a judge, but he was also human.

experience, as they are entitled to do and as is their duty, to discover the truth from suspects.

"At times aggressiveness, bluff, persistence, and guile play their part. But the court must closely inquire whether their techniques reach the objectionable standard of oppressive or unfair conduct."

They had not, said Kelly.

The judge laid bare his view of who was telling the truth about the interrogations and who was not.

"Artt is an intelligent young man whose intelligence I would say is quite above average," said Kelly. "But he told a number of lies in the witness box that belied it. Some of them affronted in their enormity. His apparent gullibility that he had no alternative but to confess to a murder which he did not do, for which he had an honest alibi and for which there was no independent or untainted evidence of his involvement, would not come from an intelligence much lower than his. Nor did his apparent acceptance that he would get out of prison in seven years if he confessed but not for 30 years if he did not. . .

"When he was taken through his confessions line by line by Mr. Appleton as to how they came to be composed and what source they came from, his string of untruths was manifest, and his demeanour underlined it all. His assertion of what he said to the police in answer to McKiernan's confrontation in the presence of McKiernan I do not believe. It contains the perfect and complete content of how an innocent man should react and I am satisfied he made it up with hindsight. . .

"I am satisfied that the detectives did not use his anxiety and these discussions to make them into a threat or promise of a favour to induce any of the confessions he made. In particular I do not accept that they threatened him with 30 years' imprisonment on the one hand and promised him seven years on the other. When they said he would possibly get life, I think they were trying to soften the blow having regard to his condition at the time. I think he did show genuine remorse at times during the interviews but I suspect that most of the tears that he shed were for his own situation and that of his wife and child and not for what is left of the Miles family. . .

"I have no doubt but that all his confessions were freely and voluntarily given, and I am satisfied that they should be given full weight. I find it incredible that a young man of Artt's common sense as well as intelligence should confess to a murder which he did not commit."

Kelly's logic offered a catch-22 to rival Joseph Heller's. It went like this:

Kevin had told the truth in Castlereagh when he admitted murdering Miles. In court, he lied about the matter. Those lies made him a liar, to be distrusted as a witness. But they bolstered his credibility as a truth-teller in Castlereagh, rendering his confession there gospel and his in-court denials of it lies.

There was still some explaining to do.

Kevin had not known the names of any of his accomplices. It was no problem, said Kelly. Kevin had just been covering for other terrorists. That was to be expected, the judge said.

"The omission from his statement of the names of his accomplices in the murder is not due to his ignorance of their identity but in accordance with the terrorist code and/ or fear of reprisal for disclosure," Kelly said. "I believe the vagueness and generality of his description in the statement of the actual shooting is in part due to his reluctance to face up to the confession to a positive and deliberate shooting."

Kelly turned to Kevin's alibi. He had offered uncontradicted testimony of being with the Keenans on the night of November 26, 1978. It counted for nothing, said Kelly. The witnesses were biased, that was all. How could they be believed?

"The evidence of . . . his former fiancée, Ms. Lorraine Kane [sic], does not raise a reasonable doubt in my mind as to his guilt," said the judge, butchering the name of Kevin's main alibi witness. "Although no longer his fiancée, I feel Miss Kane's [sic] evidence also comes from a not disinterested source. She is strongly biased against the police. Her fairly recent recall of what happened three and a half years ago does not give me confidence in the accuracy of what she says. She is deliberately or unintentionally recalling another Sunday evening."

There was no mention of whether the detectives who testified about Kevin's statements could have been not disinterested themselves or biased against a man accused of assassinating an officer personally known to at least one of them (Hylands).

Kelly summed up.

"I am satisfied beyond reasonable doubt that Artt's confessions are true, that he was one of two gunmen who were sent out and did set out to kill Mr. Miles and that he deliberately shot at Mr. Miles with that intention and assisted in achieving the common purpose of murder.

"He is therefore guilty of the offences charged in counts 90 and 91."

Carmen had believed Kevin was coming home. John and Maeve believed he was coming home. Ted Jones had convinced them of it. Now he was never coming home.

FORTY-FOUR

Lowering the Boom

Kevin felt his body go numb.

The other men in the dock had been afraid to testify on their own behalf. Kevin had taken the stand and told Kelly the truth. Kevin had believed the truth would prevail and he would walk free. Instead, he would be going to the Maze to serve what was sure to be a long prison term.

It was unbelievable.

"Against all odds, I believed the truth would prevail, I would walk from the courts a free man. I believed in justice, until I experienced that it didn't exist," he wrote in 1992.

Ironically, Kelly had acquitted Kevin of count 166, membership of the IRA. During closing argument, Higgins himself had admitted there had been no evidence to prove the charge. And so, Kevin was both guilty of an IRA murder and not guilty of being an IRA man in the first place.

"While there is evidence that Artt was interested in joining the I.R.A. and *prima facie* evidence that he committed a murder on their behalf," Kelly said, "there is no real evidence that he became a member. I hold there is no *prima facie* case in Count 166."

Kelly sentenced Kevin and McKiernan to life imprisonment for the murder of Albert Miles. For good measure, Kelly added fifteen more years to Kevin's sentence, on the firearms count.

Kelly adjourned the proceedings, rose from his chair, and slipped back through the red curtain for the second-to-last time.

On August 5, Kelly took the bench for the last day of the Irish trial of the century.

Below the courtroom, prison service officers had set up a rotation. They brought in each defendant one at a time to be sentenced, then escorted him out, then brought in the next one. Family members crowded outside the gallery, waiting for their loved one's name to be shouted out to them so they could scramble in to hear Kelly pronounce sentence. After Kelly finished pronouncing each sentence, shouted profanities of family members and relatives disgusted at the charade echoed in the halls outside the courtroom.

Kelly sentenced the thirty-five defendants he had adjudged guilty to a cumulative total of 4,022 years in prison.

Seventy-one defense witnesses had testified, either under subpoena or voluntarily. Only seven of them were defendants.[6] The remainder were third party witnesses. To Kelly, all of their testimony meant nothing.

"He'd have been better off judging butter than human beings," said Arthur Harvey in 1996.

In a daze, Kevin trudged through the tunnel back to the Crum for the last time, utterly depressed, victim of a juristic charade and fraud masquerading as a fair trial, on his way to the Maze, from whose walls he might never emerge alive.

On the morning of August 5, 1983, guards escorted Kevin out of the Crum in chains, to a waiting British Army Chinook helicopter. With him were his three fellow new

---

6. Apart from Kevin, they were Desmond Breslin, Paul Kane, Kevin Mulgrew, Patrick Fennell, Thomas McKinney, and Joseph Kelly.

lifers, Gerald Loughlin, Charles McKiernan, and Kevin Mulgrew.

The big twin-rotor helicopter lifted off and hovered above the Crum, then lowered its nose and started climbing, headed for the Maze, ten miles away.

As the Chinook picked up speed and the green landscape rolled by below, Kevin felt he was being sent to his death at the hands of Maze prison guards. In the din of the engines and rotors, surrounded by helmeted soldiers, he sat in his manacles praying silently to St. Jude, the patron saint of hopeless causes, to rescue him.

The idea of appealing crossed his mind. But his faith in the courts was destroyed. And who knew if he would be alive or dead by the time the Court of Appeal reviewed the case?

In Catholic communities throughout the north, Kelly's judgment drew scorn.

In other quarters, it played better. On February 8, 1984, in a ceremony at Buckingham Palace, as a military band played and an honor guard stood by at attention, Basil Kelly knelt before Queen Elizabeth II on a short, padded red and gold stool, and bowed his head. The queen touched Kelly's right shoulder, then his left, with a sword, and pronounced him a knight of the British Empire.

FORTY-FIVE

Welcome to Hell

At the Maze, the helicopter touched down. Soldiers handed Kevin over to a clutch of prison service officers in dark blue uniforms and peaked caps. They hustled their new prize in to reception.

There they photographed him, made him strip naked, searched him, gave him a towel, and handed his clothes back to him. The newspapers, television, and radio had all trumpeted his conviction for murdering Miles. They finally had their hands on the murderer of Albert Miles. They started in on him in the first minute.

Provie cunt. We got ye now, ye Fenian bastard.

They talked about Miles—*Bertie, Bert, our Bert.*

Ye're going straight to the boards, Barry. Welcome to hell.

Presently guards transported Kevin, Gerald Loughlin, Charles McKiernan, and Kevin Mulgrew to H-7. The men were taken straight in to see the Principal Officer of H-7, who was seated in his office.

One by one, each man took his turn in the office. The door was open.

Of the four, Kevin went in first.

Ordinarily, this exercise was routine for newly arrived lifers at the Maze. The principal officer held a brief meeting with each man and offered some cursory advice, a spiel.

Try to settle down. Don't cause trouble. Blah blah blah.

Afterward, guards would escort the men out to their assigned cells on the wing.

Loughlin stood just outside the door, awaiting his turn. The PO sat behind a desk, glaring at Kevin. After the standard spiel, the officer added one more thing.

Oh, by the way, Artt, I just want to echo the words of Inspector Hylands. I hope ye rot in here for the rest of your stinking life. I hope to make your time as hard as possible.

Kevin emerged, pale and frightened.

"Did you hear that?" he asked Loughlin.

Kevin was escorted out and taken to H-7. Loughlin went to H-8.

The billeting was unusual.

Kevin was "not like us," Loughlin recalls— "without real political connections," "totally innocent." He was in for a hard time at the hands of his new captors. They took care to treat prisoners convicted of killing prison officials or guards more harshly than prisoners who had killed mere policemen or Loyalist paramilitaries. Kevin was such a prisoner. His notoriety gave him something in common with some of H-7's other residents: Brendan Mead, Bobby Storey, Gerry Kelly, and Brendan "Bik" McFarlane, all prominent IRA men, to whom the news media had given much attention down the years. Now the lives of each of them would intertwine in a way that Kevin could not have imagined.

In his despair, Kevin retained the presence of mind to focus on the mechanical tasks necessary to take an appeal.

On August 8, 1983, three days after arriving at the Maze, Kevin and Ted Jones filled out, signed, and dated a form notice of appeal, to be filed at the Northern Ireland Court of Appeal.

ILLUSTRATIONS

*Visit **wbp.bz/atggallery** to view these and other illustrations related to this story.*

Ireland

Florence and Albert Miles, on holiday in 1976 in Godalming, Surrey, England. (Alan Miles)

Former mother-and-baby home, Kinturk convent, Castlepollard, Co. Westmeath, Ireland, photographed in 2016. Birthplace of Kevin Barry Artt. (Dan Lawton)

IRA volunteer, traitor, and British
informant Maurice Gilvarry

Police photograph of Albert Miles at 8 Evelyn Gardens,
Belfast, November 26, 1978. (Royal Ulster Constabulary)

Kevin Barry Artt, then employed as a truck driver and laborer by Robert Hart Memorials, built the gravesite and placed the stones at the resting place of Albert Miles at Carnmoney Cemetery in Newtownabbey, County Antrim, about seven miles outside Belfast. (Dan Lawton)

Watercolor of Kevin Barry Artt's holding cell at Castlereagh Holding Centre, Belfast, as it looked in 1981. (Kevin Barry Artt 1996)

During 1982 and 1983, Kevin and his co-defendants traversed this tunnel twice a day, crossing under the street from Crumlin Road Jail to the Crumlin Road Courthouse and back again, each court day for nine consecutive months. (Dan Lawton)

Sir John William Basil Kelly, the British judge who presided over the Irish Trial of the Century in 1982 and 1983. He sentenced the defendants to a cumulative total of 4,022 years in prison. Soon afterward, he traveled to London, where Queen Elizabeth II knighted him at Buckingham Palace. (Alamy)

Her Majesty's Prison Maze, known to Irish Republicans as Long Kesh Prison. (Alamy)

The main gate and Tally Lodge of the Maze, where guards and escaping Republican prisoners brawled during the escape on September 25, 1983.

Mugshot of Kevin Barry Artt, taken at the Maze shortly after his arrival on August 5, 1983. (Northern Ireland Prison Service via Press Association)

Kevin's fellow Maze escapees from left to right starting in the first row: Joe Corey, Pádraig McKearney, Seamus Clarke, Gerard P. "Blute" McDonnell, Pól Brennan, and Jimmy Smyth. (Northern Ireland Prison Service)

On the run and living underground in San Francisco in 1985, with his beard and hair dyed jet black, trying to stay incognito, Kevin felt like a kind of poor man's James Bond. (Kevin Barry Artt 1985)

Kevin Barry Artt arriving on a San Francisco Municipal Railway cable car, downtown San Francisco, California, in 1996, for a meeting with his American lawyers. (Michael Brennan)

Kevin Barry Artt and his American lawyer, James J. Brosnahan, at Brosnahan's office at Morrison & Foerster in San Francisco in 1996. (Michael Brennan)

A happy day on the courthouse steps at 450 Golden Gate Avenue in San Francisco, on October 16, 1998, the day of the release from jail of Maze escapees ordered by Judge Legge the day before. Pictured from left to right are attorneys Jim Larson and Gil Eisenberg, Maze escapees Terry Kirby, Kevin Barry Artt, and Pól Brennan, and attorney James J. Brosnahan. (Polaris Images)

A big day in the case of Kevin Barry Artt at the Northern Ireland Court of Appeal, March 5, 2020. Pictured from left to right, on the bench, are Justices Bernard McCloskey, Ben Stephens, and Adrian Colton. Pictured from behind, from left to right, are solicitor Andrew Moriarty and barrister Fiona Doherty, QC. (Dan Lawton)

Peter Heathwood at home in Killough, Northern Ireland, on October 22, 2019. (Dan Lawton)

Medical student and IRA volunteer Kevin Barry, the namesake of Kevin Barry Artt, in 1918. At age 18, after a trial by a British court-martial at which he refused to recognize the legitimacy of the court, Barry was hanged at Mountjoy Jail in Dublin.

SECTION VIII

OUT OF THE MAZE

FORTY-SIX

H-7

Kevin's new home, H-7, housed 125 Republican prisoners. Of that number, forty-four had convictions for murder, attempted murder, or conspiracy to murder. Twenty-four were doing life or the equivalent. Another eighty-eight were doing ten years or longer. Most were in their twenties. Kevin's cell was eight feet by ten. A heavy steel door separated it from the corridor. The door had a small slit which could be slid open by a guard. There was a cot, a window near the ceiling, a desk and chair, a small wardrobe, and no toilet or sink. Kevin taped up a print of Salvador Dali's Crucifixion, a surrealist portrayal of the crucifixion of Jesus, to the wall.

Allowed to mingle within his wing, Kevin soon displayed a talent for drawing. He sketched portraits of the children of Gerry Loughlin from photos Loughlin lent him. The prison service allowed Kevin a guitar, which he played. A few prisoners had known Kevin on the outside in the close-knit community of north Belfast. One was Liam Maskey, an ex-boxer who coached amateurs at a boxing club there. Kevin had once come in to the club to inquire about training there.

In the Maze, as on the street, Kevin was thought incapable of having killed Albert Miles. A few fellow prisoners razzed him about having been so naïve as to believe the detectives who promised he would be out in seven years if he only confessed in Castlereagh.

"I guess that's the Republican way of keeping morale up. But they clowned me hard," Kevin recalled in 1996.

Kevin attended Masses on Sundays in the chapel with the other men, praying to St. Jude for a chance to escape.

FORTY-SEVEN

A Plan Not So Simple

"We had a vision. We knew where we were going," recalled Gerry Kelly years later. "Thatcher had consigned ten of our guys to die. The best answer to it was to smash the H-Blocks. The way to do that was the escape."

The escape's mastermind was Larry Marley, a 36-year-old IRA man from Ardoyne in north Belfast. Marley's own multiple escape attempts had earned him the nickname Papillon, after Steve McQueen's character in the movie about a French prisoner's relentless efforts to escape a penal colony.

But how to escape the Maze? It was escape-proof, supposedly. The place was a fortress, a labyrinth on 360 acres. It was also a puzzle. No single prisoner had even seen the entire premises. Each Block was a prison within a prison, a self-contained unit within another self-contained unit, all of it sitting inside a British Ministry of Defence perimeter, adjacent to a large British Army camp, encircled by an eighteen-foot-high wall made of steel-reinforced concrete. No one knew the whole layout. The prison service made it impossible. The guards used blacked-out vans to transport prisoners within the Maze so that no one could see out.

There were four rings of security, starting with the Blocks.

Each one had its own staff of guards, with a secure communications room that lay behind two locked doors. It housed radios and telephones which connected the guards to a central Emergency Control Room (ECR). There were alarm buttons all over the place, affording any guard who felt himself in trouble a chance to summon help.

Each Block sat behind a double-gated vehicle lock and a sixteen-foot-high fence of its own, which separated it from the second ring—a segment, which also sat behind a high concrete wall.

The third ring of security was the perimeter wall. Eighteen feet high, it was made of reinforced concrete. Atop it, British Army snipers manned twelve watch towers placed at two-hundred-yard intervals.

Just walking from one of the H-Blocks to the main gate, a distance of half a mile, would take a man walking at a normal gait fifteen minutes.

Beyond the main gate lay the last, fourth ring of security, beyond a thirty-yard band of grass: coils of razor wire spread out low to the ground, nine feet across. Armed soldiers with Alsatian dogs patrolled the grass around the clock. Unless a man could get through the wire without getting entangled and cut up, there was only one other way to the outside world. That was via the external gate, manned by more British Army soldiers.

Initially, Marley favored tunneling out. The ground beneath the Maze was soft and sandy, ideal for the purpose.

But the history of tunnel escapes from Long Kesh was not encouraging. The British had seeded the ground with sensors. They were buried all over the place. Every two days, a British Army helicopter equipped with ground penetrating radar hovered overhead, scanning the earth for new tunnels. Each time the prisoners started digging a tunnel, the screws discovered it.

One day in the spring of 1983, a friendly prisoner in the kitchen greeted Marley. The man told Marley that he had only a couple of years left to do and wasn't going anywhere. But, he said, if he were still trying to escape, he had an idea.

It was the kitchen truck.

The truck made the rounds of the Maze three times a day, every day, stopping at each of the Blocks to offload food for the prisoners. What about hijacking it, loading it up with prisoners, and driving it straight out the front gate?

Marley dismissed it as impossible.

But all the other ideas seemed either bad or ill-suited to a mass escape. Tunnels were not the answer. A man or three might make it to the main gate disguised as a guard or a priest. But doing those things *en masse* seemed impossible.

The kitchen truck.

Marley warmed to the notion. Of all the bad ideas, it was the least bad one. To Marley's committee, the truck soon acquired a nickname: the Happy Wagon.

Marley dispatched watchers to study the truck closely and report back to him with answers to questions. Where did the truck go and when? How long did it take to travel between each Block? Who drove it? Who was the orderly who rode in the passenger seat?

Answers started filtering back.

The truck moved from Block to Block seemingly at random rather than at fixed times or in any predictable order. The same man always drove it: Davy McLaughlin, a prison service officer. His orderly was always Republican prisoner Desy Armstrong.

The most important bit of information that emerged was this one: on the truck's route from Block to Block, no one ever searched the truck.

Marley, Bobby Storey, Gerry Kelly, and Bik McFarlane set to work formulating a plan in secret over the course of several months. The code name for the escape would be

"S.P.," an acronym for Set Piece—IRA jargon that denoted a planned operation.

Kelly, age thirty, was tall and lean. He had a confident, commanding presence. Kelly had the respect of the men. They viewed him as capable. Kelly had been in prison continuously since 1973. He had spent nearly all of that time in maximum security and long periods in solitary confinement. He was widely read, an intellectual who devoured books by authors like George Orwell and Alduous Huxley. As an IRA volunteer, his resume was impressive.

Kelly had two successful escapes to his credit: the first from Crumlin Road Jail in Belfast during the 1960s, and the second from Mountjoy Prison in Dublin, after which he evaded detection by hiding in a tree for several days. After the second escape he returned to active service with the IRA, detonating a car bomb at the Old Bailey in London in 1973. One man had died of a heart attack in the bombing, and 180 were injured.

After being caught, tried, and sentenced to life in prison in Britain, Kelly nearly escaped a third time, from Wormwood Scrubs, a British prison outside London, before guards spotted him on top of the outer wall. During a hunger strike aimed at allowing him and his comrades to serve their time for the Old Bailey bombing in the north rather than on the mainland of Britain, the British had force-fed him 160 times.

Eventually, they relented and moved Kelly to the north in 1976. He wound up in the Nissen huts of Long Kesh, alongside the Maze. After another failed escape attempt there the British decided enough was enough. They moved Kelly to the H-Blocks. Kelly's failed escapes left him feeling like the "worst escaper in the world." Now he wanted to try again.

"He was head and shoulders above anyone in terms of his ability to think," recalled former IRA man Anthony McIntyre in 2019. "He was very strong-willed, but open to ideas. He was one of the bravest and most courageous IRA people I'd ever met."

Bik McFarlane was from Ardoyne. He was thirty-one years old. He had succeeded his good friend, Bobby Sands, as OC of Republican prisoners in the Maze when Sands went on hunger strike in 1981, and served in that role until the beginning of 1982. His nickname, Bik, had originated when he was a youngster in school, after a brand of biscuit. He had a reputation for being educated, politicized, and articulate. McFarlane was musically gifted. He sang and played guitar. He displayed confidence and skill in everything he did, including the prolific writing of comms at night by the orange light that entered his cell through a crack in the door. He was approachable and good at diplomacy.

Fellow prisoners knew McFarlane as a devout Catholic, a student of liberation theology whose morning ritual included reading a favorite Bible psalm. The men respected him.

Bobby Storey, known as Big Bob, stood six feet and four inches tall. He would be the OC of the escape. Twenty-seven years old, he had been interned at Long Kesh on his seventeenth birthday, in 1973. After his release two years later, he had endured two trials which ended in acquittals, one for blowing up a hotel and another for murder. Among Republican prisoners, Storey had a justly earned reputation for being one of the most arrested and one of the most-often-beaten men in the six counties during the period from 1969 until the mid-1990s.

Piece by tiny piece, Marley, Kelly, McFarlane, and Storey started assembling a mosaic of the entire prison. It was like putting together a giant jigsaw puzzle, only without the picture on the box that showed you what the puzzle looked like when you finished it.

There were some media photographs of parts of the prison. Marley's committee started having them smuggled in. There were other bits and pieces. The vans had the odd scrape on a blackened window or crack in a door hinge. A man riding in one of them could glimpse outside and report what he had seen. Prisoners ferried to and from workshops and the concrete yard stole furtive glances at towers, gates, the movements of the trucks and guards.

A comprehensive picture of the entire prison started to coalesce. Big blank spaces gave way as more and more pieces fell into place.

By early 1983, the committee had the basics of a plan worked out. It called for the escape to begin in H-7. It sat sandwiched between H-8, to the east, and H-6, to the west. The front gates of H-7 and H-8 faced each other. But H-8 was undergoing refurbishment and was empty, so no one would be there to look at H-7 from a few yards away.

To the rear of H-7 sat H-6. But the escapees would proceed out the front gate of H-7, putting the escape out of anyone's direct line of sight from H-6.

H-7 offered other advantages.

It housed a large number of men serving long terms, including twenty-four men serving life sentences and twenty-eight serving sentences of ten years or longer. Several were formidable IRA men: Kelly, McFarlane, Storey, Brendan Mead, Seamus Campbell, Seamus McElwaine, Sean McGlinchey, and Tony "Tank" McAllister among them. They would want to perform well and take chances in an escape. The publicity which could be realized from the escape of the Block's big names would embarrass the British.

The plan was intricate.

First, using smuggled-in weapons, the prisoners would overpower the guards in H-7 and strip them of their batons, uniforms, and keys. Captured guards would be moved around on their hands and knees, disabling them from making a move toward one of the telephones or alarm buttons which were at chest level. There were only sixteen officers detailed for duty on the wings (four per wing). The prisoners would use numbers to their advantage. Because there were no closed-circuit television cameras in the Block, no one outside would detect what was happening.

Firearms would be needed to coerce instant compliance from the guards. The guards had easy access to alarm buttons, telephones, and radios. Making sure not even one of them pushed a button or lifted a handset while the prisoners were taking down the Block would be essential. If a phone rang, a guard would have to answer it. A prisoner would have to hold a gun to the guard's head lest he alert the caller to what was happening.

Once stripped, the guards would be herded into a classroom. There a prisoner would read them a prepared statement. It would assure them they would suffer no harm so long as they cooperated.

Prisoners would put on the guards' uniforms and impersonate them at each stage of the escape—at the gate to H-7, where the kitchen truck would enter, at every succeeding gate the truck needed to clear on its way out, and beyond the main gate, in plain view of British soldiers manning the watchtowers. The soldiers, unable to distinguish guards from prisoners disguised as guards, would hold their fire rather than shoot a man who might be a guard, at least for a couple of minutes.

The kitchen truck left the prison grounds only rarely. But sometimes prison service officers borrowed it for "homers," house moves or odd jobs. It was thought possible to drive the truck straight out of the front gate without anything seeming amiss.

If it arrived at H-7 on time, the kitchen truck would roll through the Block's gate at 3:15 p.m. It was a box truck, a two-axle commercial vehicle, with a hydraulic lift and a shutter that opened and closed vertically in the back. Once emptied of its food and supplies, its cargo hold was big enough to accommodate nearly forty men, who would be loaded into it after the prisoners commandeered it from the driver.

In all, the truck would have to pass through six manned gates: the H-7 gate lock, segment gate 1, the administration gate, the main gate, a pole barrier, and the external gate. Davy McLaughlin, the prison service officer who drove the truck every day, would be coerced into driving it. A prisoner would lie on the floorboards of the truck, unseen by everyone but McLaughlin, and aim a pistol at McLaughlin's head during the journey, to ensure his cooperation. McLaughlin had to be convinced to cooperate and display an unruffled demeanor while driving the truck.

After traveling north across about half a mile of the prison grounds, the truck would reach the Tally Lodge. It was a small one-story building at the prison's main gate, the funnel through which all traffic into and out of the prison passed. McLaughlin would park the truck in its parking lot.

The timetable would put the kitchen truck at the main gate at 4:00 p.m., just before there was a shift change.

A team of nine armed prisoners dressed as guards would dismount the truck and approach the Tally Lodge just before the shift change. Instead of storming the building, they would approach calmly, staying in character until the last possible moment. They would arrest and stand guard over all guards in the Tally Lodge and those who happened to enter or exit during the shift change. Then they would open the main gate, allowing the truck to drive through. Those on foot would follow in cars stolen from guards who had been forced to turn over their car keys during the seizure of H-7.

The last barrier was the external gate, separating the British Army base within which the prison sat and public land. It was manned by a prison guard and British Army soldier. Outside it lay the Halftown Road. Beyond was a housing estate and open country.

At a rendezvous point about ten miles away, a team of the IRA's South Armagh, South Down, and Tyrone

Brigades would receive the escapees. They would have Kalashnikov rifles and a specially modified truck mounted with a Browning .50 caliber machine gun. The team would spirit the escapees away in vehicles to safe houses in south Armagh before the army and police had a chance to catch up.

A Rear Guard of thirty men was largely comprised of prisoners with little time left to serve on their sentences. They would have much to lose by going on the escape and getting caught. They would remain behind in H-7. There they would mind the guards, burn photographs and records which could be used to ascertain who had escaped, and, once the guards regained control, lock themselves into their cells and fling the keys away.

If, at any point, guards discovered the ruse, the verbal signal would be: "The balloon's up."

Then it would be every man for himself.

By June, Marley had a final plan, written out on fifty sheets of toilet paper. His chief co-author was McFarlane.

Now all Marley and his committee needed was the approval of the IRA's Army Council and its support, in the way of weapons, escape vehicles, clothing, and other materials.

In June 1983, the Army Council gave S.P. a green light.

Kevin Barry Artt, who had never held a gun in his hand, the odd man out, a taxi driver from Jordanstown imprisoned alongside the hard men of the IRA, knew nothing about it.

FORTY-EIGHT

We Can Escape and We Will Escape

The escape would take place on the last Sunday in September, a week after the championship game of the All-Ireland Senior Football tournament. Sundays were lazy days at the Maze. There were no visits and fewer guards on duty.

It was August 1983. Marley's fifty sheets of toilet paper now appended photographs, maps, and diagrams. All of it got rolled up into a bullet-shaped package, wrapped in cling film, and gingerly eased up the rectum of a prisoner who carried it into H-7.

Outside the walls, the IRA was busy procuring weapons and planning logistics getting the prisoners away from the Maze and into safe houses as quickly as possible on the big day.

To lower the risk of detection, information about the escape would be shared with other prisoners only on a need-to-know basis. Many of the 125 men in H-7—something less than half—would have no idea what was happening until it happened.

In the meantime, the prisoners had spent months cultivating easy ways with the guards, engaging them in casual conversations about soccer, families, women, cars, booze, gambling, music, family news, movies. During the friendly chats, some prisoners gleaned unsolicited bits of information which they reported back to the escape leaders. All the while, the prisoners maintained their charm offensive, buying themselves more goodwill by the day.

It worked. Guards loosened formalities and protocols. In return, they got politeness and cooperation from prisoners, down to *please* and *thank you* from the likes of Bik McFarlane himself.

It made for an easy shift, a far cry from the times of the blanket and dirty protests.

By September 1983, incidents of confrontation between prisoner and guard had dropped off to zero. An order from the prison governor, Stanley Hilditch, forbidding prisoners from having more than one picture board per cell, even in a cell occupied by two men, went down without a peep of protest.

Out of 125 men imprisoned in H-7, who would go?

The truck could hold only forty, including the man on the floorboards of the cab holding a weapon on McLaughlin, the driver.

The Army Council supplied the answer.

It wanted certain men out—men who could be expected to return to active service. There were over twenty lifers in H-7. They would be given high priority, unless they had been an informant while in custody. No one with fewer than twelve years left to serve would be allowed to go unless he had further charges pending against him.

Marley's committee duly sent out a comm with a list of names. The IRA edited it and sent it back in. The process repeated itself several times.

On the morning of Saturday, September 24, Kevin enjoyed a visit with Carmen. She deposited some cash in the tuck shop under Kevin's name. She also brought in a cake she had baked, his favorite, with cherries in it. To Carmen, Kevin seemed in good spirits, in brilliant form, better than she had seen him since his arrest in 1981.

That night, Bobby Storey surreptitiously circulated a message to all potential escapees before lock-up. Rab Kerr distributed it. It read:

We've broken the prison security. We have infiltrated the ranks of screws. We can escape and we will escape. Do the part assigned to you and we will succeed. We will grasp victory.

Kevin Barry Artt did not get the word. He drifted off to sleep in his bunk, oblivious to what lay in store. At that moment, his name still was not on the list.

FORTY-NINE

Steve McQueen in Ireland

On the morning of Sunday, September 25, Gerry Kelly and the other leaders worked painstakingly to solve last-minute problems. In cell 26, they discussed the list of escapees for the last time.

The name of Kevin Barry Artt came up.

"He's doing life," said Bobby Storey. "Let him go."

Kevin sat in the dining room eating his lunch. It was about 12:30 p.m.

Another prisoner approached him.

"Barry," he said. "They want you in cell 26."

In his short time at the Maze, Kevin had earned a reputation among fellow prisoners for being likeable. But the IRA men disapproved of his friendly relations with a couple of INLA men. Kevin and the two men had celebrated his twenty-fourth birthday a week earlier, on September 18, with some hashish smuggled in by Carmen.

A trio of serious-looking men received Kevin in cell 26.

Kevin assumed the worst. He was expecting a beating or reprimand. Kevin knew of the IRA's disapproval of recreational drug use but had made no secret of smoking the hash.

"There's an escape on today," said one. "As a Republican prisoner serving a life sentence, ye're entitled to go if you want."

Kevin hadn't had the slightest inkling there was an escape on. By now, he had resigned himself to the prospect of years in the Maze. IRA men had always treated him standoffishly. Now they were inviting him on an escape.

It was an easy call. Kevin was doing life plus fifteen years. If he got captured, how much more time could the court give him?

"What do I have to do?" Kevin asked.

"Come to the circle when we call ye, around 3 p.m. Ride in the back of a lorry to the Tally Lodge. There'll be some cars waiting there," came the reply.

Kevin could not believe his good fortune. *All he had to do was get in the back of a truck and ride out the front gate.* For a moment, he flashed on a Hollywood film, "The Great Escape." In it, Steve McQueen had played an American airman imprisoned in a German POW camp during the Second World War. During a daring escape, McQueen steals a Triumph TR-6 Trophy motorcycle and rides it across the German countryside toward the Swiss border, chased by astonished German soldiers. At the climax of the chase scene, McQueen jumps the bike over a barbed-wire fence. *Steve McQueen in Ireland!*

In their cells, the leaders and escapees began final preparations. They fashioned masks, gave themselves haircuts, shaved off mustaches, closed windows, and turned up record players and radios so that they would blast music at maximum volume. The din rang through the wings.

The escape team had constructed its arsenal out of component parts of weapons painstakingly smuggled in over the course of months by wives, girlfriends, and accomplices. There were three Titan .25 caliber semi-automatic pistols (one fitted with a silencer), a Raven .25 semi-automatic, a Sterling .22 caliber semi-automatic pistol, and several rounds of ammunition loaded into clips. A replica looked like a sixth handgun. There was a miscellany of hand tools—chisels, screwdrivers, and a hammer, purloined from the workshops and hidden in the hollowed-out frames and legs of tables in the cells.

At 2:30 p.m., to all outward appearances, the normal Sunday routine prevailed in H-Block 7. Most of the 125 prisoners moved between wings freely. Some played soccer outside. About twenty-four men employed as orderlies cleaned and did routine maintenance work. The weather was overcast, the air dry and chilly.

A full complement of twenty-four prison guards was on duty. There were two senior officers in charge, sixteen officers supervising inmates in the wings, and six officers manning fixed posts controlling movements within the Block. A medical officer was on duty too.

At the moment the operation began, only nine of the sixteen guards in the wings were at their stations. Four were in the tea room and three in the lavatories, reducing the number of guards patrolling three of the four wings to just two.

The IRA now had exactly the men it wanted in H-7.

The choreography of the escape started to unfold.

The guards' canteen would be taken first. Initial targets were the five guards in the circle area who might press an alarm button.

Brendy Mead, Tony McAllister, Gerry Kelly, and Bik McFarlane moved out to the circle, all armed with pistols, headed for the store room as though to retrieve supplies. All were capable and experienced IRA men. Each was a lifer.

It was time for the go code—the word, *bumper*, the nickname for an electric floor polishing machine used by orderlies to polish the floors in the Block. Kelly would be the man pushing the bumper. *Bumper* would be the signal that would beckon Bobby Storey, the OC of the escape, to the circle, and trigger a silent ninety-second countdown before everyone started to move.

In C-Wing, Big Bob stood at a sink, washing a shirt. It was nearing 2:30 p.m.

With each passing minute, Storey grew more worried. The plan required control of the Block by 3:00 p.m., so they could load the truck, travel the half mile between H-7 and the Tally Lodge, and get there before 4:00 p.m., when the shift change happened. Time was rolling by. *What the fuck could be taking so long?*

At 2:30 p.m., McFarlane's deep baritone rang out from near the circle.

"A and B Wing, is the bumper down there?"

Thirty-seven other men felt adrenaline surge through their bodies. It was on!

Sean McGlinchey shouted back an answer: "It's not here, Bik."

McFarlane repeated the code, shouting into the C and D side from the circle: "Is the bumper down there?"

He knew everyone would hear him. A guard who heard McFarlane repeated it, unwittingly passing the signal to anyone who hadn't heard McFarlane.

On cue, the men now moved into positions that would enable them to take down every guard on the wings.

Storey went into the food hall and got the bumper. He started pushing it toward the circle. Before arriving there, he ducked into a storeroom. Mead, McFarlane, Storey, Kelly, and McAllister had converged there. Storey greeted them, asking how they were doing.

"Shiting ourselves," Kelly replied with a jaunty grin.

Storey laughed. The five men fanned out.

Bik McFarlane approached the circle-guard, who was standing in the locked and gated lobby at the entrance to the Block. McFarlane asked to be allowed in to sweep the lobby. The guard unlocked the gate and let him in. McFarlane produced a handgun, ordered the man to lay on the floor, and speedily stripped him of his baton and keys.

Gerry Kelly approached the steel door to the Block's communications room. The door was supposed to be shut. But, on this day, as it often was, it was ajar. Poor ventilation made the room uncomfortable to work in. The officers inside found it easier to communicate with their colleagues in the circle with the door open. Through the open door, Kelly spied a guard, John Adams, at work. Adams had his back turned to Kelly.

Storey and McAllister entered the officers' canteen. There, four guards were on a break, having some tea. McAllister was there on the pretext of ordering a cup of tea for a guard outside.

Soon after, McAllister emerged and announced to the guard that his tea was ready. The guard went into the canteen. Kelly and Storey then moved into the circle. Storey slipped in behind the guard entering the canteen. Kelly stood at the welfare office between the front hall grille and the canteen—alone in the circle area, waiting for Storey to re-emerge.

Now all stationed in the positions dictated by the plan, the prisoners made their first big move.

In the guards' canteen, Storey and McAllister drew their weapons. They were small, .22 and .25 caliber handguns.

In a bit of theater, Storey and McAllister adopted firing poses, pointing the weapons at the officers.

"Get on the floor and do it quietly," rasped Storey in a loud whisper.

The guards' facial expressions displayed shock and disbelief. Soon a fifth officer entered, called in there by McAllister. All got down on the floor, except one, Harry Reynolds. Reynolds stood about 5'7" in height and was grossly overweight. Among the prisoners he was known for sleeping during his shift. The prisoners generally had seen "little harm in him." Storey pulled a chair over and motioned to Reynolds.

"Sit on that and don't move or he'll shoot you," said Storey, pointing at McAllister.

Two orderlies, one brandishing a revolver and the other a screwdriver, quickly overpowered guards who had been manning the gate locks leading from the wings to the circle. In another area, another orderly stabbed a guard with a handicraft knife. Another used a hammer to club a guard in the back of the head.

Three guards who emerged from staff toilets immediately found themselves faced by prisoners wielding guns. They quickly submitted to their new captors.

Most of the hard work still lay ahead. There were twenty emergency alarm points, seven telephones, and two intercoms and two-way radios to be covered. There was the communications room to secure, along with every other nook and cranny of H-Block 7. One lapse, one stray telephone or radio call, one alarm bell or siren, would ring down the curtain on the whole business.

The first shots of the Maze escape were fired, by a Republican prisoner—Gerry Kelly. In a struggle to prevent a guard in the communications room, John Adams, from locking himself inside and raising the alarm, Kelly had fired two shots at Adams. The second shot had wounded Adams in the head, just above the left eye.[7] He lay alive and conscious on the floor. The sound of the shots had echoed

---

7. In his published firsthand account of the escape (published in 2013), which otherwise brims with names of witnesses to the escape, Kelly took pains not to name himself as the shooter of Adams, identifying the shooter only as "the prisoner."

During a later interview with a journalist who asked Kelly whether he had shot Adams, Kelly offered a painstaking circumlocution, admitting only to having *pointed* a pistol at Adams and threatened to shoot him, without denying having shot him. A court found Kelly not guilty of attempting to murder Adams. Two published reports have named Kelly as the shooter.

throughout the Block. Kelly's gun had been fitted with a silencer, but it had failed.

Storey and Kelly looked at one another. Had Adams had enough time to raise the alarm? They thought not.

The sound of the shots did not travel through the closed doors of the Block to the guard manning the gate lock at the entrance to H-7, an officer named McFall. He stood at his post, looking bored, oblivious to the situation inside.

Presently, McFarlane ambled toward McFall. McFarlane now had the keys he had taken from the guard in the entrance lobby. He had used them to let himself and two other prisoners out of the Block.

"Excuse me, McFall," said McFarlane. "I'd like to get into the sentry box and sweep it out. Can ye unlock the gate so I can get in there?

Thinking nothing amiss, McFall complied.

McFarlane now displayed a gun and relieved McFall of his keys.

The two other prisoners escorted the astonished guard inside H-7 and took him to the officer's tea room. There, two other prisoners quickly hooded him, stripped him, and tied him up.

In the communications room, John Adams lay on the floor. Gerry Kelly knelt over him.

"Are you OK, John?" asked Kelly.

Adams managed a whisper. "I think so," he rasped.

In the twenty minutes that had passed since McFarlane asked where the bumper was, the Republican prisoners of H-7 had taken down the Block without raising a single alarm.

FIFTY

The Kid Invited to the Party that Nobody Knows

The twenty-four guards who had been on duty inside H-7 now lay face down on the floor, gravely shocked. Some were trembling. All were wondering what the hell might happen next.

Prisoners guarded eleven of them in the wings. The rest were in the circle or administration area, prone, with pillowcases over their heads, hands tied tightly behind their backs, under the guard of edgy, glowering IRA men who felt no love for them.

At this moment, there were both guards and prisoners in the Block who had no idea what was happening. Not all prisoners had been briefed or even told about the escape. The guards, helpless and blinded, feared that the operation now underway was the beginning of a revenge attack in retaliation for the cruelties they had inflicted during the five years of protests that ended in 1981. Some expected to be killed.

Storey wielded a clipboard, like a football coach on the sideline during a game. On the clipboard was a painstakingly prepared checklist. Big Bob shouted down each wing, asking for reports of any injuries and reminding everybody within earshot that the Republican prisoners were now in charge of H-7.

The only injuries to guards in the A-, B-, C-, and D-wings were minor—a stab wound to the shoulder of a guard who initially resisted, and a contusion suffered from the hammer blow to a guard's head.

A team of prisoners loaded Adams onto a makeshift stretcher (a futon) and removed him from the control room.

In each wing, prisoners now herded the guards who had been arrested there toward cell 26, the double cell of each wing.

As each guard entered, prisoners stripped him to his underwear. The prisoners dumped the uniforms into brown bags, marking each bag "small," "medium" or "large," depending on the size of the guard, the better to fit the uniforms to the prisoners who would soon don them.

Each guard's personal belongings went into a pillowcase with his name scrawled on it. Observing Kelly's strict order to treat the guards humanely, the prisoners helped the guards who struggled to breathe underneath their hoods, by fluffing the pillowcases up and down to draw in air and using ping-pong paddles as fans. They tied the guards up to one another.

The cacophony created by record players and radios playing rock music at high volume continued to reverberate through the Block.

Scores of prisoners now converged on the circle.

One of the leaders read out a prepared statement to them: the IRA was now in charge of the Block. There was an escape on, but only a subset of the prisoners was going. The others would go back to their cells.

The statement was intended, in part, to provide cover for the men who stayed behind, so they could claim they had declined to go on the escape, something that might help them later.

Men took up stations as lookouts, for the kitchen truck and any guards who might approach the gate. Former blanket man Pól Brennan walked from wing to wing, alert to any sign of trouble.

Now it was time to move all of the guards (except the Principal Officer) to a central point. Prisoners escorted them out of the four big cells on each wing (cell 26) and into the education room. It was off a hallway which connected the C- and D-Wings. Guards were bound together by the wrist, in pairs. All wore their makeshift hoods. The prisoners' Rear Guard seated them in the chairs, classroom-style. One prisoner hastily created a seating chart, so that if a phone call came in for one of the guards the man could be brought to the phone quickly so as to keep the ruse going. The Principal Officer was tied to a chair in his office. A member of the Rear Guard was detailed to watch him in the event of a phone call.

By now, the circle was crowded with prisoners and the floor littered with guards' shirts, pants, boots, belts, and shoes. Thirteen prisoners started sorting and putting on guards' uniforms. They worked deliberately and unhurriedly, taking care to match the size of each uniform to the body type of each man who would wear it, so as to preserve every appearance of normality to the searching eyes of the guards who would soon study them outside.

Kieran Fleming entered the classroom. He read out a prepared statement to the stunned audience of guards assembled there. Marley's committee had carefully crafted it, in the hope it might reduce the likelihood of guards brutalizing the prisoners left behind after the escape.

"What has taken place here today was a carefully planned exercise to secure the release of a substantial number of POWs," Fleming declared. "The Block is now under our control. Anyone who has been assaulted or injured was as a result of his refusal to cooperate with us. It is not our intention to settle old scores, ill-treat, or degrade any of you regardless of your past. Though should anyone try to underestimate or wish to challenge our position, he or they will be severely dealt with. Anyone who refuses to comply with our instructions now or in the future will feel the wrath of the Republican Movement.

"Should any members of the prison administration ill-treat, victimize, or commit any acts of perjury against Republican POWs in any follow up inquiries, judicial or otherwise, they will forfeit their lives for what we will see as a further act of repression against the Nationalist people.

"To conclude we give you our word as Republicans, that none of you will come to any harm providing you co-operate fully with us. Anyone who refuses to do so will suffer the ultimate consequence—death! Allow common sense to prevail. Do not be used as cannon fodder by the prison administration or the faceless bureaucrats at Stormont and Whitehall."

Fleming walked out, leaving the statement on a desk, for authorities to find later.

Outside, at the gate to H-7, Corey and McGlinchey, doing their best not to fidget in their borrowed prison service uniforms, waited for the kitchen truck. At 3:15 p.m., the truck was twenty minutes late and nowhere to be seen.

Inside H-7, escape team members were busy removing documents from the communications room and office, including mugshots of the escapees. Others were showing the escapees a map of where the truck would be going and making them memorize the route.

Some prisoners were euphoric. Others, fearing the truck's tardy arrival would doom the escape, were depressed.

At 3:25 p.m., Corey and McGlinchey spied a pretty sight: a white, Bedford box truck trundling toward H-7.

Doing their best to mimic the movements of guards following the endless repetition of tedious routine, they opened the outer gate, allowing the truck into the airlock. In the cab were the two men expected: the driver, Davy McLaughlin, a prison service officer, and prisoner orderly Desy Armstrong, who knew nothing of the plan and sat in the passenger seat. McLaughlin observed that there were two guards inside the airlock rather than the usual one. He mentioned it to Armstrong, calling it odd. Armstrong, too, had noticed it. He shrugged it off.

McLaughlin eased off the brake. The truck crept forward, into the airlock. As Corey and McGlinchey locked the outer gate and then opened the inner one, they did their best to look away from McLaughlin, to avoid being recognized. McLaughlin, following muscle memory in familiar surroundings, did not look at their faces, or, if he did, he did not recognize the men as prisoners. Armstrong sat in the passenger seat, looking bored.

From inside the front door of H-7, Marcus Murray spied the truck. He told Storey it was on its way.

Out came Kelly, McFarlane, and Storey, all dressed in guards' uniforms and peaked caps. Following protocol, the truck did a U-turn in the yard, then slowly reversed toward the hall entrance door, where unloading and loading took place. In a move they had choreographed in private, Storey coolly opened the driver's side door and brandished a gun at Davy McLaughlin. Kelly reached inside and grabbed McLaughlin by the right arm. Kelly pressed his pistol to McLaughlin's head and gripped his right arm. On the passenger side, McFarlane seized Desy Armstrong.

Kelly frogmarched McLaughlin inside, to the circle. There, McLaughlin saw an unbelievable sight: a busy beehive controlled by armed Republican prisoners, some in guards' uniforms, the others wearing masks, pistols and ammunition lay out in the open, strewn about on tables.

The escape planners had intended the sight to inspire shock and awe in McLaughlin. It did. Kelly took McLaughlin into the medical room. Covering its walls were finely detailed, hand-drawn maps and clandestinely taken photographs of the escape route. Bobby Storey entered and addressed McLaughlin.

"IRA POWs have taken over the Block," Big Bob declared. "We're in charge. Do as ye're told, and you'll be

OK. The guards who have cooperated have gone unharmed. The one who didn't has been shot already. This man will ride in the cab with ye on the way out. He is serving multiple life sentences and has nothing to lose. He'll shoot ye without hesitation at the slightest sign ye're not cooperating fully. Even his Republican friends think him a ruthless bastard. He is one."

Storey pointed out the half-mile route McLaughlin would drive to the main gate.

"Ye will drive the truck along this exact route. Study it carefully.

"Yer foot will be tied to the clutch with a length of cord. One of us will lie on the floorboards close to ye. He will be armed with a loaded pistol and pointing it at yer head. He will be vigilant to the slightest false move that ye might make. Underneath yer seat there will be a grenade. The pin will be tied to another length of cord. The inside door handle on the driver's side is being removed. Ye won't be able to exit the cab on your own.

"If the man guarding ye detects any effort on yer part to signal other guards during the journey to the front gate, or deviate from the prescribed route, he will shoot ye and pull the pin on the grenade.

"The grenade has a seven-second delay. It will allow the man guarding you time to exit the cab after he shoots you. After the explosion, ye'll be dead, and our operation will continue.

"This is happening, Davy. It is going to happen the easy way or the hard way. I recommend the easy way."

The easy way meant everybody would live and the prisoners would escape.

The hard way meant McLaughlin and some of his colleagues would die in a grenade blast and the prisoners would escape anyway.

Kelly closely observed McLaughlin during Storey's lecture. McLaughlin's body language suggested he understood and was going to go along without any trouble. Storey turned on his heel and walked out. Kelly stayed with McLaughlin.

Outside, the truck's new cargo was being loaded—thirty-seven Republican prisoners, who now packed themselves into the cargo hold. Storey checked each man's name as he boarded the truck.

Among them was Kevin Barry Artt.

There were sentimental goodbyes. One man, who had lost his leg in an explosion, wept at not being able to go.

Last to board were the prisoners wearing guards' uniforms. They would ride in the back and be the first to exit at the Tally Lodge. Escapees and Rear Guard members exchanged back slaps and handshakes, but few words. Some escapees could not help worrying about what would happen to the Rear Guard once enraged authorities started exacting revenge for their imminent public humiliation. Rear Guard members wondered whether the escapees could make it out the front gate, and, if they did, about their futures.

They were behind schedule and there was still a long way to go. It was 3:55 p.m.—five minutes before they were due at the Tally Lodge, a half mile away. By 4:00 p.m. they were supposed to have gotten out just ahead of the shift change and been ten miles away from the Maze.

Gerry Kelly and Harry Murray escorted McLaughlin back out to the truck. They put McLaughlin in through the passenger's side and ordered him to climb over to the driver's seat. One of the escapees, Marcus Murray, had broken the handles off of the driver's side door, inside and out.

As promised, a cord was visible on the floorboards of the cab. The cord ran underneath the seat and out of sight. There was no grenade.

Kelly tied McLaughlin's foot to the clutch with another piece of cord. Then he lay on his back in the well of the cab. McFarlane guided Desy Armstrong, the orderly, into the passenger seat and told him to sit up straight.

McLaughlin raised the hydraulic tailgate at the rear of the truck. A prisoner hoisted the shutter down and slammed it shut, plunging the thirty-seven men behind it into darkness.

After Kevin boarded, he hunkered down among his comrades. To him it looked like the whole Block was in there with him. Everybody got down onto the floor.

Kevin felt like a stranger among friends who knew each other well.

"I didn't know anybody in there, just Billy Gorman," recalled Kevin. As boys, Gorman and Kevin had been classmates at St. Patrick's primary school. "There were mostly a bunch of strangers I didn't know. It was weird. I was the kid invited to the party that nobody knows."

Just before McLaughlin started the ignition, the OC of the Rear Guard, Seamus McDermott, rapped on the side of the truck in a last gesture of support for his comrades. He did not know if he would ever see them again.

McLaughlin turned the key in the ignition. The engine coughed, then coughed again, then died.

McLaughlin tried a second time.

Still nothing.

With pulses pounding, thirty-eight Republican prisoners held their breaths as McLaughlin tried a third time. Now the Happy Wagon's diesel engine rumbled to life. McLaughlin put it in gear and eased the truck and its cargo toward the inner gate of the airlock.

Just before the truck rolled away, bound for the front gate, the members of a thirty-man Rear Guard started executing their instructions, directed by McDermott.

In the circle, they started burning all the photographs of prisoners which had resided in the office, as well as the cell cards which correlated each prisoner to his cell. For fuel, they used contraband lighter fluid. Acrid smoke filled the air. When the authorities regained control of H-7 and began trying to learn who had escaped, they would find piles of smoldering ashes instead of photographs and records of escaped prisoners. As the escapees sped away from the Maze, their former captors would still be trying to figure out who they were, delaying their broadcast of names and photographs of their quarry.

As the truck advanced, guards waved it through three consecutive manned gates. Kelly, supine on the floorboards, pointing his pistol at Davy McLaughlin's head, guessed they must be passing the prison hospital. There Bobby Sands and nine others had died of starvation two years earlier. Kelly remembered the day Albert Miles had told him the only way he would ever leave the Maze was in a box. Ironically, Miles had been right, just not in the way he had meant.

In the darkness of the cargo hold, adrenaline pumped and hearts pounded. The men's eyes had adjusted to the darkness. Tiny slivers of light allowed the men barely to discern one another's faces. The men's body heat accumulated inside the box. It was hot. The men were sweating. Jackets lay over the small holes in the bed of the truck, to keep any guards who might run a mirror underneath from seeing inside.

One man, Peter Hamilton, whispered the lyrics of a Leonard Cohen song, "Bird on the Wire":

> Like a bird on the wire
> Like a drunk in a midnight choir
> I have tried in my way to be free.

Storey told him to shut the fuck up.

As the truck approached the Tally Lodge, a guard spied Davy McLaughlin in the driver's seat.

The guard called out, "You're always doing Sundays, Davy. You must love this job!"

McLaughlin waved, then turned into the Tally Lodge parking lot.

Kelly, now sitting up in the passenger seat in his guard's uniform, told McLaughlin to back the truck up at an angle which would obscure the back of the truck from the British Army soldiers above.

Quickly, smoothly, out of the back of the truck came the Tally Lodge team, clad in guards' uniforms, complete with peaked caps: Jimmy Burns, Denis Cummings, Rab Kerr, Bik McFarlane, Sean McGlinchey, Brendy Mead, Harry Murray, Eddie O'Connor, Bobby Storey. They paused a moment, to straighten up and smooth out their uniforms. They had five pistols and one replica among them.

Storey approached the driver's side window and spoke to McLaughlin, distracting him. Kelly handed his pistol out of the passenger side window to a comrade who handed Kelly a wooden replica crafted by Gerry McDonnell. The replica looked good. Another man pulled the rear shutter door of the truck back down.

The Tally Lodge team now clustered at the side of the truck.

No one inside the Tally Lodge had seen them.

Storey counted the men, to make sure there were nine as planned. He asked if everyone was ready. The men nodded yes. Kelly ordered them into their designated groups.

Nine IRA men, doing their best impressions of prison guards, walked calmly, deliberately, and in character across the parking lot toward the Tally Lodge.

It was almost four o'clock.

The men expected six guards to be in the Tally Lodge, maybe a couple more. The numbers weren't bad—nine on six. A tenth man, armed with a pistol, walked toward the officer manning the inner vehicle gate, where he would order him to open it before escorting the man into the Tally Lodge.

If there were a place to turn back, the thirty-eight men of H-7 had left it behind.

FIFTY-ONE

The Balloon's Up

The Tally Lodge was the funnel through which all guards passed while coming on and off their shifts at the Maze. Strangely for a structure that straddled the one part of the prison which gave access to the outside world, it was no fortress. It was a one-story, prefabricated building, known in the British Isles as a portacabin, made largely of plywood and glass. The doors were ordinary domestic doors, neither locked nor fortified. Alongside the building, a single turnstile controlled pedestrian traffic. Inside were the principal officer's office, a tea room, a room known as the tally room, and search areas.

About halfway between the truck and the Tally Lodge, Storey turned and tipped his cap in Gerry Kelly's direction. It was the signal for Kelly to start driving slowly over the last fifty yards between the truck and the main gate.

The inner and outer main gates were massive—eighteen feet high, as high as the concrete wall through which they gave passage. The inner gate had vertical bars through which one could see to the other side. The outer gate, painted dark green, had a fifteen-foot-high blind made of security mesh. The blind made it impossible for anyone either outside it or in the airlock to see what was on the other side. It opened and closed via a hydraulic system controlled by guards manning a control panel inside the Tally Lodge.

The Tally Lodge team, all in guards' uniforms, now split into two groups. One would control the building's interior, the other its exterior. If all went according to plan, the kitchen truck would pass through the inner and outer gates as the guards in the Tally Lodge lay powerless on the floor, held captive by the interior team.

Following protocol for passage of prison vehicles through the main gate, a guard, Samuel Scott, emerged from the Tally Lodge as the inner gate began to open automatically. Sean McGlinchey, acutely aware of the presence of a British soldier manning the watch tower which overlooked the gate, accosted Scott with a casual greeting. McGlinchey held a newspaper which concealed a pistol.

Keeping his body between the line of sight of the British soldier and Scott, McGlinchey flashed the weapon at Scott.

"Do what I say or I'll shoot you," he told Scott in a low voice. "Behave normally." McGlinchey then broke into a grin, in case the soldier above was looking at his face—the better to seem as though he were engaged in a pleasant conversation with a fellow guard.

"We're goin' inside," McGlinchey told Scott. "Come on."

The two men walked together into the Tally Lodge.

Murray took over for McGlinchey. He waved McLaughlin forward, into the airlock. The inner gate closed behind it.

The plan now called for Kelly to resume his place on the floorboards, McLaughlin to continue driving, while Goose Russell and Harry Murray, both in uniform, would sit in the passenger seats, holding three security passes lifted from inside the Tally Lodge. The truck would then drive out, turn right, drive east for about six hundred yards, breach the external gate, and drive to freedom.

Jimmy Burns, Dennis Cummings, Rab Kerr, Brendy Mead, and Eddie O'Connor would stay in the Tally Lodge until after everyone had escaped. Then they would use the keys they had taken from a guard in H-7 to drive to freedom themselves. Miles away, a crew of the South Armagh Brigade was standing by to meet the escapees, bundle them into cars, hustle them away, and disperse them into safe houses.

Mead and McFarlane strode into the Tally Lodge, then exited it toward the guard manning the pedestrian gate. At the same time, Burns, Cummings, Kerr, and Bobby Storey entered the Tally Lodge through a door on the other side. It was the exit door of the corridor through which incoming guards came onto their shifts.

Burns went straight to the closest room. It was the Principal Officer's office. There he stuck his pistol in the face of the Senior Officer, Wright, who had been sitting at his desk alone with his head down looking at some papers.

"Down on the floor, now," Burns told Wright. "Face down."

Storey seized two guards and deposited them in the tally room. Kerr and Cummings had already corralled several other guards there. Bik McFarlane and Brendy Mead, in their guards' uniforms, surprised the guard manning the pedestrian gate and relieved him of his duties. Mead took the man's place there.

Among the guards, there was confusion and bewilderment. Some thought what was happening was a drill. Then Bobby Storey took off his peaked cap and glasses, exposing the extraordinary reality: armed IRA men in guards' uniforms now controlled the Tally Lodge.

As more guards began arriving for their shifts, Brendy Mead admitted them through the pedestrian gate. Following routine, the guards passed through, not bothering to look closely at Mead, who kept the bill of his cap pulled down low. The guards walked into the Tally Lodge, directly into the arms of the team awaiting them there.

In the tally room, Rab Kerr was busy tying pairs of hands with strips of bed sheet and ordering the guards to lie on the floor. He struggled feverishly to keep up with the ongoing influx of bodies in the jam-packed tally room, which was the size of a townhouse kitchen.

The arithmetic was inexorable. The interior Tally Lodge team was getting outnumbered fast. The floor space given over to their captives began to dwindle. It was like the stateroom scene in "A Night at the Opera," minus the comedy. More bodies piled in every minute. Only two members of the Tally Lodge team were there to guard them—Dennis Cummings and Rab Kerr. As the minutes ticked past, Cummings and Kerr were gradually losing control. There were thirty guards piled up inside the room, then forty, higgledy-piggledy, practically on top of one another.

The guards in the tally room started muttering to one another. Some started sitting up. Burns, McGlinchey, Murray, and O'Connor—the exterior team—kept adding to the agglutination of men on the floor, bringing in more freshly-captured guards coming off duty. McFarlane and Storey were doing the same with the guards coming on duty through the pedestrian gate.

The guards started fighting back.

A newly captured guard who had not yet had his baton impounded drew it and attacked one of his captors, drawing a swift counter-attack. A prisoner stabbed him in the side with a narrow chisel. Two other guards, also freshly arrested, followed suit and drew their batons, then were stabbed themselves before prisoners controlled and disarmed all three.

Provoked by the attacks on their colleagues, other guards started yelling and trying to rise from the floor. Cummings and Kerr yelled at the guards, told them to shut up, pointed their guns at them.

But the guards had the numbers now.

Prison guard Jim Ferris looked out the window and saw what was happening at the external pedestrian gate. Each time his captors' gaze drifted away from him, he edged closer by a degree toward an exit which led outside. Then he managed to rise and run outside.

"Secure the gate!" he yelled as he ran. "Secure the gate! Raise the alarm!"

In hot pursuit was Rab Kerr, with pistol in hand. Nearby was Brendy Mead, who was conversing with a newly arrived guard who had entered the pedestrian gate. Mead joined Kerr in the chase. Ferris was running toward the pedestrian gate.

Mead grabbed Ferris from behind and hauled him back. When Ferris resisted, Mead punched him. Alarmed by what they had seen on the closed-circuit TV monitors inside, McFarlane and Storey came rushing out. Mead told them to haul Ferris inside the Tally Lodge. They did.

Peering down from his perch in the nearest watch tower, a British soldier saw the commotion.

What the . . .? Why were the guards fighting each other outside the Tally Lodge?

It was a bizarre sight—guards fighting one another just outside the Tally Lodge.

Ferris lay inside the Tally Lodge for the next hour, conscious and talking, before he suddenly stopped breathing. He had had a heart attack. He would be the sole fatality of the escape.

Outside, Davy McLaughlin and Gerry Kelly sat in the cab of the kitchen truck, its engine idling. McLaughlin had driven the truck right up to the main gate, on Kelly's order. He had seen Mead punch the guard in the passageway outside the Tally Lodge that led to the pedestrian gate. Now he peered upward at the British soldier in the watch tower, straining to see if he was making a radio call.

More and more guards coming onto their shifts or returning from breaks trickled into the Tally Lodge.

One, Reginald McBurney, felt something was wrong. The pedestrian gate was closed, the vehicle gates open, and approaching him was a man in a guard's uniform who looked unsettlingly familiar.

It was Bik McFarlane, in the passageway that led to the pedestrian gate.

"McFarlane, you bastard, what are you doing here!" McBurney yelled.

Then he put his whistle to his lips and started blowing it as hard as he could.

Following their training, other guards joined in, creating a shrill chorus of whistles. It was 4:12 p.m., just twelve minutes after the kitchen truck had rolled to a halt near the Tally Lodge. In a matter of minutes, the RUC and British Army would begin throwing up roadblocks around the prison.

McFarlane walked past the cab of the truck, where Gerry Kelly sat in the passenger seat. The window was down.

"The balloon's up," McFarlane said quietly as he walked past Kelly.

FIFTY-TWO

Ram the Gate

One hundred minutes had passed since Tony McAllister and Bobby Storey had pulled their weapons in H-7's canteen, initiating the escape. Inside the Block, the alarm sounded at last—a din of buzzers, barking on intercoms, telephones ringing, echoing, bouncing off the concrete surfaces, clashing with the racket created by the radios in the cells.

Inside the Tally Lodge, Seamus McElwaine was trying to get the outer gate open so the truck could drive out at last. The guards had succeeded in stalling McElwaine for a few minutes. A single prison officer who sat inside a locked cage controlled the gate from a control panel. The gate operated hydraulically. The officer controlled it via a lever. It could be activated only with a metal key. Alongside the lever was a sealed welded box with a narrow slit. If something went wrong, the officer was supposed to dump the key through the slit, making it impossible to open the gate.

At first the guard tried to pull the key out so he could dump it in the box. But when McElwaine pointed a gun at his head and told him to open the bloody gate, he complied.

The outer gate started swinging open.

McLaughlin eased the truck forward, into the airlock.

Reginald McBurney, the guard who had recognized McFarlane and blown his whistle, now realized what was happening. He yelled to another guard, William McKane, who was parked just outside the main gate, to drive his car in front of the gate and block it. McKane pulled up to the gate, then got out of his car, locked it, and drew his baton.

Another guard, William Gallagher, heard McBurney. He did the same with his own car. If IRA prisoners meant to escape out the main gate in broad daylight, McBurney, McKane, and Gallagher were going to do their best to stop them.

Kelly jumped out of the cab and met McFarlane and Storey at the back of the truck. There the three had a quick chat. They agreed it was time to open the shutter and tell the men inside that it was every man for himself.

Sitting in the dark of the box of the truck, Kevin heard the sounds of the growing commotion outside. No one dared utter a peep from within. Kevin's heart sank as he began to resign himself to capture and a beating.

Suddenly, the shutter at the rear of the truck shot up. Light flooded in. As the men's eyes adjusted to the light, they could see the silhouette of a tall, uniformed guard. It was Bobby Storey, in a guard's uniform. The tone in his voice conveyed urgency.

"The ball's busted, boys," he said. "Everybody out. It's every man for himself."

The men started tumbling out of the truck, jumping down to the ground awkwardly, trying to shake the numbness out of their legs after crouching in the dark during the ride from H-7.

Inside the Tally Lodge, all of the guards were scrambling to their feet and going after the prisoners now. It was a melee. Guards and prisoners were fighting hand-to-hand. Two guards jumped on Bobby Storey and started wrestling with him. One managed to knock his gun away. Other guards went after Rab Kerr. In the scrum, Kerr, worried that a guard might seize his gun and shoot him with it, flicked on the safety as he fell to the floor. Another guard, Campbell

Courtney, wrestled one of his captors' guns away from him, then hit him with it before being struck in the back of the head by another prisoner. As he reeled from the blow, Courtney could not believe the sight he glimpsed out a window: dozens of Republican prisoners clambering out of the back of the kitchen truck and running toward the main gate.

Storey yelled, "Okay, you win, we lose!"

It momentarily calmed the guards down and bought a few more seconds as the prisoners outside ran for it.

A siren sounded, its long rising wail audible to anyone within a mile of the prison, clashing with the ringing of alarm bells.

The outer gate swung open at last. Gallagher's and McKane's cars were blocking the truck from exiting the vehicle gate. But there was enough space for a man on foot to squeeze through. The prisoners started to scoot out the gate, between Gallagher's and McKane's cars. Others dashed through the pedestrian gate. Some crouched low as they ran, trying to make themselves smaller targets for the soldiers above. Some were in guards' uniforms, some were in their own clothes. Finding no transport awaiting them, most of the escapees scampered toward the razor wire perimeter fence that was the last barrier between them and the outside world, with enraged guards trailing in hot pursuit.

Just inside the main gate, it was bedlam.

There were guards all over the place, blowing whistles, screaming, fighting with escapees, wrangling guard dogs. Other guards seemed passive, or so stunned by what was happening they let prisoners race right by them toward the wire.

To the soldiers in the watch towers above, the sight was surreal—dozens of men, running willy-nilly, some of them appearing to be guards chasing other guards. There was no precedent for the situation. Unsure of what to do without running afoul of their rules of engagement, and afraid to do the wrong thing and possibly kill a guard by mistake, the soldiers held their fire.

Kieran Fleming got tangled up in the barbed wire of the perimeter fence but managed to extricate himself and plow his way through. He gashed his hand in the process. He, Padraig McKearney, and six others hijacked a passing car, left its bewildered driver by the side of the road, and sped away.

Some of the soldiers started shooting.

Inside the Tally Lodge, Rab Kerr, Denis Cummings, and Edward O'Connor were still trying to contain the guards for as long as possible so their comrades could get away. Three guards lay on the floor, wounded. A wailing siren, clanging alarm bells, screaming whistles, shouting, and gunshots created a mad cacophony.

Instead of going for the perimeter fence, some escapees turned right and dashed into the guards' parking lot just to the north of the perimeter wall.

There, prison guard William Gallagher, who had blocked the main gate with his car only minutes before, was parking his car, a yellow Toyota Celica. An officer had told him to get it out of the way so the main gate could be shut again. Just as Gallagher backed into the guards' parking lot, he saw the incredible sight of men running pell-mell out of the Tally Lodge.

Before Gallagher could exit his car and lock it, an onrushing Jimmy Donnelly threw the driver's side door open. He roughly pulled Gallagher out. Gallagher had seen Donnelly coming and taken the keys out of the ignition an instant before Donnelly could lay hands on him. Now Gallagher flung the keys away, toward a group of other guards nearby.

Mead and another guard now lunged for the keys, which lay on the ground.

Mead got there first, inches ahead of the guard. Mead feigned bending down to pick up the keys. Then he rose out of a crouch, balled his fist, and hit the guard in the throat as hard as he could. The guard dropped to the ground as though poleaxed.

Mead scooped up the keys and dashed back to Gallagher's car.

Kevin's heart was racing as he came upon the scene. He felt like it might explode out of his chest. He caught a glimpse of the open green fields beyond the perimeter fence.

In front of him was a yellow Toyota Celica, a two-door coupe. Kevin saw escapees piling into it. He dove in the passenger-side window, a split second before Brendy Mead shouted at everyone to lock the doors and roll up the windows. Mead and Jaz McCann were in front, with Mead at the wheel. Kevin lay on the laps of the three in the back seat—Jimmy Burns, Jimmy Donnelly, and Paul Kane.

It was time to go!

Mead could not get the car to start.

The others laughed.

Mead shouted at them to shut up. After all the running and fighting he was hyperventilating, covered in sweat, amped up. He heard someone outside the car shout, "Smash the windscreen!"

As he fumbled with the stick shift, Mead heard the tap of metal on the window. Mead turned his head to see the barrel of a pistol pointed at his head. The guard holding it was trying to fire it, but the weapon had jammed.

Mead jerked his head away and tried to start the car again. Now, at last, the little four-cylinder engine came to life.

The guard, enraged, now reversed the pistol in his hand. He wound up and slammed the butt against the windshield. Other guards were surrounding the car, drawing batons. In the instant before Mead hit the gas and burned rubber, their baton blows fell on the car, shattering the side windows and showering the men inside with cubes of safety glass.

Off they went, toward the external gate, a third of a mile away, as the guards' shouts receded behind them.

Mead slowed to drive over a ramp below one of the watch towers, the first of three they would pass on their way to the external gate. Resisting the urge to put the pedal to the metal, he tried to maintain an air of calm.

To their left, north of the perimeter wall, Kevin could see prisoners scrambling through the barbed-wire fence. He saw a fleeing prisoner go down near the fence, shot in the leg by a British soldier from a watch tower. It was Harry Murray, who had been part of the Tally Lodge team.

Brendy Mead drove along the perimeter wall toward the external gate. If the soldiers thought of firing plastic bullets from their riot guns, they discarded this option, or Mead drove out of their short range before they could load, aim, and fire them.

Mead barreled past three watch towers, picking up speed as the Celica closed the gap between the six desperate men inside and the exterior gate.

As he drove, Mead kept hugging the perimeter wall, which stood to his right. Kevin looked out to the left side of the car as the little Toyota gained speed.

In the rearview mirror, Mead spied a red sedan, a Czech-made Skoda, gaining on them. The driver was William McClure, an officer who had just arrived to go on his shift.

McClure liked to eat his lunch in his car, where he could read the newspaper and listen to the radio in peace. He first spied the chaos unfolding outside the main gate while munching a sandwich. It looked like some prisoners had hijacked a yellow Celica and were heading toward the external gate. An astonished McClure dropped his half-eaten sandwich, started up his car, hit the gas, and took off after them.

As McClure gained on Mead from behind, he started honking his horn and flashing his headlights, trying to warn the guard at the pole barrier, Thomas Aiken, who now saw the strange sight of two speeding sedans approaching in what looked like a drag race, one of them honking its horn and flashing its headlights.

Mead floored it. They were hauling ass now. The red and white poles were pointing straight up—all clear ahead. Aiken had just lifted the pole, to allow the wife of a prison officer through. He stood aside, amazed, as the two cars zoomed past. As he drove by, McClure yelled out the window at Aiken, to make sure all the exits were sealed.

The two cars raced toward the external gate. Behind them, at the pole barrier, Aiken was shouting and waving, trying to get the attention of the soldiers and guards manning the external gate.

The little yellow sedan hurtled on, gaining speed, but McClure had overtaken it. Now the little red Skoda was out in front.

As they passed over the ramp parallel to the second British Army watch tower on the perimeter wall, the six men in the car wondered why the British had not riddled the car with bullets. The men tensed up, expecting rounds to strike the car at any moment. A soldier leaned out of the watch tower, clearly looking at them. But he did not raise his weapon. If he thought about doing it, maybe he hesitated because the only vehicles which ever passed this way were driven and occupied by prison guards.

There was one more gate to go—the sixth one, the last one, the external gate. Soldiers and guards opened and shut it manually. It was a double gate, made of corrugated tin, with a skeleton of three-inch box metal. To its right sat a sentry box manned by a soldier.

Accelerating toward the gate, Mead aimed for dead center. Beyond, he could see green hedges and fields.

Everyone in the car was shouting at Mead now.

"Ram the gate! Ram the gate, Brendy!"

At the last instant, McClure swerved his car to the left to avoid ramming the gate himself.

At the external gates, telephones were ringing and radios crackling. The order came over both: *stop all movement.*

Kevin grabbed the seat in front of him and lowered his shoulder into it, bracing for the impact which lay just ahead.

FIFTY-THREE

What Are Ye Doing Out Here?

As Mead sped toward the external gate, he could see a British soldier and two prison officers struggling to close it.

"Hold tight!" Mead yelled.

Just before Mead could get there, the two officers dropped the vertical bar which secured the gate into the ground and scampered aside.

Mead aimed the hurtling Celica for dead center where the gates met. The throttle of the little four-cylinder engine was all the way open.

Anticipating the crash, the men, packed together like sardines, braced themselves in various positions.

The British soldier stood at the gate, seemingly frozen, between the onrushing car and the gate. He waited until the last instant to dive out of the way.

Mead shut his eyes just before the moment of impact.

The car smashed into the left-hand side of the gate, sending it flying open. The impact threw the rear of the car sideways, crashing into the right-hand side of the gate, which flew all the way open. The car came to rest between the two gates, jammed into a gap between them, with the left gate at a 45-degree angle against the right front fender. The impact knocked Mead out momentarily.

When he came to, he felt pain in his scalp—he was being dragged out of the car by his hair. His alertness returned. He shouted to the others that he was caught. The others were scrambling out.

"Let go of me hair, let go," Mead yelled. "Take me arm. I'll go quietly."

Fucking right ye will, ye bastard, said a guard. He grabbed Mead by the arm. Mead waited for the instant when the man's grip loosened, then punched him, hard, in the ribcage. The guard staggered back.

Mead leaped onto the hood and hopped down onto the ground on the other side, before he turned right and took off running down the Halftown Road. Ahead of him he saw Paul Kane running too. Beyond he saw houses. Maybe there was another car to hijack there.

In the Celica, Jimmy Donnelly seemed frozen.

"Come on, Jimmy, come on!" shouted Kevin as he scrambled out.

Donnelly shook his head. The sound of shots being fired might have discouraged him from trying to run. To Kevin it seemed Donnelly had "given up the ghost" and resigned himself to being captured.

Everybody but Donnelly bailed out, scrambled over the hood of the little car as it sat jammed in the gate, and took off running.

Guards descended on Donnelly. He went quietly, surrendering without a fight.

Off went Kevin out the passenger door, following Paul Kane. As he scrambled out the gate, he saw the soldier who manned the gate unholster his pistol.

Kane was running in a crouched position, down the Halftown Road. Kevin saw a guard hot on Paul Kane's heels, or so Kevin thought before the trailing man's hat fell off and long hair fell out. Kevin realized it was Brendy Mead disguised as a guard.

Kevin could not catch up with them—they were too far ahead, running too fast.

Mead and Kane flagged down a car. They hijacked it and sped off, unable to hear Jimmy Burns behind them, shouting at them to wait up for him.

Meanwhile, Jaz McCann, at first stunned and shaken from the collision, had taken off running down the Halftown Road. He got off it and turned left, down the Bog Road. He was wearing a brown leather bomber jacket and brown trousers. Burns, in a guard's uniform, had run off too, shouting to the two guards and British soldier that he was chasing the escapees. Kevin heard two gunshots. He saw McCann go down and assumed Jaz had been shot.

The yellow Toyota rested, wedged in the still-open gate, its doors thrown wide open, trunk smashed, its hood slightly ajar.

By 4:25 p.m., just thirteen minutes after sirens started wailing, the Army, UDR, and RUC were activating Operation Vesper, the code name for a coordinated effort to capture escaped prisoners. A cordon of vehicle checkpoints swiftly went up on all roads leading away from the Maze, two-miles-distance from its walls.

Kevin Barry Artt was still inside the cordon. He was dressed in civilian clothes—a pair of blue jeans, a dark blue denim shirt, the clothes he had put on before breakfast in his cell that morning.

He was running as hard as he could.

He had turned right—south—on the Halftown Road, then gotten off the road to his left, jumped a hedge, and turned down a farm lane. In the distance, a housing estate beckoned—*might be some cars there*.

Kevin's mind raced to his next steps, but he couldn't think of any.

He kept on running—down an embankment. Getting closer to the housing estate, he saw British Army jeeps entering it. Kevin hit the deck. He crawled into some bushes, then made his way into a hedge that ran along the foot of an embankment. In the distance he could hear gunshots. He was huffing and puffing, completely winded after going from zero to a full run over hundreds of yards, and pouring sweat. On a late September afternoon in Northern Ireland, there was still plenty of light out.

Kevin breathed and tried to hide himself from the soldiers he was sure would be swarming the area any minute. He still had no plan. He had exited the Maze without one, had never thought to plan an escape route away from it. He was still only about 150 yards outside the perimeter wall.

What to do now?

He took deep breaths, trying to control his breathing.

Kevin heard the rumble of vehicles. They were British Army Jeeps. They came to a halt only fifteen yards from where he lay below the hedge. He heard Jeep doors slamming shut, soldiers talking, English accents, the crunch of boots on pavement. A group of soldiers departed on foot toward the housing estate. Two stayed behind.

Kevin burrowed into the earth, pulled weeds and brambles close around himself, then lay prone, his head resting on his arms, waiting, waiting for the soldiers to go away. He overheard the soldiers' desultory conversation. They were bitching to one another about sore feet and double shifts.

At 5 p.m., news of the escape hit the radio waves. In H-7, cheers echoed throughout the Block. They could hear other Republican prisoners cheering in the neighboring blocks.

Outside the Maze, the RUC men were in a mood of hysteria. Armed IRA criminals were on the loose.

Kevin lay still and quiet, breathing, waiting, doing his best to meld into the earth and be invisible, like a rabbit hiding from a predator in its hole. The IRA team in Armagh had bugged out anyway after hearing reports that the escapees were on foot and in the open.

Kevin lay underneath the hedge. When, at last, the soldiers mounted up and drove away, it was nearly 8 p.m. With the sun nearly gone, it was getting cold. In his single layer of light clothing, Kevin felt hypothermia coming on.

Kevin lay there still another half-hour, shivering, afraid there might yet be soldiers lurking nearby, hoping they could lure him out after pretending to have left, itching for a chance to shoot him.

Kevin rose. It was dark. It was a cold dry night. Not a drop of dew lay on the ground.

He looked around. There was no sign of anyone.

Kevin crossed the road, into the housing estate, after clothes and any mode of transportation he could lay hands on.

He slipped into the back garden of the first house he came to. There were two vehicles parked in the driveway. Kevin stole up to the driver's side door of the first one, planning to hot-wire it if it were unlocked. It was locked. So was the second car. There was no shed in the back.

Kevin moved on to the next house, then a third. It had a small shed in the back garden. Kevin tiptoed toward it, with his head swiveling around and his eyes darting from house to house, alert to the sight of anyone who might see him. There was no one. Everything was still. Kevin eased the shed's door open. It was on the latch, unlocked and Kevin eased himself inside.

It was dark in there. But there was enough ambient light to discern the shapes of bicycles leaning against the wall. Kevin's heart leapt at the sight of them.

Just as he moved toward them there was a sudden burst of light outside the shed. Kevin crept toward the door to peek out. Inside the house, a man had gone into the upstairs bathroom and turned on the overhead light. It shone partly out into the back garden. Kevin heard the man gargling. He knew it meant the man had not seen him.

Leaving the shed door ajar, Kevin let the light from the bathroom into the shed. It fell on the bikes. Kevin selected the biggest one. Moving as stealthily as he could, he maneuvered it to the door. Then he spied a button-up woman's cardigan hanging near the door.

Perfect. On it went.

The gargler switched off the bathroom light, plunging the back garden back into darkness. Kevin noiselessly eased the shed door shut. He was still within 200 yards of the main gate of the Maze prison.

Kevin walked the bike down the side of the house, out onto the street. There were kids playing out there under the streetlights, shouting at one another. Kevin acted casually. He mounted the bike and started to pedal down the street. In about half a block, Kevin came to where the kids were. He waved at them as he pedaled past. It wasn't quite Steve McQueen, but it would have to do.

Then he rode on, toward the Halftown Road. It was about 9:00 p.m. Kevin rode directly past the exterior gate the little Toyota had smashed through a few hours earlier. A crew of men was working there, repairing the gate. The smashed-up Celica was gone. When Kevin reached the Blaris Road, he knew it led to Lisburn, the nearest town. He veered onto it.

In the darkness, with the aid of the streetlights on either side, Kevin saw fields on both sides of the road. He chuckled to himself, wondering if another escapee who did not recognize him might jump out, knock him off the bike, and commandeer it for himself.

Presently, Kevin glided over a rise. As he accelerated down the other side, there it was: an RUC vehicle checkpoint. Two Jeeps, an unmarked car, and eight to ten uniformed constables. It was too late to stop or bail out and run. Turning around seemed stupid.

Kevin rode directly into the checkpoint, taking care to slow down as he neared the officers.

Kevin dismounted, play-acting already, a local citizen, surprised and mildly pissed-off at being inconvenienced.

A constable approached Kevin warily but did not unholster his weapon.

The officer looked Kevin up and down.

What are ye doing out here?

At the same moment, across the Irish Sea, Alan Miles was in Scotland, near a radio. He listened, astonished, as the announcer broadcast the news that a number of Republican prisoners had escaped late that afternoon from the Maze prison. He wondered whether one of them might be Kevin Barry Artt, the man convicted of murdering his father.

FIFTY-FOUR

I Know Someone

Kevin put on his best poker face.

"I'm a student at Queen's. I heard about the escape from the Maze, I came out to have a look."

"What's yer name?"

On the spot, Kevin concocted a fake name, something that sounded good and Protestant.

"William Johnson," he replied. "Ye can call me Billy."

"Let's see some i.d. then."

"Sorry, I haven't got it on me."

"What's yer date of birth?

Kevin paused a beat, then said, "December 6, 1962."

"Where are ye going?"

"Back to Belfast."

"Stay where ye are."

The officer walked away to converse with his sergeant.

After the two men had a word, the sergeant approached Kevin.

"Can ye repeat the date of your birth, please."

"December 16, 1962."

"I thought ye said December sixth."

The sergeant cocked his head, eyeing Kevin closely.

"We're taking ye to Lisburn Police Station."

Kevin put on a mask that bespoke concern and a trace of annoyance.

He assumed the officers would impound his bicycle and put it in the trunk.

"Don't scrape my bike," he told them.

"Yer bike's staying here. Don't worry about yer bike," replied the sergeant.

The officers let him lay the bike on a footpath that ran aside the road. As he placed the bike there, he asked the other officers nearby to watch the bike.

"It's nearly new," he said.

The officers seemed relaxed. Everyone's weapons were in their holsters.

Maybe I'm selling it.

But could he keep it up? And would it matter once his photo was broadcast and someone in the station matched it to the polite young man sitting in the reception area?

Kevin's heart was beating like a trip hammer. He worried the officers were putting him through a routine which would end with their beating or shooting him.

Play along.

Kevin was going to ride it out as William Johnson. He felt he had no choice. He had gotten this far. He wasn't about to throw up his arms and say, "OK, ye got me.'"

Inwardly, Kevin found it mildly encouraging that the constables had referred to it as "your bike"—words they might not have used had they believed he'd stolen it.

Kevin sat in the back, the constables in front. The sedan rolled along in the darkness. Kevin tried to make small talk. The police radio was alive with chatter.

They rolled into the parking lot of the police barracks in Lisburn. Kevin thought the game was up.

Still gotta play along. You don't know.

The officers deposited him in the "hatch," a small reception area. There they left Kevin by himself.

Kevin perceived barely-controlled pandemonium within the station—radio chatter, telephones ringing incessantly, a lot of people moving around.

Over the next hour, Kevin Barry Artt played the role of earnest, innocent, civilian Protestant university student. He made no move to slip away, despite his fear of being discovered and set upon by officers at any moment. He wondered if the police were having him on, just waiting for him to bolt, so they could shoot him dead and claim he had been trying to assault them. His mind whirled with scenarios and options.

What to do? What to do?

Kevin sat there coolly, listening to the nonstop ringing of telephones, watching officers coming in and out. He had noticed the jersey he was wearing was a woman's. Did it stand out like a sore thumb? He hoped no one would notice.

Kevin averted eye contact with anyone, stayed hyper-vigilant, coached himself inwardly: *Just breathe, just breathe, just breathe. Play it cool.*

When he thought he could steal a look without anyone noticing, Kevin glanced at the clock on the wall.

All over the north, the biggest manhunt in the history of the province was underway. Thousands of RUC men and British troops were searching for him and the other escapees still at large.

Through a small window that joined the reception area to the main office, Kevin could see an officer talking on the telephone. The officer was not looking at Kevin.

Kevin recognized the man from an encounter he had had with him while driving for Ace.

Please don't look at me, Kevin thought as he studied his lap.

The officer ended his phone call, then disappeared from the little window. Twenty minutes passed. No one came out.

They've got me now.

The two officers who had driven him to the station at last emerged. Time seemed to slow down as they approached the bench where Kevin was sitting.

"Ye're comin' with us," said one. "We're taking ye back to your bike."

Kevin wondered if their game was to dare him to run so they could shoot him down in cold blood. Things seemed to be happening in slow motion as they walked to the car and Kevin got inside.

Keep playing along, keep playing along. Play it cool.

There was more small talk. Kevin kept up the act, asking his hosts how many prisoners had escaped and how many had been caught.

The car slowed to a halt as they returned to the vehicle checkpoint. There lay the bicycle, nestled in the grass alongside the road, safe and sound.

Kevin now put on a little cockiness for the sergeant, acting put out by the officers' interruption of his evening.

"Am I free to go now?" Kevin asked, a trace of sarcasm in his voice.

"Get on your bike," the sergeant replied, echoing the punch line of a popular TV ad that had entered the local popular lexicon. Hearing it, the other officers all laughed.

Kevin mounted up and rode off, headed for Lisburn.

Behind him, the roadblock remained in place.

As he pedaled away, a four-door sedan loaded with officers overtook him. It was a gold Hillman Avenger. Kevin gave it a sidelong glance. He saw the upraised hand of an officer emerging from the window. In an instant, Kevin mistook the silhouette of the man's gloved hand for a gun, and nearly dove off the bike before realizing the man was just waving at him.

The RUC vehicles vanished into the night.

As he pedaled along, Kevin reflected for a moment on the poetic justice of his situation. He had been innocent, falsely convicted. At the last minute, only ninety minutes before an escape that was months in the planning, escape organizers had invited him to come along. He had made it out. Police had arrested him and taken him to the station, not realizing who he was. Then they had *let him go* and joked with one another as they did it.

"I fell onto the Lisburn road after that," recalled Kevin in 2019. "My sense of direction finally kicked in, and I knew where I was."

Approaching south Belfast, he reached the Finaghy Road crossroads at about 10:00 p.m. On the way, he had passed through three UDR roadblocks after the soldiers waved him through.

Kevin Barry Artt had been a free man for nearly six hours. He was nine miles away from the main gate at the Maze.

The area was familiar to him, from his days driving for Ace. His parents and other family lived within a half mile of where he was. But there was no time to waste and no upside in taking dumb chances. He knew the net had to be closing fast.

Kevin's first stop was the local Sinn Féin headquarters, in Connolly House, on Andersontown Road. It was Sunday night. The place was closed and dark. The next stop was Downtown Taxis. Kevin remembered it had operated a small taxi depot next to a greengrocer, the Busy Bee, also on Andersontown Road.

Kevin rolled up. Two drivers stood outside. It looked like a slow night. Kevin dismounted and approached them without introducing himself.

"I need to talk to a Sinn Féin councillor," he said.

"Connolly House is right there," one replied, pointing up the street.

"You don't understand," Kevin said. "I really need to talk to a Sinn Féin councillor right now."

Then a long pause.

The two drivers looked Kevin up and down, then looked at one another.

"I know someone," said one driver.

He beckoned Kevin toward his car. The two men got in. Kevin sat in the back seat.

As the driver started the engine, he said, "What about your bike?"

"You can have it," Kevin replied.

Once they were underway, Kevin spoke to the man.

"Listen, I escaped from the Kesh today. I need to make contact with someone right away."

The driver smiled at him in the rear-view mirror.

"Relax, man," he said. "It was rather obvious."

On both sides of the Irish Sea, news of the escape had come as a thunderclap out of a bright blue sky, dominating front pages, television screens, and radios. British prison officials, and Margaret Thatcher herself, expressed shock and embarrassment at the brazenness of the escape of some of the most notorious men in the IRA. IRA units who hadn't been in the know were going out on covert patrols, searching for men who might be hiding, hungry, wet, and cold, in bogs and ditches, afraid to contact local people for fear of being turned in.

A few hours after the escape, British soldiers and RUC men raided escapee Terry Kirby's home. The raid left the house in a shambles, as usual.

"If that bastard ever comes back, he's dead," the soldiers told Kirby's mother, Bridgette, before leaving.

FIFTY-FIVE

Underground, I Am a Ghost

The someone arrived within a few minutes.

He was tall, thin, matter of fact, a few years older than Kevin, or so it seemed.

"What's the story?" he asked.

"I escaped from the Kesh today. I'm on my own. I'm not in contact with anyone. I rode up here on a bike. I need a place to stay, a safe house."

"This better not be bullshit. If ye're not telling the truth about this, ye're in a world of trouble."

"No problem."

The IRA soon moved Kevin to a safe house on the outskirts of Andersontown.

The area was mixed, borderline Protestant—a place that security forces might not comb as carefully as hardcore Republican areas elsewhere in the city. For the next two months, Kevin laid low there. All the while, British Army soldiers, RUC constables, and Irish Gardaí searched the island for him and the other eighteen escapees who remained at large.

Kevin's hosts treated him like a king. The lady of the house cultivated marijuana plants in her garden. She and her husband were a nice old couple, and in the evenings she smoked a little reefer while he sipped a pint.

The lady helped Kevin to change his appearance.

Kevin grew a beard and dyed his hair black—all of it, even his body hair. His hosts gave him a pair of eyeglasses. Kevin felt he now resembled Gerry Adams, the leader of Sinn Féin and former IRA man. He wondered if he might be stopped by security forces who mistook him for the Republican leader during transit to his next stop.

The next stop was the outskirts of Derry, seventy miles northwest of Belfast.

Two men drove Kevin there. Kevin rode in the back seat. They told him they were taking him to a safe house. During the ride, the men gave Kevin four different names and dates of birth to memorize. Kevin struggled to keep them all straight.

At the safe house, Kevin stayed overnight.

The following morning, he was told he was going to go for a jog with a group of people. The group routinely crossed the border during their workouts. The plan called for Kevin to peel off once they were south of the border. Then the rest of the group would return without him. Kevin's next stop would be a chapel in Burt, a tiny coastal village in northeast Donegal, at the base of the Inishowen Peninsula above the Lough Swilly. Someone would pick him up there.

His hosts outfitted him in some running gear and shoes.

"What they didn't tell me was it was a three-mile fucking jog," Kevin recalled, laughing. "They didn't show me any mercy. I was dying."

When they reached the border, Kevin was bringing up the rear, breathing hard, struggling to keep up. A British Army checkpoint loomed. The soldiers waved the joggers through into Donegal without hesitation.

When they were out of sight of the soldiers, one of the runners slowed, then gave Kevin directions to the chapel. There two women in a car would pick him up, he said.

The group of runners disappeared, leaving Kevin alone as they headed back toward Derry.

Following instructions, Kevin jogged to the outskirts of Burt to a small Catholic chapel, St. Aengus'. The chapel, built in 1967, had a round base made of cobblestones recycled from the Derry docks. Above was a ring of stained-glass windows, capped by a conical steel roof. Atop sat a glass-and-steel steeple, topped with a cross. Kevin hid himself in some trees just off the property. As night fell, Kevin, clad only in a single layer of running clothes, started shivering. It was late December in northwestern Ireland, just above the 55th parallel of latitude, where the average nightly temperatures routinely hovered in the mid-thirties.

Eventually, a sedan approached. Kevin, feeling the cold, stepped out toward the vehicle, which slowed as a window rolled down.

"Are you here to pick me up?" Kevin said.

"Yes, get in the car."

Kevin got in.

Off they went, headed north, toward Buncrana, a resort town on the Lough Swilly. Kevin felt like the rest of his life was just beginning.

The IRA started shuttling Kevin from safe house to safe house.

The first stop was a farm in Donegal, where Kevin's host was a nice old bachelor farmer. The man billeted Kevin in a small stone bungalow furnished with a collapsible cot. The closest town was Dungloe, a village overlooking Dungloe Bay. Fewer than a thousand residents, mostly Irish speakers, lived there.

From news reports, Kevin knew security forces were scouring Donegal for Bik McFarlane. While still at large, McFarlane had kidnapped a supermarket executive, Don Tidey. The kidnapping had ended in a deadly shootout in nearby Leitrim and McFarlane had slipped away.

Kevin fretted about being found despite his remote hiding place. Even while in prison and on the run, he had always done calisthenics to stay in shape. Now, afraid of attracting attention by steaming up the windows in the bungalow, he stopped doing the exercises.

Using scrap lumber, he built a makeshift wardrobe for his few clothes, hiding the cot behind it in case anyone looked in through the windows, which had no curtains. From time to time his host invited him into the main house, where he tended a peat fire during the chilly evenings. The décor was raw and simple.

Whether planned or not, the location lay near a hotel where Maeve and John Artt vacationed over the holidays, the Ostan Na Rosann in Dungloe. Kevin asked his handlers if he could see John and Maeve.

They readily agreed and organized a visit.

On Christmas night in 1983, Maeve and John heard a knock at the door of their hotel room. John opened it and found a man standing there.

"Barry wants to see you," the man said. "We'll bring you up to him."

John fetched a bottle of vodka and off they went.

The reunion was emotional. The three embraced and held one another for a long time. Kevin looked different with his hair dyed black.

"I told them I would probably never see them again," Kevin recalled later. "I was leaving the country."

Kevin told Maeve and John he thought Sweden could be his next destination. There, he said, he could apply for asylum. He had no intention of ever returning to Ireland. He had had enough of jail, prison, and narrowly avoiding assassination. He said that if he hadn't escaped he would have wound up being carried out of the Maze in a box someday. The guards' threats against him during his seven weeks incarcerated there had been unmistakable, he said. His captors had told him they were just waiting for the right opportunity to kill him.

The little family spent the entire night together.

In the morning, they said goodbye, wondering whether they would ever see one another again.

Everybody cried.

"We knew he couldn't stay in one place too long," remembered Maeve in 2019. "But it was still so sad."

Soon after, Kevin's handlers moved him to another part of Donegal. It was important to keep moving. In rural Donegal, local strangers and Belfast accents stood out. Staying too long in one place risked arrest by the Garda, Ireland's national police force, who could be counted on to imprison a fugitive from the six counties until the court processed the inevitable extradition request. Settling down permanently was out of the question.

Kevin's new host was also a farmer, a younger man, with a young family. He raised sheep and cattle. It was lambing season. Kevin was put to work mucking out the barn, tending sheep, delivering newborn lambs, and building pens for them.

In Belfast, Pat Finucane, the Belfast solicitor and brother to Kevin's co-escapee Dermy Finucane, kept Carmen apprised of Kevin's whereabouts. After asking permission of his host, Kevin contacted John McMorrow, an uncle who lived in Dublin. Carmen and Barry Paul met McMorrow in Dublin and rode the train from there to Donegal. At McMorrow's direction, Carmen was careful to pass through a retail store before their rendezvous in Dublin, to minimize the chance of her being followed by security forces. When she arrived at the farm, the weather was freezing. Snow covered the ground.

After about a month, Kevin's handlers reappeared and told him it was time to leave the country.

SECTION IX

LAMMING IT

FIFTY-SIX

Now Boarding

By 1985, Kevin Barry Artt's life underground had taken him to Donegal, Dublin, Sweden, and the Canary Islands. Interpol and the British were after him and every other one of the sixteen Maze escapees still at large. Gerry Kelly and Bik McFarlane were hiding in the Netherlands. Dermy Finucane was headed to the Irish Republic. The IRA had supplied help, but, conscious of Kevin's outsider status, had hit up John and Maeve rather than go into its own pocket for the money that had made its way across the Channel to Kevin and his three fellow escapees, Dermy Finucane, Terry Kirby, and Tank McAllister while they hid in Uppsala, Sweden.

For Kevin, the choice was easy. It was America. He had seen images of the Statue of Liberty, beckoning immigrants from all shores.

Kevin had imagined the worst-case scenario, in which the British eventually caught him. He knew there were Irishmen who had successfully resisted extradition in the U.S. courts. If he wound up there, he reckoned, he could expect a fair shake.

Pat Finucane broke the news to Carmen.

"I couldn't understand why he picked the States. Dermot and the others picked down south," Carmen recalled ruefully in 2019.

In Dublin, everything went smoothly. A man appeared at the safe house. Kevin had never seen him before. He was obviously IRA.

The man handed Kevin an Irish passport issued in the name of one Peter Thomas Daly, airline tickets, and some cash. He told Kevin he would fly to New York, clear immigration and customs in Kennedy airport, and fly on to San Francisco. There, Kevin's fellow Maze escapee Jimmy Smyth would pick him up at the airport, drive him into town, and help him get set up. If anything went wrong when he landed, the man said, the rally point was a pub in town, Ireland's 32, on Geary Boulevard. The owner, Jack Webb, an American, was sympathetic.

The man left without having told Kevin his name.

Kevin caught a cab to the airport the next morning.

As the big Aer Lingus 747 lumbered down the runway and lifted off from Dublin airport, Kevin Barry Artt, his hair dyed jet black, sat in a window seat, over the wing.

Flight attendants plied the charming young Irishman with miniature bottles of Irish whiskey. Kevin downed them. He stared out the window at the engine and the flat sea of white clouds that stretched to the horizon below the airliner. He forgot about fear. The whiskey took over, numbing him. High above the Atlantic Ocean, the airliner flew over the north Atlantic, chasing the sun as it headed west. Everyone who had wrecked Kevin's life—Norman Cromie, William Hylands, Charles McKiernan, Basil Kelly, every cop, soldier, and prison guard who had ever hit him or screamed at him—fell away, receding farther into the past with every passing second.

Kennedy airport was the biggest place he had ever seen. Kevin breezed through the checkpoints with scarcely a look from customs and immigrations agents, then spent the five-hour layover wandering the concourses.

Kevin boarded his second flight. Once the plane reached cruising altitude, he looked out the window. Ireland was 150 miles wide. The U.S.A. was massive. From his seat, the Great Lakes looked like big blue seas. The flat green expanses of Wisconsin and Minnesota spread from horizon to horizon. The Badlands of South Dakota were a kind of moonscape. Kevin, buzzed and sleepy from the whiskey, was too mesmerized by the landscape to shut his eyes.

After a long glide in over San Francisco Bay, Kevin was in California.

As he walked up the jetway to the terminal, the awe and wonder which Kevin had felt while airborne evaporated.

Kevin was alive. But his life was all he had left, and that was upside-down. He had lost his wife and son, his parents, his whole family. What he had to show for every day he had spent on the earth since being born was nothing. What he owned fit into a duffel bag. He felt miserable.

Kevin emerged at the gate area. It was March 22, 1985. The weather was clear, bright, and chilly. Kevin looked around for Jimmy Smyth, the man who was supposed to pick him up. What little time Kevin and Jimmy had spent together was less than thirty minutes on September 25, 1983, in the dark in the back of the Happy Wagon, on the way from H-7 to the main gate. As families and loved ones embraced the arriving passengers, Kevin stood alone, looking around.

Jimmy Smyth was nowhere to be seen.

Kevin walked through the concourse to the baggage claim area and then outside to the curb. It was late afternoon, a cool sunny day in San Francisco. Standing on the sidewalk with his duffel bag, Kevin felt self-conscious of his appearance, faintly ridiculous, comically out of place. His hair was dyed jet black, but dirty blond roots poked out from his scalp. He wore a large pair of dark sunglasses.

Kevin felt like some kind of low-rent James Bond. Instead of the Aston Martin, he had a driver who had left him standing at the curb.

Maybe he's just late, thought Kevin.

After an hour, Jimmy Smyth had still not appeared.

Fuck it, thought Kevin.

He hailed a taxi.

It was a long ride into town: fifteen miles, a twenty-dollar fare.

The driver dropped off San Francisco's newest Irish refugee at the rally point, Ireland's 32, an Irish pub on Geary Boulevard, on the west side of the city, north of Golden Gate Park. The place had a wide following in the local Irish diaspora. The owner, Jack Webb, a former San Francisco police officer, was known for his sympathy with the Republican cause.

Kevin entered the bar, which was roaring with conversation. He could smell the Guinness. Kevin paused to let his eyes adjust to the light. He approached the bar and politely hailed the bartender.

"Excuse me," Kevin said. "I'm looking for Jimmy from Belfast. Do ye know him, or know where he is?"

The barman tilted his head toward the end of the bar and motioned in that direction with his eyes.

In the dim light, Kevin saw a man sitting at the end of the bar. He seemed to be holding court with a small group of friends and nursing an Irish whiskey.

As he neared the man at the end of the bar, Kevin's ear detected a broad Belfast accent.

The man holding court was visibly drunk.

It was Jimmy Smyth.

Kevin walked up.

"Hey there, Jimmy," he said.

Smyth's eyes widened at the sight of his fellow Maze escapee.

"Fuck me, Barry! I thought it was tomorrow! How did ye get here?"

Smyth laughed. He offered no apology.

Kevin rolled his eyes.

"Let's have a drink," he said.

Kevin had worked nearly every day of his life since the age fifteen. Now he wasted no time finding a job. Jack Webb helped him find work with a small private detective agency. Soon Kevin was serving summonses and subpoenas.

Kevin got a California driver's license and U.S. passport, and immersed himself in his new life in San Francisco. He fixed automobile brakes, bartended in South San Francisco, drove an airport shuttle, kept a low profile. Kevin had heard tales of other Irish fugitives snared by the FBI after being discovered in Irish pubs. His long-term plan was to get out of San Francisco, away from its large population of Irish immigrants, as soon as he was able.

The plan became urgent when, in 1986, Kevin walked into Ireland's 32 and saw some people from Belfast. He feared they would recognize him.

In Europe, the British were still hunting down Maze escapees who remained at large. In January 1986, aided by Dutch police, they had found Gerry Kelly and Bik McFarlane hiding in a flat in Amsterdam with a load of rifles, ammunition, and explosives, and arrested them. Three months later, SAS commandos ambushed Seamus McElwaine and another IRA man, Sean Lynch, as they prepared a roadside bomb in County Fermanagh, near the border. After wounding the two, the soldiers approached McElwaine, who lay wounded and immobile on the ground. They questioned him for a few minutes and then shot him dead.

No doubt the British were still searching for Kevin and Jimmy. Possibly they were even closing in, about to pounce.

Kevin packed up his belongings and said goodbye to Jimmy Smyth. Off he went to Los Angeles. From there he ventured south, to San Diego. It felt smaller, with a more relaxed vibe than L.A. or San Francisco. The weather was nice, the Irish population small.

Kevin decided it was home.

Kevin got a job right away, at a Lotus dealership, selling new and used sports cars. He worked hard, usually seven days a week, and stayed out of trouble.

On May 8, 1987, the British crossed one more escapee's name off the list. It was Pádraig McKearney's. In Loughgall, a rural village about thirty miles southwest of Belfast, McKearney and the seven other IRA men, all heavily armed and clad in boiler suits, began an assault on a lightly manned RUC barracks there. Nearly three dozen SAS and RUC men were nearby, waiting in ambush. Within a few minutes, they fired over six hundred rounds at McKearney, his comrades, and a luckless civilian who happened to blunder into the kill zone, killing them all. Afterward, one witness likened the piles of spent bullet cartridges scattered on the killing ground to confetti at a wedding. Back at their barracks, the troops and soldiers cracked bottles of champagne and whooped it up.

It was the largest single loss of life the IRA had during the Troubles.

News of the ambush flooded the airwaves and headlines in Northern Ireland and the Irish Republic. In San Diego, the bloody deaths of McKearney and his comrades didn't make the local newspaper.

FIFTY-SEVEN

Kevin Keohane

In a city which embraced people who had come from somewhere else as its own, Kevin had a new life. Newly self-christened as Kevin Keohane, he was a San Diegan now. Transplants from all over the U.S. and the world were welcome in "America's Finest City." Kevin fit in well in the town's laid-back culture. He loved San Diego. In his spare time, he wore tank tops, cargo shorts, and flip-flops. He lived a beachy lifestyle. During his off hours, he chilled out with friends.

To them, the idea that Kevin was a murderer or hardened terrorist would have seemed far-fetched. He was gentle, sweet, caring, funny, kind. He acquired a dog, a mutt whom Kevin nicknamed Beggar O'Malley. When the poor animal got hit by a car one night, Kevin held the dog in his arms for hours, nursing it, before taking it to the veterinarian to have it put down.

At social gatherings, Kevin entertained friends by playing a twelve-string classical guitar and singing. "Greensleeves" was a favorite. Using watercolors, he created paintings, seemingly in the style of Salvador Dali, the same artist whose print had once graced Kevin's cell in the Maze. He gave them away to friends. To his friends, Kevin was a gentle soul—a pacifist, who never got angry or agitated. Everyone knew him as Kevin Keohane, the name that was on his driver's license. He stayed out of San Diego's few Irish pubs.

Like countless other immigrants in California, Kevin worked. He cleaned carpets. He worked as a private investigator, at Cartel 1000, Inc., a firm run by ex-San Diego Police Department sergeant Connie Zimmerman, even giving testimony in court during a homicide trial in downtown San Diego. He applied for a license to sell used cars. He had had some misgivings when asked to give fingerprints. But there was no way around it. DMV demanded it as a condition of granting the license. Kevin submitted his fingerprints. After getting the license, he sold cars, first at East Auto Sales in San Diego and later at Mossy Ford in Pacific Beach. There he worked long hours, evenings, and weekends. One month, Kevin sold twenty-eight cars in a month, earning $9,800 in commissions on the sales.

Kevin's income gave him the buying power to taste American materialism. He bought furniture, clothes, a motorcycle, a boat.

Across the Atlantic, Kevin's name appeared in an article on page one of the *Belfast Telegraph*, above the fold, in 1987. The story placed Kevin in a courtroom in Paris, France after having supposedly been arrested aboard a freighter, the *Eksund*, a boat laden with tons of arms munitions meant for the IRA. Kevin, said the article, was Britain's most wanted man, and the leader of a five-man "killer squad" who would be aiming to assassinate Margaret Thatcher at the Tory conference at Blackpool within three weeks' time. *The Sun* and *Daily Mail* tabloids repeated the story on November 4, 1987, adding that Kevin had attended "'refresher' courses in terrorism in Libya."

FIFTY-EIGHT

You'll Never Believe Who's Here

Except for the occasional article which the *San Diego Union-Tribune* picked up from wire services, Kevin did not keep up with the Troubles. He thought he had left them behind forever the moment he landed at Kennedy airport.

By 1992, Carmen Artt had given up waiting for word from Kevin. She remained an unemployed single mother, tainted by association with her notorious husband.

"He totally ditched me," Carmen bitterly recalled in 1992.

Convinced she would never hear from Kevin again, Carmen petitioned the court for a divorce, on the grounds of his absence for five years. The court granted it.

Kevin moved aboard *L' Attraction*, a thirty-six-foot houseboat docked at Seaforth Marina, at Quivira Basin on Mission Bay. There he spent much of his free time fishing. Mossy Ford had fired him for chronic tardiness.

Kathleen Mills was a comely, thirty-seven-year-old redhead who worked as a paralegal. Freshly divorced, she shared a rented house with her boyfriend, Peter Duffy, at 1767 39th Avenue, in the Sunset District of San Francisco. The neighborhood was home to many Irish, both with legal status and without. Duffy was a native of Coleraine, a town in the north of Ireland, located between Derry and Belfast.

His fellow Irishman and drinking companion Geordie Markey, of Belfast, slept in a guest room.

One night, Duffy and Markey returned home late after a night out at the bars. Their barhopping was a pet peeve of Mills'.

"You'll never believe who's here," Duffy declared to Mills.

"Who?" she asked.

"Long Kesh escapees," said Duffy.

Like some Irish before and after them, Duffy and Markey found it hard to keep such a tidbit secret. While nursing pints in Irish watering holes nearby, they talked. The FBI had learned that trolling such places for fugitive Irishmen could yield results. This night, one of its agents had been there, listening.

SECTION X

THE LONG ARM

FIFTY-NINE

It's Not Every Day We Bag These Sort of People

In February 1991, ten Maze escapees remained at large.

The morning of Wednesday, June 3, 1992, found one of them, Kevin Barry Artt, snoozing aboard his houseboat on Mission Bay. Below decks, the only sounds audible were the gentle lapping of the water against the hull and the occasional cry of a seagull overhead.

Kevin's onboard telephone rang. It was about 9 a.m.

During the prior two weeks, Kevin had felt uneasy, looking over his shoulder. Friends had been telling Kevin they felt they were being watched and followed by police. Kevin suspected the long arm of Great Britain might be nearing him at last.

Kevin answered the phone.

The caller was the harbor master, Fred Daugherty. His voice conveyed distress. Police had arrived and told Daugherty that several cars had been broken into in the parking lot overnight. Could Kevin come out and check to see if his vehicle was among them?

Daugherty liked his Irish live-aboard tenant. Kevin was quiet and polite. He never forgot to slip Daugherty $100 in cash each month to look the other way while Kevin lived aboard *L'Attraction*.

The car, a white 1980 Toyota Celica convertible, was Kevin's baby, a car that embodied his beach bum lifestyle.

A little groggy, Kevin thought it was strange. The Celica had a state-of-the-art Viper alarm system, with a field disturbance sensor that detected anyone touching or reaching into the car. When triggered, the sensor triggered an automated voice which said, *Warning! Protected by Viper! Stand back, or I will sound my alarm!* Then three loud honks of the horn, and *I've been tampered with!*

The alarm was loud enough to be heard from the boat. Kevin wondered why he had not heard it.

He threw on a pair of camouflage shorts, a ball cap, and flip-flops. In his haste he did not don a shirt. Emerging from the cabin, he alighted from the vessel onto the dock and trotted up the ramp to the parking lot. To Daugherty, Kevin looked like he had just gotten out of bed, a little dazed and sleepy. As Kevin hustled up the ramp, he noticed an old couple sitting on a bench nearby.

There was something weird about it.

Kevin approached the little convertible. It looked all right. Kevin felt relieved.

Swoosh, swoosh, swoosh. Cars zoomed into the parking lot, converging on Kevin. Their doors came flying open. Out poured agents in plain clothes, pointing guns, shouting.

"Put your hands on the vehicle! Hands on the vehicle! Now, goddammit!"

Perhaps there were eight of them. All were pointing guns at him. The old couple on the bench had been working undercover. They had alighted from their seats on the bench. Now they were pointing guns at him too.

There was a cop there too, standing back. He looked like a San Diego Police Department officer.

Kevin put his hands on the car, setting off the alarm.

Protected by Viper! Stand back!

The agents kept yelling.

"Stop the alarm! Turn it off!"

It was hard to hear the agents over the din of the horn honking and the disembodied voice of the alarm yelling at everyone.

Warning! Protected by Viper! Stand back, or I will sound my alarm! I've been tampered with!

"I can't turn it off, I don't have the keys!" Kevin shouted. He had left them aboard the boat.

"Let me go back aboard for a minute," Kevin said. "I'll get the keys and turn the alarm off. I'd like to put on a shirt too."

The answer was no.

One agent handcuffed Kevin. Another fastened manacles to Kevin's ankles, hobbling him.

"You're under arrest," said one of the agents. Another agent read Kevin his *Miranda* rights.

Then they bundled him into a sedan and drove off, toward downtown San Diego, ten minutes away.

Frank Green's breathless story appeared two days later in the *San Diego Union-Tribune*. About the arrests of Kevin and another Irishman, Jimmy Smyth, Green wrote:

> British officials say Artt, 35 [sic], is an Irish Republican Army (IRA) commando who escaped from a British maximum-security prison in 1983 while serving a life sentence for the murder of a Northern Ireland prison official in 1981 [sic]. . .
>
> "We're extremely pleased by the apprehensions," said a spokeswoman at the Royal Ulster Constabulary in Belfast, noting that the arrests had been coordinated by British special agents and Interpol. "It's not every day we bag these sort of people."

Alan Abrahamson of the *Los Angeles Times* assumed both men were terrorists, writing: "If convicted, both terrorists could draw up to five years in a U.S. prison."

The agents drove Kevin downtown to the Metropolitan Correctional Center, where they transferred custody of Kevin to the guards at the MCC. Kevin asked for an attorney. They put him in a cell.

The cell looked like something designed for Hannibal Lecter. It was the only one of its kind in the MCC, with an all stainless-steel interior and no window or natural light. There was a toilet, but no sink. The bed was welded to the floor.

What the fuck is this? Kevin wondered.

A few days after he arrived, a guard told him jail administration had designed the cell to hold "the devil himself" after an incident in which a prisoner had overpowered a guard, dragged him into his cell, forcibly sodomized him, and held him hostage for a brief period.

Kevin would spend the next three weeks there in solitary confinement, without bail.

The court appointed attorney Marc Geller, a private-bar lawyer who was on a panel of attorneys who accepted pro bono cases, as Kevin's counsel.

On June 10, 1992, a magistrate, Roger McKee, denied a bail application filed by Geller. At the urging of federal prosecutor Robert Lauchlan, Jr., McKee deemed Kevin a danger to society and a flight risk.

The British government wasted little time in announcing its intent to extradite Kevin Barry Artt and Jimmy Smyth.

"We expect the extradition course to be taken," said an unnamed RUC official. Both men, he said, were "dangerous criminals." The British would do everything within their power to ensure that the fugitives were delivered into RUC hands.

I called Geller soon after the story of Kevin's arrest broke in the *San Diego Union-Tribune*. I explained that the law firm where I worked, Luce Forward, did asylum cases on a *pro bono* basis for refugees. Would Geller mind if I visited his client and spoke to him about pursuing an asylum application, so he could help avoid deportation?

"Not at all," he replied. "I'm getting out soon anyway. They're moving him up to San Francisco."

The MCC was a hulking, 23-story skyscraper operated by the Bureau of Prisons, with capacity for 1,000 prisoners. One prominent architectural feature were narrow vertical windows on all four sides of the building. They were wide enough to afford a prisoner a small view of San Diego Bay and the city's downtown. The exterior façade was drab brown concrete. As they still did in 2018, the design and materials screamed early 1970s.

After clearing security and riding the elevator up to a visiting room, I heard the jingling of keys, the creaking of hinges, the clank of chains, enough chains to rival those of Jacob Marley's ghost, or so it sounded. Here was Kevin Keohane, wanted international fugitive and escaped murderer, the would-be assassin of Margaret Thatcher, clad in an orange jumpsuit. Three guards accompanied him.

"He's got a three-man hold on him," said one. "That's because he's a dangerous man. Isn't that right, Keohane?"

KO-hane.

An officer at the jail had told him the marshals viewed him as the number one security risk in San Diego.

Chains hobbled Kevin's feet, which were shod in plastic slippers. Shackles bound his handcuffed hands at his waist. Kevin had dark reddish hair and deep blue eyes.

He seemed wary, wide-eyed. I guessed he had enough bad experiences with attorneys to be wary of them on general principles.

"I'm Dan Lawton," I said. "I'm a lawyer. I talked to your lawyer, Marc Geller, on the phone. He said you might be interested in going for asylum."

I handed Kevin a business card. He studied it closely.

"The law firm where I work does a lot of asylum applications for refugees," I said. "I've done a few of them, mostly for Central Americans. We do the work pro bono."

I asked Kevin his name.

"Kevin Barry John Artt," he said.

Showing the naiveté of a civil lawyer unaccustomed to interactions with the criminally accused, I got straight to the bottom line. Had he done it?

"No," he replied. His dark blue eyes stared evenly back at me.

"How did you get convicted?"

"I confessed," he said.

I had no criminal law experience. What I did have was a reflexively American reaction to hearing that a defendant had confessed to a crime. Why would anybody confess to something that he had not done?

"I didn't do it," he added.

There would be time to sort all that out.

We talked about McKiernan, Castlereagh, the Black trial, his escape from the Maze, his time on the lam, his entry into the United States. His demeanor was unguarded, his answers spontaneous and given without hesitating.

When it was time to go, and with tongue in cheek, I cautioned him against trying to escape the MCC.

"I've already thought about it," Kevin said, without missing a beat.

I put a hand up.

"I don't want to hear it," I said.

"You'd just need some explosives up here. Blow a hole through the wall, then shinny down a rope ladder to the street. Someone on a motorcycle waiting."

"Good night," I said, pretending that I hadn't heard him. Kevin laughed.

Later that night, Kevin composed a note in pencil about his suddenly changed circumstances. "Being arrested in California is a blessing in disguise," he wrote. "It is a weight lifted off my shoulders, an opportunity to reveal the truth, a forum to bring to light the degradation of human rights of not only myself but my fellow countrymen. . .

"The support of those that know me has given me the heart, and the light at the end of the tunnel. I owe them the truth. I owe myself and family the truth and all the innocents in the British justice system deserve exposure."

SIXTY

He's a Cowardly Murderer

In San Francisco, Mark Zanides was the U.S. Attorney's Office's international extradition specialist.

Zanides was a formidable prosecutor. Among defense lawyers, he had a reputation for cockiness. Of Greek ancestry, he had black hair and dark eyes, and stood about 6'3". Flamboyant of dress, sometimes he sported a calf-length black leather coat, which he had gotten in Argentina while working on an extradition case there. He drove a Porsche, an unusual vehicle for a federal prosecutor. Rumor had it a framed, autographed glossy photograph of Margaret Thatcher hung on the wall of Zanides' office at 450 Golden Gate Avenue.

Zanides had a track record of success in extradition cases. He had been practicing nearly nineteen years. He had undergraduate and law degrees from Stanford and the University of Chicago, respectively. Perhaps he thought this one would be like all the others. The extraditee would fight for a while, gin up some fuss, and delay. Then the marshals would put him on the plane which would carry him back home.

Sara Criscitelli was the newly appointed assistant director in the Department of Justice's Office of International Affairs, headquartered in Washington, D.C. She was forty-four years old and a graduate of Hofstra University School of Law in Long Island. She spoke with a distinct New York City accent. In appearance she was bespectacled, bookish, schoolmarmish. She wore cardigan sweaters. Unlike Zanides, she did not stare Kevin or the defense lawyers down or make faces during court proceedings. In appearance, she and the flamboyant Zanides seemed polar opposites. The two made an odd couple.

Zanides' and Criscitelli's clients were a gaggle of officials who served at the highest levels of the British government and military. Their number and titles suggested a high degree of interest in Kevin Barry Artt in London. There was British Army lieutenant general Alistair Irwin, commander of the 39th infantry brigade in Northern Ireland, who would later serve as general officer commanding all British forces in the north. From the Crown Solicitor's Office in Northern Ireland, there was British attorney James Conn, who would later be knighted by Queen Elizabeth for "services to justice." Jonathan Powell, a diplomat, represented the British government's Foreign Office and the British Embassy. From the British government's Northern Ireland Office, there was Sir John Chilcot, permanent under-secretary of state for Northern Ireland, and his subordinate, career civil servant Anthony Beeton.

Paul Hamlin, a native of England, was the RUC officer in charge of the extradition. He would serve as the prosecutors' primary point of contact with the British government and attend court hearings in San Francisco.

In court, Zanides was given to make theatrical facial expressions—rolling his eyes and snickering at arguments made by Brosnahan, seemingly trying to telegraph his views to the bench from his seat at the counsel table.

An article published in a legal trade magazine in 1997 quoted Zanides as saying this about Kevin: "He's a cowardly murderer. Go to some guy's house and shoot him, that doesn't take any great courage."

"He was an angry, vindictive prick," Kevin remembered. "He went out of his way to be vindictive on every level."

SIXTY-ONE

Setting the Stage

The first page of the certificate of conviction duly forwarded by the Home Office in London bore the royal coat of arms in the upper right-hand corner. Appended was a twelve-page statement attesting to Kevin's conviction of the Miles murder as well as possession of a firearm and a recitation of the extraditable character of the offenses.

In the way of politics and mindset, Kevin could have drawn better than the judge assigned to his case, Charles A. Legge.

Legge was 61 years old, a San Francisco native born during the Great Depression, with impeccable credentials, including two degrees from Stanford University.

Legge fit the mold of conservative judges nominated to the bench by President Ronald Reagan. In an interview given to a writer for a legal newspaper, he described himself as a "moderate Republican." His biography in the *Los Angeles Daily Journal* listed "Protestant" on a line next to "religion." Physically, he seemed straight out of central casting, with thinning, neatly cut salt-and-pepper hair, metal frame glasses, and a genial, gentle manner. He belonged to the ultra-exclusive, all-male Bohemian Club, whose members had included U.S. presidents, cabinet officials, university presidents, CEOs of large corporations, national media figures, and accomplished artists, most of whom had to wait fifteen years for an opening before gaining entry.

Early on, Legge developed a reputation for maintaining a distance from attorneys and abstaining from much dialogue during hearings.

"You're arguing before him and you have no idea whether you're persuading him," said one criminal defense lawyer.

Attorneys gave high grades to Legge for fairness, courtesy, even-handedness, a knack for grasping complexity, work ethic, and intellectual energy. Criminal defense lawyers thought him a good listener, not the best you could draw, but far from the worst. The printed card the judge kept nearby his seat on the bench paraphrased the first verse of chapter 15 of the Book of Proverbs: *A soft answer turns away wrath, but a harsh word stirs up anger.*

Kevin's lawyer, the famous trial attorney Jim Brosnahan, was working pro bono. Tall and genteel, bespectacled and balding, rangy, with an oval head that seemed slightly oversized, the fifty-eight-year-old Brosnahan was a formidable physical presence, something he offset with a folksy, disarming manner and toothy smile that seemed part-Irish street corner pol, part genuine. He stood six feet and five inches tall. Behind the lenses of steel-framed glasses, his blue eyes sometimes revealed a twinkle. Fond of the U.S. constitution, he carried a pocket-sized copy of it with him at all times. It was a habit possibly inspired by the late U.S. Supreme Court Justice Hugo Black, who famously did the same thing. Family photos and sports memorabilia cluttered his corner office at 345 California Street. Brosnahan lived in Berkeley, a city more closely attuned with his iconoclastic and sometimes-anarchic political leanings than San Francisco.

Brosnahan had chosen law as a career after watching a trial and speaking to one of the trial lawyers afterward. The lawyer had told him that if he became a lawyer, he would not make much money but at least he would have some terrific stories to tell.

The lawyer had been right.

Legge was a "good guy," Brosnahan recalled in 2018. "But he saw things from the English point of view, maybe without even knowing he was doing it." Legge was personal friends with John Mortimer, the acclaimed English barrister, screenwriter, and author, most famous for inventing the character of Horace Rumpole of *Rumpole of the Bailey.*

Inside Santa Rita County Jail, twenty-six miles southeast of Oakland, Kevin Barry Artt, clad in a bright yellow jumpsuit and red plastic sandals, passed the days in his cell, without bail and with no bail hearing or trial date on the calendar. He did calisthenics, drew landscapes and surrealist images with colored pencils, read paperbacks, wrote letters to family and friends, mingled with the other prisoners.

The British press had always taken keen interest in Kevin's case. They had published stories branding him as Albert Miles' murderer. Now they took it a step further, circulating a wild tale, unattributed and unsubstantiated, that Kevin was a member of a "hit squad" stalking Margaret Thatcher and a generally dangerous international terrorist, a sort of Irish Carlos the Jackal or Abu Nidal, who had lived underground somewhere in the Republic of Ireland, with cash and weapons supplied by Libyan dictator Muammar Gadhafi, seeking revenge for the SAS ambush of IRA members at Loughgall in 1987.

SIXTY-TWO

Bearing Witness

On November 12, 1996, Kevin Barry Artt, dressed in a sober gray suit, the one proper suit he owned, finally rose and walked to the witness stand. He had spent much of the last four-and-a-half years in jail without bail in Pleasanton, a federal prison twenty miles southeast of Oakland, awaiting this day.

Two and a half weeks earlier, in private, Brosnahan and his team had assembled a mock jury, put Kevin in front of it, and questioned him as Mark Zanides might, putting their client through the paces of a simulated cross-examination.

In advance of the mock sessions, one of Brosnahan's lieutenants had written a memo listing topics which Zanides could be expected to probe:

- *Kevin's desire to become a member of the IRA . . .*
- *Why would a smart, intelligent, and articulate person like Kevin admit to such a heinous crime, no matter how much they verbally and physically abused him?*
- *Kevin testified he confessed because he was afraid of losing his family, yet he totally abandoned that family when he escaped, and has had little to no contact with them since (i.e. no longer with Carmen, doesn't support or have much contact with son, etc.)*

Another Brosnahan associate, Julia Alloggiamento, had prepared a memo too, listing anticipated cross-examination topics of her own:

- *Kevin's trip to America*
- *Connections with IRA members to get him here . . .*
- *Left wife and child behind . . .*
- *No contact with wife or child once in America*

Not all of the mock jurors had been impressed. Kevin's explanation of why he had confessed ("I had no choice") had failed to persuade some of them.

"We need to explain why you thought you had no choice, and that it was the detectives who were telling you the only choices were 7 years or 30 years" wrote one of Brosnahan's lieutenants afterward. "You need to convey why you would have trusted the detectives, especially if your attitude on the street to the RUC was one of disdain. Don't just say 'they forced me to sign a confession.'"

Today, Kevin was in front of the real audience: Charles Legge.

Brosnahan walked Kevin through his early years, his experiences as a teenager, his suffering at the hands of security forces during 1976, 1977, and 1978, and his escape from the Maze.

Then he opened the subject of Kevin's arrest in the wee hours of December 12, 1978:

Q. Did they talk to you about the Miles murder?
A. Yes, they did.
Q. What did you say about that?
A. I told them I had no involvement in it.
Q. Mr. Artt, was that true?
A. Yes, it was.
Q. Did you kill Albert Miles?
A. No, sir, I did not.
Q. Have you ever killed anybody?
A. No, I haven't.
Q. You are not guilty of this charge?

A. Absolutely not guilty.

Q. As God is your witness?

A. As God is my witness.

Brosnahan yielded his witness and sat down. It was the moment every trial lawyer dreads and must suffer— the instant in which he must sit down quietly while the opposing lawyer rises to begin trying to destroy his client on the witness stand, an experience he must mostly watch in silence while pretending calm and indifference.

Zanides started chipping away.

His was a workmanlike cross-examination, the sort to be expected from a savvy prosecutor confronting a witness who had confessed to murder but now claimed innocence. Zanides peppered Kevin with a series of questions aimed at undermining the credibility of the man who was now on trial for his life and limb.

Had not Kevin been represented by an eminent lawyer, Michael Nicholson, at the trial in Belfast?

Did not he sign a confession which acknowledged he had done so of his own free will and allowed to add, alter, or correct anything he wanted to before signing it?

Wasn't Kevin essentially saying that he should be believed over all of the detectives who had testified about his confession and that the court should view those detectives as perjurers?

However coercive the setting in Castlereagh in 1981, the detectives had not tortured Kevin. Wasn't that right?

Had Kevin not tried to join the IRA, knowing that it was bombing and shooting people in pursuit of its political goals?

There were witnesses in the north who knew of Kevin's supposed innocence, like Fyfe, an RUC inspector who'd told Kevin in 1978 that detectives knew he was innocent, and Charlie McNutt, Kevin's father, who'd heard Fyfe say it. *But they weren't in court in San Francisco to testify to it.*

Kevin had been stopped a lot by police while driving his unlicensed taxi, Zanides said. But he was driving it during the height of the Troubles in Belfast, where police and Army units had thrown up vehicle checkpoints all over the city to try to intercept bomb-laden vehicles which might explode and kill or injure innocent people. *And so it was normal and natural that he was stopped a lot, was it not? And, rightly or wrongly, did not the police view Ace as an IRA front, a sort of delivery service whose cargo was munitions meant to kill and maim the IRA's targets?*

Zanides pointed to inconsistencies in Kevin's testimony. Kevin had testified to the barrel of a long rifle emerging from the window of the car that had backed up suddenly that night, but somehow forgotten to include the detail in the written statement he had made at the Oldpark Road RUC station. *Wasn't that right?*

And his alibi—Lorraine Keenan had testified to it in 1983, Kevin's lawyers hadn't called her parents, Brian and Gladys, and her brother, Stevie, who could have corroborated what Lorraine had said, to do it from the witness stand in Kelly's courtroom. *Wasn't that also true?*

However bad detectives' treatment of him had been at Castlereagh, he had not filed any complaint about it, despite having the opportunity to do so if he wished. That was correct, too, wasn't it, even as to the bit about Hewitt hitting him in the head with a bullet?

Kevin had to admit the answer to each of these questions was the same: yes.

SIXTY-THREE

The Moths Come Out

At 1:30 p.m. on December 11, 1996, all attorneys and parties convened in Judge Legge's courtroom for closing arguments.

Brosnahan went first. He would speak for the next three hours, most of the time without looking at his notes.

It was a climactic moment in a stellar legal career, a chance to address the court in a historic case on behalf of an innocent client wrongly convicted of murder. Most defense attorneys only dream of having one such case in their careers. Spectators crammed the gallery. I was one of them.

For the rest of the afternoon, Brosnahan delivered a summation as formidable, eloquent, and thorough as he had given in thirty-two years of practice, painstakingly walking through the facts proven at trial and explaining how the governing law, the treaty, now required Legge to refuse Kevin Barry Artt's extradition to Northern Ireland.

By turns it was disjointed, sentimental, rigorously logical, lawyerly, passionate, tied closely to exhibits and testimony duly received into the evidence by Legge, at once scholarly Socratic method and corner-bar common sense.

Brosnahan punctuated it with literary allusions and small detours devoted to witness credibility and government gaffes, little litotes in which he disclaimed an effort to create drama when he was doing that very thing. He tailored it to his audience, echoing back to Legge's concerns which the judge himself had voiced during the trial, and appealing to Legge's subtle Anglophilia. It was vintage Bros, a closing argument both textbook in its legalistic soundness and utterly idiosyncratic, a piece of work worthy of the man who had literally written the book on how best to try a case in a California courtroom.[8]

Kevin Barry Artt was no IRA murderer, Brosnahan said. There was no logic to the notion that he could have been one.

"He was . . . kind of a red light. He was a little bit too outspoken, he was a little too combative, and they followed him, they recorded him and all of that.

"There is no way that he would be picked to do an IRA murder. It would not make the slightest bit of sense. Not only is he not from an IRA family, not only is there no showing that anything would cause him to do that kind of thing, but, beyond that, he is a young driver of an automobile that is known to the officials."

But that had not prevented the RUC, acting in concert with a shadowy Loyalist paramilitary group, from deciding they would be better off without Kevin Barry Artt above the ground any longer.

"So there is Kevin Barry Artt. He is in Belfast. He is 19 years of age [sic]. And on a Sunday night—and this has nothing to do with him except it has shaped his life like some kind of wild, wind-driven Sierra tree. It has been everything to his life.

"If I cannot convince your Honor, it will be everything that is in the future of his life.

---

8. J. Brosnahan, *Trial Handbook for California Lawyers* (Bancroft-Whitney Co. 1974).

"And having nothing to do with him, on a Sunday night at ten-past-eight on a street in Belfast, Albert Miles, the number two person in charge of the Maze prison, is at home with his wife and son. They are both witnesses.

"There is a knock on the door. And in Belfast they are careful. But she opens the door. There is a shooting. Albert Miles dies, and, no doubt, Mrs. Miles' life is changed forever. No question about it . . .

"The people with motive to kill Albert Miles in Belfast on November 26, 1978, are legion. I don't know what the number is. But I do know that at the Maze prison where he works there is great turmoil. There is great political unrest. The prisoners are adopting positions which they believe are correct, and the authorities are trying to break them.

"So the number of people that might have gone in that Sunday night and shot Albert Miles is unlimited. The IRA is presumptively responsible for the shooting. And where is the evidence as to who did the murder?

"No matter what else we think about this case, this must be the moment where I am entitled to ask that question. Because my client faces the charge, and there is no evidence that he did the murder.

"You could have fingerprints, for example, you could have forensics; you could have hair samples or scrapings from the fingernails; you could have the car or guns or whatever; you could have an eyewitness on the street.

"Your Honor heard nothing from the officials in Northern Ireland about the murder. They did not seek to present it. They don't want to talk about it. They are not going to talk about it.

"They're going to suggest in the vaguest of all possible ways that somewhere—somewhere else there was some other judge that looked at it. And they will say, you know, we really shouldn't retry this case. . .

"If they feel righteous about this, if they feel that this should happen, if they feel this is a treaty partner that should respond, if they feel they are fighting terrorism . . . none of which is an issue to me. But if they feel all of that, this is the United States. That's the witness stand. Where are the witnesses?

"Silence."

Brosnahan wove in a glaring peculiarity in the McKiernan confession that police in Castlereagh had used to convince Kevin he had no choice but to confess.

"A .38 and a .45 [were] used, evidently, from the bullets that were there, not linked in any way to Mr. Artt. And when Mr. McKiernan avows as to how he thinks he did the murder, he said he had a 9-millimeter gun. . . A 9-millimeter is not a .38 and is not a .45.

"There is not only no evidence, but every time we look a little bit under the cover of this case to see what might be underneath, the moths come out, troubling moths, terrible moths, frightening moths. . .

"What does it take in Castlereagh? What does it take? And I am going to presume that those officers also are kind of a prisoner of Northern Ireland in their own way, and I won't dwell on it. But what does it take for one of them to say, 'We don't have any evidence. We have nothing.'

"Well, what kind of court can you go to with no evidence and get by with it?

"There is only one answer in Christendom, and that's the Diplock court. You can't go anywhere in Europe and get by with it. There is no evidence of this murder."

What it really all boiled down to was the confession, Brosnahan said. That had been the issue for Basil Kelly. That was going to be the issue for Legge.

"If a man decides in the misery of Castlereagh that he has two choices left to him in his life, and one is thirty years stipulated where his family will be gone, basically, or, on the other hand, seven years in which he has some hope of getting out, then when the officers have told you all these things, he can repeat them back. And that is what occurred at Castlereagh.

"Beyond that supply of information is nothing coming from Kevin Barry Artt about this murder. He cannot give them anything new."

The trial Basil Kelly had conducted in 1982 and 1983, Brosnahan said, had been a show trial, an exercise so unfair that not even Kelly's own colleagues had been willing to uphold its results. The Northern Ireland Court of Appeal had reversed Kelly in 1986, quashing the convictions of 22 defendants, citing Kelly's erroneous reliance on Christopher Black's unreliable testimony.

"Judge Kelly listens to the testimony of Christopher Black, and at some point, announces that he is one of the most credible witnesses that he has heard. . .

"It will have to be your Honor that decides that on the 30th of November, 1981, what they did in that room in Castlereagh, away from cameras and recordings, away from witnesses and lawyers, away from . . . anyone else, was fair."

Ironically, the evidence that the police, acting in collusion with Loyalist paramilitaries, had tried to murder Kevin Artt, said Bros, was much stronger than the case against Kevin for murdering Albert Miles.

"They were going to kill him. *Kill him.* What words will they use to de-personalize him so that this seems like that's just something that he's got to endure? . . .

"The authorities know there's a group that wants to kill him. He says what any human would say: Who are they? Where are they? What can you tell me to help me protect myself? Nothing. Silence. Any protection you can give me? No. Nothing. It's policy. . .

"It's policy that blots out responsibility. It's policy that makes collusion possible. It's policy that prevents criticism if, in fact, details have been leaked to Loyalist paramilitaries."

The effort to kill Kevin had not ended with the Heathwood shooting. It recurred with no warning, on December 30, 1980, as Kevin walked down a darkened street with Al Sloan, headed to a Chinese restaurant in the middle of the night.

"I will stake the case on this, on this point, right here, right now. I'm not trying to be dramatic, but this is it, this is really it. There's a man with a gun, he's chasing Kevin Barry Artt. Mr. Sloan is terrified. Mr. Sloan has run up this street. This street exists in the world. He runs up this street, he dives through the glass of the window, he cuts his nose and his forehead . . . he thought he was going to be assassinated and killed. That's what he testified to.

"So what was that all about? What is that testimony? What does that show? Who were those men? Are those Loyalist paramilitaries? No. Are they the figment of Mr. Artt's and Mr. Sloan's imaginations? No. No, they are four RUC officers at 12:30 or 1:00 at night, who are in a car with their uniforms on the bottom, the recognizable RUC pants, and civvies, I would call them, or regular dress over, so that they don't look like police officers, in an unmarked car, with guns. . .

"Prejudice, to a Catholic, and to a nationalist, gets no worse than men in police uniforms chasing him with a gun, without justification, on what the form calls the nature of the complaint, discreditable conduct."

All of it, warned Brosnahan, portended a dark future for Kevin Barry Artt if returned to Belfast. Brosnahan did not quote Thomas Hobbes, the English philosopher, in this passage, but he might have. An extradited Kevin Barry Artt would live a life permeated by constant fear and the danger of violent death. It would be solitary, poor, nasty, brutish, and short. Now, Brosnahan's voice rose.

"Does the court have any idea what will happen to Mr. Artt . . . when they have him in custody in [the] Maze away from the sight and sound of any protective legal cover?

"I am not here intense because I don't know how to be calm. I think I argue for a man's future. And I think he did not do the murder. And I think they were trying to kill him.

"And you know what, your Honor? I think our case against the RUC for attempting to murder Kevin Barry Artt is far stronger than any case they ever had against him for killing Albert Miles. We have evidence and documents and events.

"And it doesn't do the officials from Northern Ireland any good . . . for them to make minor distinctions and minor points when their own people chased him with a gun.

"Silence on that issue from them. Nothing said. No explanation, nothing. . . .

"They beat him; they chased him with a gun; . . . they withheld protection from him and information in the face of knowledge that he would be assassinated by a paramilitary organization. They investigated but never solved a shooting at the Heathwood house about which there is considerable evidence of implication or at least strong support by some police authority. And now they come to your Honor and say, 'Give him to us again. Give him to us again.'"

Brosnahan summed up.

"A long time ago the English system was our system. We have grown up from that. We have advanced it. We have gone beyond it.

"We are not lording it over anybody, we are not engaging in triumphalism, but they have come to test your Honor's soul. They have said, 'Here. Send him back.' And they have hoped that your Honor will not be moved to see what needs to be seen.

"And all I can do—and it may be inadequate to the task, but I hope that it is not—as an American lawyer is to call down American principles and to say, 'Here. This is what we are. We can't do this for you. Sorry. We can't do it.'

"So I ask your Honor to find in this case from all the evidence and in ways that your Honor will find to phrase it so that it's quite appropriate and based on the evidence and all of that—I ask your Honor to find that Kevin Barry Artt cannot be sent back to Northern Ireland."

With that, Brosnahan thanked Legge and sat down.

It was Mark Zanides' turn.

Zanides had spent much of the last four-and-a-half years trying to extradite Kevin Barry Artt. The case had not been the cut-and-dried exercise to which Zanides had become accustomed in prior extraditions. The travel, depositions, briefing, hearings, appeals of bail rulings all had been exhaustive and exhausting. America's most vital ally had entrusted the extradition of its most wanted fugitive to him.

The content and tone of Zanides' argument soon left no doubt that his gloves were off.

Zanides started with the sheer magnitude of the Troubles and the devastation they had caused in the ranks of police and soldiers in the north. Over 3,400 people had been killed. Over a third of them had been members of the security forces. There had been over 35,000 injured and 41,000 shootings and bombings. Using ratios based on the small population of Northern Ireland, proportionately, it was as if 68,000 people had been killed (24,000 of them police and soldiers) and 700,000 injured in California, with 820,000 shooting and bombing incidents in the same twenty-five-year period. The numbers were staggering.

And it was all the fault of the IRA—an organization which Kevin Barry Artt had wanted to join, Zanides said. He was just what the British had always said he was, a terrorist. The same was true of his own witnesses, IRA men like Brendan Hughes, Bik McFarlane, and Séanna Walsh, who had given testimony by deposition in Belfast.

The entirety of the case, Zanides said, turned on Kevin's confession in Castlereagh in 1981. Basil Kelly had held a seven-day hearing on the admissibility of the confession and listened at length to both the detectives who heard the confession and Kevin Barry Artt himself. Kelly had devoted thorough study to the matter and held the confession entirely admissible. Now there was no reason for Legge to second-guess his British colleague.

As for Brosnahan's argument that the Miles murder charge had been trumped up, it was frivolous, absurd, a product of a distorted view of the record and disregard of the facts.

McKiernan had incriminated Kevin and signed a confession naming him as his accomplice. Afterward, McKiernan had not recanted it, despite having the chance and despite recanting another statement he had made in Castlereagh. Nor had he testified on Kevin's behalf in this trial, in which multiple other men convicted in the Black trial *had* testified. By itself, his statement gave probable cause to police to arrest Kevin in 1981.

Yes, Kevin had withstood seven days of interrogation in Castlereagh in 1978. In 1981, the difference had been not ill-treatment or false promises of urging a lighter sentence to Kelly at trial. It had been Charles McKiernan. McKiernan was all the Crown needed to send him away to the Maze for life, whether Kevin cooperated or not, and Kevin had known it before putting pen to paper on the night of November 30, 1981.

"Artt knew the government had Charles McKiernan. He knew that he was going to get convicted and he made his choice. And his choice was that he would confess, put himself in the best possible light before the court, and see what resulted."

Kevin was a liar as well as a murderer, Zanides said. Kelly had so found, and he had been right.

SECTION XI

ROLLERCOASTER

SIXTY-FOUR

Washing His Hands

On August 11, 1997, Judge Charles Legge issued his decision in *In re Requested Extradition of Artt.*

The matter of Kevin's confession vexed Legge hardly at all.

Kevin had had an "exhaustive" suppression hearing during the Black trial, Legge wrote. During it, he and eleven RUC detectives had taken the stand and testified about what had happened to him inside Castlereagh. Kevin's statements were clearly his own, said Legge, and they had "obviously not" been fed to him by police. Indeed, wrote Legge, Kevin had admitted he invented some of his statements in order to placate detectives.

In 1997, Legge's logic embedded a catch-22 to match Basil Kelly's in 1983.

In Castlereagh, Legge wrote, Kevin had told the truth about murdering Albert Miles, but lied about other things. The lies he told about the other things did not undermine his credibility as a truth-teller about the Miles murder. In San Francisco, Kevin had lied under oath about having told the truth about the Miles murder, making his confession in Castlereagh true and his recantation a lie.

Legge paused to consider the matter of Kevin's innocence.

In a lengthy decision which discussed history, precedent, and the cases' long backgrounds, Legge devoted four lines to the topic.

"In this proceeding," he wrote, "Artt introduced evidence to attempt to establish his innocence of the crime of which he was convicted. Artt presented certain evidence which might indicate his innocence, or which at least questions his guilt. But under the Supplementary Treaty, it is not the function of this court to simply retry Artt, either with the old evidence or with new. Rather, the issue is whether he was convicted because of the protected factors.

The rest of it was a series of perfunctory dismissals of every argument Brosnahan had made.

Yes, the Black trial had been a mass trial in which the evidence about Kevin had occupied only a week. But it had been "commensurate with basic standards of fairness in criminal cases." Yes, the Northern Ireland Court of Appeal had overturned twenty-two convictions of Kevin's co-defendants. But evidence of Kevin's appeal was "not clear," and even if he had appealed, he had himself to blame for escaping and not staying in Northern Ireland to see his appeal through to conclusion. If Basil Kelly was a member of the Orange Order, there had been no direct evidence of it presented.

Besides, Legge wrote, it seemed like Kevin was an unsavory character in the first place. Twice he had been charged with abusive conduct toward police.

The judge had washed his hands, realizing Kevin's worst fears. Legge did not see it as his place to question the Diplock court system or to find fault with the work of a British colleague it employed. If an innocent man had to go back to Northern Ireland, possibly to be killed, definitely to be imprisoned, so be it. The infirmities of British emergency laws and courts were not Legge's problem.

SIXTY-FIVE

A Good Friday

Later that day, Kevin surrendered to the marshals at 450 Golden Gate Avenue. By 4:00 p.m., he was behind bars at Pleasanton, twenty miles southeast of Oakland, in a red jumpsuit.

Even so, he was dejected, crushed. This one felt worse than 1983. He deserved to win. He was innocent. He had Jim Brosnahan, the best trial lawyer in the world. The American courts would give him a fair shot, or so he had thought. But now he faced another long stretch in a cell and, unless the Ninth Circuit took his side, an airplane ride back to Belfast with the smug Paul Hamlin and his perfectly coiffed hair.

Barring some kind of *deus ex machina*, as of October 1997, it looked like Kevin Barry Artt could expect to sit in jail for two years or more while his appeal unfolded in the Ninth Circuit and, failing that, the U.S. Supreme Court.

The *deus ex machina*, or what might be one, appeared on April 10, 1998, the Friday before Easter, with the announcement of the Good Friday Agreement in Belfast.

The IRA and all other paramilitary groups would disarm and decommission all weapons. The hated emergency laws would be repealed, troops withdrawn to levels "compatible with a normal peaceful society," and security installations (such as fortified barracks and watch towers) removed from the landscape. The RUC would be re-constituted and re-named the Police Service of Northern Ireland and be subject to an independent commission. The six counties would stay part of the United Kingdom until majorities in both north and south elected otherwise. There were guarantees of "rigorous impartiality" in law enforcement, equality in civil rights, freedom from discrimination, and just and equal treatment for minority as well as majority in the north. Direct rule from London would give way to a power-sharing executive and a local assembly.

The GFA had the approval of the governments of Great Britain and the Republic of Ireland, as well as all major political parties in the north, including Sinn Féin. Voters would decide to enact it into law, or not, in island-wide elections held on May 22, 1998—the first all-island vote in eighty years.

On election day, ninety-five percent of those polled in the south approved. Seventy-one percent in the north did.

After thirty years, an end to the Troubles seemed at hand.

So long as their paramilitary groups maintained ceasefires, prisoners convicted of scheduled offenses would be released no later than July 28, 2000, so long as they did not support any proscribed organization, were convicted before April 10, 1998, had been sentenced to serve more than five years in custody, and were not a danger to the public. There were four hundred twenty such prisoners in the six counties. Two hundred of them were expected to be out by Christmas.

But what about men like Kevin Barry Artt, who were fugitives on the run from British authorities? Did the Good Friday Agreement cover them or mandate their release?

The GFA didn't say.

SIXTY-SIX

Celtic Amistad

The U.S. Court of Appeals for the Ninth Circuit was a sprawling judicial district spanning nine western states. In August 1998, it was the largest federal appeals court in the nation. On October 9, 1998, two of its judges, Dorothy Nelson and Betty Fletcher, reversed Legge, held that Kevin could not be extradited, and remanded the case for a new trial.

It was, at long last, a win for Kevin Barry Artt in a courtroom.

Nelson took pains to compliment Legge on his thoughtful and thorough disposition of the issues. He had correctly held that Kevin had failed to prove prospective persecution on account of his religion or political beliefs, wrote Nelson.

Where Legge had erred, she said, was in construing the "Aquino clause" of the extradition treaty. It forbade extradition if the respondent proved the U.K. extradition request was made "with a view to try or punish him on account of his race, religion, nationality, or political opinions[.]" Legge had limited his inquiry to evidence of prejudice in the men's individual cases but refused to let them prove broader systemic bias in the Diplock system. This had deprived Kevin of a fair hearing, Nelson reasoned.

"We believe that the district judge defined the scope of inquiry too narrowly. The existence of bias is not always readily apparent from an individualized inquiry, particularly where, as in Northern Ireland, procedural safeguards have been eliminated. After all, a trial judge or detective is unlikely to memorialize the fact that his or her decisions were motivated by political or religious bias.

"As a result, a defendant, lacking the panoply of procedural protections typically accorded the accused in the Anglo-American system, is left vulnerable to the silent prejudices of judicial and law enforcement officers. Absent an opportunity to present more generalized evidence of bias, the defendant shoulders the impossible burden of identifying clear signs of individualized prejudice within the opaque procedures employed by the Northern Ireland justice system."

Across the Atlantic, the BBC broadcast news of the ruling, displaying photographs of Kevin, including his mugshot taken by the RUC early on that chilly December morning in 1981. The story quoted Brosnahan, who called on Mo Mowlam, Britain's secretary of state for Northern Ireland, to drop the case in the spirit of the Good Friday Agreement.

"It's a big victory," said Brosnahan. "It's like a Celtic *Amistad* for us. It is justice long postponed."

In Northern Ireland, the Rev. Ian Paisley, equal parts Unionist demagogue, religious minister, and carny barker, was beside himself.

"This is absolutely horrendous," Paisley told the BBC. "What happened to American cooperation? It really is a disgrace.

"The American authorities are in breach of the spirit of the Good Friday Agreement themselves by not following through on extradition proceedings."

Other Unionist officials agreed. One, Ken Maginnis, was indignant at the very idea of an American court questioning Diplock justice.

"It is unhelpful when an American court calls into question the integrity of a justice system which has served the people of Northern Ireland well during thirty difficult years," Maginnis said.

Which people of Northern Ireland Maginnis was referring to, he did not say.

Throughout 1999 and the first half of 2000, the case hung in limbo. Voters across the Atlantic had approved the Good Friday Agreement by wide margins, but the document's provisions had not yet been codified into law. Likely cognizant of the fact, the Ninth Circuit seemed to be taking its sweet time.

Kevin applied and re-applied for permission to leave the Bay Area to visit Incline Village for three weeks. But, after Criscitelli told the INS to revoke his work permit, he was flat broke. As the months passed, he found himself at loose ends, restless. Over his head, there was a sword of Damocles hanging by a thread. Each morning he awoke to the possibility that the Ninth Circuit or the INS might suddenly do something that turned his world back upside down in a twinkling. Desperate for cash, he started doing car repairs on the street in front of the apartment at Joost Avenue, just to make the $900 rent each month. He did body work, mechanical repairs, oil changes.

In August 1999, the Ninth Circuit seemed mute, paralyzed. It had been over seven years since the morning FBI agents arrested Kevin in San Diego. The Ninth Circuit had given, then taken away. Now no one was willing to hazard a prediction of what it would do. What in the world was taking so long?

Brosnahan's team was preparing for the worst in case the Ninth Circuit delivered bad news. An internal memo to Brosnahan's team circulated on August 3, 2000, listing what had to be done if the Ninth Circuit affirmed Legge and ordered Kevin extradited after all. Included was a petition for certiorari in the U.S. Supreme Court.

The bolt of lightning which came out of a clear blue sky in October 2000 made all it unnecessary.

SIXTY-SEVEN

Her Britannic Majesty's Embassy

By August 1, 2000, in accord with the GFA, the British had released every prisoner convicted of a terrorist offense. Jimmy Smyth and Joe Doherty, both extraditees returned to the Maze by American courts, had been among the first prisoners released. So had men convicted of murdering police and others after serving only a fraction of the time Kevin Artt had. The last one had walked out of the Maze on July 28, 2000. The Crumlin Road Jail was obsolete. The Maze, once the crown jewel of the British prison system, was empty, derelict, a candidate for redevelopment as an auto race track, museum, or industrial park.

The order that came from the Ninth Circuit on October 13, 2000, was short and pointed:

> The Government is hereby ordered to show cause within 42 days from the date of this order, why proceedings in this court and in the district court should not be dismissed as moot. See, The New York Times International, Saturday, September 30, 2000; A6, which reports that Northern Ireland Secretary Peter Mandelson said fugitives from British jails will be freed; and also see, the Statement [dated 29th September 20000] by Secretary of State, Peter Mandelson MP on

Extradition of Convicted Fugitives, released by the Northern Ireland Information Service [a copy of which is attached hereto].

SO ORDERED.

Six days later, an unnamed British official transmitted a diplomatic note to the U.S. Department of State. At its bottom, no name or signature block appeared, only the great seal of the United Kingdom, around which appeared the words BRITISH EMBASSY WASHINGTON. It read:

> Her Britannic Majesty's Embassy present their compliments to the Department of State and have the honour to inform them that the British Government will no longer pursue the extradition of those individuals who have been convicted of offences committed prior to the Good Friday Agreement but who, as a result of the accelerated release scheme under the Agreement, would have little if any of their original sentence to serve if they were returned to Northern Ireland. The case of Kevin Barry John Artt falls into this category. The British Government hereby formally withdraws the extradition request in respect of [him] . . . as the Secretary of State for Northern Ireland informed the Attorney General in a letter on 29 September 2000.

After over eight years of bruising litigation against Kevin Barry Artt in the federal courts, the case was ending with a whimper. The British were *giving up*.

SIXTY-EIGHT

Hung Like A Horse

In December 2000, the end of the case of *In Re the Requested Extradition of Artt* coincided with two other humbling events in the life of Mark Zanides. He found himself out of his office at 450 Golden Gate Avenue and across the Bay, working in the U.S. Attorney's office there. The move followed unfavorable media coverage about a drug case in which Zanides unwittingly exposed a cocaine trafficking network run by cash-strapped Nicaraguan rebels backed by the CIA. Whether Zanides fairly deserved any blame in the scandal or not, he wound up across the Bay when it was over.

Too, there had been a personal humiliation.

In December 2000, Zanides had attended a crowded, boozy lawyers' Christmas party in San Francisco. Zanides and his girlfriend, a deputy district attorney, quarreled. Then the woman, who had driven Zanides to the party, had wound up going home with Patrick Hallinan, a criminal defense lawyer, leaving Zanides stranded. Joseph Morehead, a friend of Zanides, gave the distraught prosecutor a lift home.

Morehead lent a sympathetic ear while Zanides bemoaned his girlfriend's public desertion of him. Zanides wondered aloud why she would do it.

"Maybe because Patrick Hallinan is hung like a fucking horse," Morehead replied.

As if all of that were not bad enough, during the week after Christmas, Kevin Barry Artt appeared at 450 Golden Gate Avenue in downtown San Francisco, to have his electronic ankle bracelet removed by the Marshals Service on the 20th floor.

Kevin felt in a good mood. The case was over at last. Criscitelli, Zanides, and the British were out of his life. His last physical connection to all of them was about to be severed.

Kevin boarded the elevator in the lobby. Just before the doors slid closed, another passenger boarded—Mark Zanides, on his way to his own office on the 18th floor.

Zanides greeted Kevin with a silent scowl.

It was the first and only time the two men had been alone together.

As the car ascended, Kevin broke the awkward silence.

"I was sorry to hear about your demotion, Mark," he said.

"It *wasn't* a demotion," Zanides snapped. "What happened was –"

The elevator doors opened. The car had stopped at the 18th floor, Zanides' stop. Zanides got off.

"Oh, and I was sorry about the Patrick Hallinan thing," Kevin said. "I heard he's hung like a fucking horse."

Zanides turned, with a look of shock on his face. Before he could muster a response, the doors closed. Up went the elevator, to the 20th floor.

There Kevin reported to the Marshals and got his ankle bracelet removed at last.

SECTION XII

PUTTING GHOSTS TO REST

SIXTY-NINE

In the Royal Courts of Justice

In 2017, Kevin Barry Artt remained a peaceful, law-abiding San Francisco resident—not quite Ward Cleaver of "Leave It to Beaver," but little different than countless American dads. He drove the kids to and from school and basketball practice, admonished them to do their homework. He shared household chores with Fiona, his wife. He went about the never-ending and exhausting business of supervising his construction crews who worked throughout the Bay Area, dashing from job site to job site in a pickup truck.

In Northern Ireland, Kevin had filed an appeal in 1983, just after arriving at the Maze, with the help of Ted Jones. But it had become ornamental seven weeks later, on the day Kevin and thirty-seven other desperate men came tumbling out of the Happy Wagon just inside the front gate of the Maze. After that, pursuing his appeal from safe houses in Ireland, Sweden, and California had been out of the question. What better way would there have been to alert the British to his whereabouts abroad?

And so, the appeal of Kevin Barry Artt had lain on the books of the Northern Ireland Court of Appeal for 34 years, from 1983 to 2017. It was lost in the stacks, inert, buried in a file cabinet. If a Crown solicitor or court clerk had thought about getting it off the books, he had shrugged and forgotten about it.

In 1995, during Kevin's marathon extradition case, Brosnahan had inquired privately about resurrecting Kevin's Irish appeal. If an Irish court threw out Kevin's conviction, wouldn't it obviate the whole extradition? Bros had asked for the opinion of a learned Irish lawyer, Barra McGrory, on the subject. McGrory had thrown cold water on the idea immediately. Irish law didn't allow fugitives to litigate appeals *in absentia*, he told Brosnahan. An effort to rejuvenate Kevin's appeal would not only fail; it would be laughed out of court.

But that had been then. This was 2017. Kevin Barry Artt still had a murder conviction hanging over his head and was at risk of deportation by the Department of Homeland Security. That had been one thing when he had been a poor bachelor during the 1990s. But now he had an American wife, their two young children, the life they had built together in San Francisco, and a thriving construction business.

Kevin called up Peter Madden, his solicitor in Belfast.

"I want to get my appeal going again," he told him. "Can I do that?"

In a stroke of fortuitous timing, by 2017, Irish law had changed, as law sometimes does. A new court decision had come down in the case of a fugitive, Martin McCauley, who had litigated his own appeal *in absentia* from the Republic of Ireland. The Northern Ireland Court of Appeal had allowed it and quashed McCauley's conviction for possession of firearms.

The answer, Madden said, was yes.

This happy bit of news prompted a second question.

"If I hire you to do my appeal, can you be paid at public expense?"

"We'd have to ask the court's permission," Madden replied. "But I think we would get it."

Madden asked one of his partners, Fearghal Shiels, to re-start the appeal of Kevin Barry Artt.

Shiels was a strapping lawyer in his mid-forties. He had craggily handsome features, a small paunch on a big frame, an easy smile, a nice head of salt-and-pepper hair. He was proud to work at the law firm that still bore the name of the late Catholic solicitor Pat Finucane, whom Loyalist thugs had murdered in front of his family in 1989. For the next three years, Shiels would play the role of dogged and tireless advocate on Kevin's behalf.

Shiels assembled a small team to help dig into the case. He recruited Aodhan McCavana and Eamonn Rea, two bright young law students, to work on it full-time. He enlisted two distinguished barristers, Fiona Doherty and Andrew Moriarty, to do the work in court.

For Fearghal's team, there would be plenty of work to go around both inside and out of court.

Kevin had had two long trials, one on each side of the Atlantic. The volume of paper exceeded 135 banker's boxes, generated in the 1980s and 1990s, when imaging technologies were not what they are today. Now all of it had to be pulled out of storage, assembled, read, understood, mined for what was useful. Shiels, Doherty, Moriarty, and their team started retrieving and organizing the reams of paper that lay in file drawers, on courthouse shelves, in boxes tucked away in warehouses, and in computers in San Diego, San Francisco, and Belfast.

On April 1, 2019, three Justices of the Court of Appeal would take the bench in Belfast, to discuss preliminaries with Doherty and her opponent, Crown counsel Gerald Simpson, QC, a courtly and genteel prosecutor. Simpson and the solicitor he instructed, David McClean, would be the ones to tell the court that Basil Kelly had been right all along and that Kevin Barry Artt's conviction should stand. It would be the first court hearing in the case of *R v. Artt* in Belfast since the Black trial.

Early that morning, I awoke in my hotel, had a quick workout in the big staircase down the hall from my room, and fixed breakfast in the kitchenette. Then I walked the few blocks' distance to the Royal Courts of Justice building on Victoria Street.

It was a big, square, four-story building, clad in a Portland stone façade and fronted by Corinthian columns. British architects had designed it in the Classical style. Workers had erected the courthouse shortly after the partition of Ireland. It had opened in 1933 as a shining example of the Orange State's grand new public buildings. Outside the entrance, barristers in robes converged on the reception area, toting their wigs and briefcases, hurrying along as lawyers do, to their hearings and appointments and trials.

It was just after 9:30 a.m. when I cleared security and entered the marbled central hall. It was as grand as the building's exterior, forty-five yards long, with a coffered ceiling that rose thirty feet above the floor. Listed in the glass-enclosed display case at eye level was the day's schedule of hearings.

The courtroom was what an American visitor might expect. Handsome dark wood wainscoting climbed fifteen feet high on the walls. In the center of the ceiling, diffused natural light glowed through a skylight. High above the bench was the Great Seal of the Realm, in high relief, edged in gold trim: three passant guardant lions, a harp (representing Ireland), a medley of other lions, and a unicorn above a thistle, rose, and shamrock. The words adorning the banner read: Dieu et mon Droit. *God and my Right*, the same words that had proclaimed Basil Kelly's power over the men and women in Courtroom No. 1 in 1983.

I took a seat in the gallery.

A clerk wheeled a dolly loaded with three-ring notebooks onto the narrow bench.

A few minutes later, his voice rang out over the black speakers mounted alongside the bench.

All stand, please.

Out came three Justices of the Court of Appeal—Lord Chief Justice Declan Morgan, Lord Justice Seamus Treacy, and Justice Mark Horner. In their scarlet robes and white wigs, they looked almost regal.

Morgan got down to business, turning to Simpson. Where, asked Morgan, did the Crown stand on the merits of the appeal?

I was eager to hear what came next. Would Simpson be strident? Self-righteous? Pleasantly confident?

Simpson seemed a little sheepish.

"We're still not sure where the full documentation is, my lord," he said. "What we need to do is find out if we're ever going to find the original signed statements of the detectives. An outstanding response is awaited from the Home Office. We must liaise with these third parties, as it is understood the appellant wishes to perform ESDA testing on the original notes."

ESDA, an acronym for electrostatic data apparatus, was a forensic tool for examining questioned documents. ESDA testing had first come into widespread practice during the mid-1990s, long after the Christopher Black trial had ended, and the Queen had knighted Basil Kelly.

When a detective writes notes on a pad using a pen or pencil, he leaves indented impressions on the pages underneath. Later, if there are questions about whether he destroyed or fiddled with notes presented as authentic originals, an examiner can resolve them. First, he lays the underlying pages on a metal plate, face up, and places a sheet of thin plastic film on top. Then he applies an electrical charge via a rod, by passing the rod over across the surface of the plastic sheet. Afterward, he dusts the plastic sheet with toner. The toner settles on the plastic, migrating to areas where the paper has impressions, drawn to the higher electrostatic charge they emit.

The resulting image reveals to the eye the impressions which otherwise would have been invisible. If the overlying sheet, or what is said to be the overlying sheet, is available, the image of the underlying page's impressions can be superimposed on top of it. Then one can see if there is a close match or variances. A close match proves the authenticity of the original. Variances prove the overlying page presented as the original to be a fake, switched in later after the original has been destroyed.

Every detective who had testified against Kevin at the Black trial had looked at his notes about what had happened inside Castlereagh before entering the witness box. Each had sworn he'd made the notes contemporaneously, without tampering with them later. In 2019, ESDA would enable examiners to see if this was actually true. Any tampering would have left an indelible forensic trail which, in 1981, detectives would never have known they were creating. The trail might show something exculpatory that the tamperer deemed inconvenient to the prosecution. Moreover, it would make liars out of the detectives—the sole witnesses who had testified against Kevin.

With that, the hearing was over. Kevin's appeal was going forward.

The next day, the headline in *The Irish News* read:
MAZE ESCAPEE KEVIN BARRY ARTT (59) SECURES RIGHT TO RENEWED LEGAL BID TO OVERTURN IRA MURDER CONVICTION

"A convicted murderer who fled to the United States after taking part in the mass IRA Maze prison escape 36 years ago has secured the right to mount a renewed legal bid to clear his name," read the opening paragraph.

Six days later, an email landed in my inbox. It would turn the British crown's case against Kevin Barry Artt upside down.

SEVENTY

I Would Like to Know the Full Facts of My Father's Murder

It was an email from Alan Miles, written in his quirky style, which resembled E.E. Cummings':

A few thoughts/questions
I most certainly cannot confirm one way or other
if kevin artt is guilty or not of my fathers murder
If not guilty I hope it is proven and the guilty
person known
If he didn't do it concerted campaign to put him
in the frame
Intelligence immediately after
Mckeirnan naming him
So if innocent he was set up from inside pira
Why? . . . .
I still would like to meet kevin artt
I am in new York in september

I opened the attachment.

It was an undated, confidential police report, forty-six pages long. It was entitled "Historical Enquiries Team Review Summary Report, Concerning the murder of Albert Miles."

An email accompanied it. It was dated April 5, 2012. The author was someone named Mike McErlane, senior investigating officer of the Historical Enquiries Team in Lisburn. It was addressed to Alan Miles. McErlane's email said this:

> *Alan please find the report into your fathers murder attached.*
>
> *I know you will find this very difficult.*

I opened the report and started flipping pages.

The Historical Enquiries Team (HET), it said, had a structure with separate investigative units, some of whom had no prior connection to the former RUC. Its mission was to help bring "a measure of resolution" to families of victims whose murders were attributable to the Troubles. It would carry out this mission by "thorough and exhaustive examination" of such murders when asked by bereaved families.

Alan Miles had asked, on February 7, 2012, writing, "I would like to know the full facts of my father's murder."

Two months later, the government had answered, with this report.

It was the first new piece of information about the Miles murder anyone had seen in nearly thirty years.

Much of the report regurgitated old, familiar data. That night in 1978, Alan had spied a man "just inside the front door with a dark gun in his right hand which he was holding at arm's length and pointing" in Albert's direction. Four shots had struck Albert. The last one, a .45 caliber bullet, had killed him. A neighbor had seen a blue sedan speeding away after hearing shots fired. And so forth.

What caught my eye was this passage:

> On January 5, 1979, an explosion occurred in Northwick Drive Belfast, killing two Provisional IRA men, Lawrence Montgomery and Francis Donnelly. They died when an improvised explosive device (IED) they had been moving to a car, exploded prematurely. The security forces responded to the scene and recovered other

bomb-making equipment and five handguns in a follow-up search of a house near the explosion. Neither of these men had been named in the previous intelligence about Bert's murder.

One of the guns found was a .45 calibre Colt automatic pistol, serial number 816045. It was identified as one of the weapons used in Bert's murder. *Another gun found in this house was a Colt .38 revolver. It is very likely that this was the second weapon used, but the bullet heads recovered after Bert's murder, were too badly damaged for comparison purposes.*

Could this be the .38 that Kevin had described to detectives in Castlereagh? Did it have a "barrel that spun," a "silver-coloured" finish?

The report didn't say.

After thirty years in law practice, I'd read too many stories of suppression of exculpatory material by prosecutors and police in the U.S. courts. What had happened seemed obvious: the RUC, or Ronnie Appleton, or both of them, had suppressed the gun and never told Kevin's defense team it existed, neatly disposing of any conflict between the gun's appearance and Kevin's made-up description of it.

The .38 found at Northwick Drive had to be dark in color.

Alan Miles had seen it for himself that night at Evelyn Gardens and said so to the RUC.

Had it been "silver-coloured," I thought, Ronnie Appleton would have brought it to Kelly's courtroom in 1983, held it up high for all to see, brandished it in front of Basil Kelly and the defense lawyers, and told all there assembled it matched Kevin Barry Artt's own description of the gun he had used to shoot Albert Miles, further proving his guilt.

I emailed the HET report to Kevin, triggering a torrent of text messages:

Have to take kids to b ball so I have only scanned doc They are certainly not trying to clear my name quite contrary however their complete lack of forensic evidence that was certainly available to them I wonder is there some exculpatory evidence they are not saying? . . .

Jeez Dan they had hair guns rounds a witness who seen the killers ammo and finger prints how come we didn't know any of this for the trial or the extradition? . . .

Had we this knowledge back in the day even Kelly would have had a tough time convicting me

It is malicious to bury someone in a prison for the rest of their life for a crime they did not commit I got lucky and got away but thats not the point

Kevin forwarded the report to Fiona Doherty and Fearghal Shiels in Belfast.

And so it came to pass that Albert Miles' son, who had seen his father shot down in cold blood by IRA assassins, handed a document to the lawyers for the man convicted of doing it that would help undo his conviction.

SEVENTY-ONE

I Am Fighting to Get My Life Back

I felt I knew in my bones what was going to happen.

When asked, the Crown's lawyers, Simpson and McClean, would say they had contacted the PSNI and Home Office but no one had gotten back to them. As time passed, the appeal hearing would draw nearer. When it came at last, the Crown would not have produced anything out of the HET's files, wherever they were. The Crown would run out the clock. In the end it would tell the court, "Nothing new to see here."

The Justices would affirm Kevin's murder conviction. Then they would exit the bench at a stately walk, return to their chambers, and wonder in disgust why Kevin's lawyers had wasted their precious time. Everyone who had always believed Kevin Barry Artt guilty would say, *See. I told ye he done the business.* And Kevin Barry Artt would remain under the sword of Damocles until the day federal agents arrived at his house to take him to the airport for the flight to George Best Airport in Belfast.

By the end of the month of May 2019, the Crown had produced nothing.

It seemed to me it would be simple enough for David McClean or Gerry Simpson to schedule an appointment at PSNI headquarters, ask to see the files on the Miles murder, and read them. They hadn't bothered, or, if they had, the PSNI had winked and then ignored them.

Precious time is slippin' away, goes the lyric of the Van Morrison song. So it seemed to me in the late spring of 2019.

So it seemed to Kevin too. He feared the worst: the Crown was sitting on exculpatory evidence, just as they had in 1982 and 1983, to doom his appeal.

He wrote this email to Fearghal Shiels' paralegal:

I am fighting to get my life back . . . this appeal is winnable and we are going to have the appellate court reverse this conviction. I do not trust the crown or its agents, they will do nothing for us without being forced through the courts [sic] direction, no matter how nice they are to your face. I experienced their hatred on both sides of the Atlantic a decade apart, the passage of time will not change that fact, period.

I want the court to direct the crown to produce the documents we request, otherwise, and please excuse my vernacular, may as well be pissing in [to] the wind. . .

Please excuse my boarding house manner, or directness, life has left me tainted and I take everything head on . . .

"IRA Maze escapee Kevin Artt will have bid to quash conviction heard next year," said the headline in the *Belfast Telegraph* on December 2, 2019.

The two photos accompanying the story were Kevin's mugshot taken at the Maze in 1983 and an aerial photo of the sprawling pentagonal prison.

"His lawyers have prepared fresh grounds on which they contend the conviction should be quashed," the story read. "In court today it was revealed that contemporaneous notes have now been discovered and disclosed."

As 2020 opened, new evidence kept trickling out of the offices of the Public Prosecution Service.

There were records of the weapons and ammunition seized by the RUC at Northwick Drive in 1979 after the premature explosion that killed Francis Donnelly and Lawrence Montgomery, the two IRA men who had tried but failed to load a bomb safely into their car. A constable had heavily redacted the forms, concealing . . . what?

For the first time, there was this: constables had recovered a *fifth* handgun at Northwick Drive, on the street alongside one of the dead Provos. There was no photograph of it, of course. But an RUC forensics man, John Milburn, had described it on a form: ". . . a Colt 6 shot revolver calibre .38 S & W serial number 325304. The revolver was in good condition and when test fired proved effective." Another police official had written this: ". . . an American made .38 COLT 'Police Positive' serial number 325304."

I guessed it was dark—black or dark blue.

How could it not be?

A quick Google search yielded some data about the Colt Police Positive .38. It came in two finishes—"polished blued" (nearly black), and nickel-plated.

Maybe the gun could be matched to the bullets recovered at Evelyn Gardens. If its color could be determined, it could be both tied to Albert Miles' murder and eliminated as the "silver-coloured" weapon which Kevin Barry Artt imagined for the detectives in 1981.

In February 2020, Kevin, as he often did, had a good idea that hadn't occurred to anyone else.

Why not contact the weapon's manufacturer, the Colt Manufacturing Company, provide the weapon's serial number, and ask what color it was? Maybe Colt would have a record of it.

In early February 2020, Kevin made the call himself. The man who answered put him on hold, pulled up a record, and came back on. He told Kevin what the record showed.

He added that, for $300, Colt would prepare a certified record describing the weapon in detail and mail it to Kevin.

Kevin dashed off an email reporting this startling development to Fearghal Shiels:

> *I can pull a full description of this weapon from the Manufacturer, so far I have been told that it was made in 1929 and was more than likely Blue not nickel . . .*
>
> *Bottom line this evidence was hidden from the defense, then, and we only discovered it by pure chance, is it only I that see's [sic] the significance of this?*

The research of Mark Mastaglio, a gun expert, confirmed what Colt had told Kevin. The Colt .38 Police Positive came in two alternative finishes: "blued," and nickel-plated. The blued models were more common than the nickel-plated. The gun on which Colt had engraved serial number 325304 was a .38 caliber revolver with a four-inch barrel and a dark blue finish. In 1929, Colt had shipped it to the Railway Express Agency in New York City. How the weapon had found its way across the Atlantic and into the hands of an IRA quartermaster was not explained.

Shiels reported this momentous bit of news in a letter to the court on February 13, 2020:

> The manufacturer has provided a description of the weapon as manufactured that is inconsistent with the description given by the Appellant during interview. The Appellant will now make a fresh evidence application which will include Mr. Mastaglio's report . . . in support of his admission that his admissions are not reliable.

Meanwhile, each side's document examiners had their turns with the detectives' original notes. The Crown had managed to locate them at last.

The ESDA work done by the Crown's expert, Brian Craythorne, agreed with that done by Kevin's expert, Stephen Cosslett.

Independently, each man had come to the same conclusion: The detectives had tampered with their own notes of their interrogations of Kevin Barry Artt at Castlereagh.

In the prim, precise lexicon favored by expert witnesses, Craythorne noted the variances between the indentations he found between multiple sets of underlying pages and pages that lay on top of them:

> *It was not possible to find handwritten entries corresponding to these indentations within the interview notes.*
>
> *Very faint illegible indentations of text were found which could not be read and has [sic] no obvious source within the Artt interview notes.*
>
> *Indentations were found . . . no source of which could be found within these interview notes.*
>
> *Faint indentations found upside down with respect to the interview notes which do not appear to be part of these interview notes.*

Here was another way to say it: "The authors of the notes threw away what they wrote originally. Later, they wrote something else to replace what they threw away, then called the something else their original interview notes."

Craythorne didn't name the tamperers. He hardly needed to. He correlated each tampered-with batch of notes to the date, time, and interview number of the interview with which it correlated. The RUC's own records listed each detective who had conducted each session.

Juxtaposing them with Craythorne's report yielded the detectives' names, as well as the content of each interview:

Interview number	Date and time	Detectives	Content
6	Nov. 29, 1:50 to 4:20 p.m.	Caskey, Whitehead	Charles McKiernan confrontation
11	Nov. 30, 7:30 to 9:35 p.m.	McLaughlin, Turner	Kevin signs written confession
14	December 1, 3:35 to 5:40 p.m.	Hill, McLaughlin	Kevin describes .38 caliber as "silver coloured," with a "round barrel"

The three sessions were the pivotal ones out of thirty-two total hours of interrogation spanning five days.

In 1983, from the witness stand, RUC detectives Caskey, Whitehead, McLaughlin, Turner, and Hill had told Basil Kelly that their notes were pristine originals, correctly reflected what had happened in the interview rooms, had been created "at the time," and hadn't been changed after the fact.

At the time, there hadn't been any way for Kevin's trial lawyers, Michael Nicholson and Arthur Harvey, to prove them wrong.

I thought of Alan Dershowitz's warning to young lawyers of what they could expect once they emerged from law school and into the courts. It was the sight of policemen lying through their teeth to convict people they believed to be guilty but whose rights they had violated in order to secure the evidence of their guilt. And it was judges who pretended to believe them in order to avoid freeing someone they also believed to be guilty.

SEVENTY-TWO

These Convictions Are Not Safe

On Thursday, March 5, 2020, at about 9:45 a.m., a little bleary and jet-lagged, I settled into my seat in the gallery of the Court of Appeal in Belfast.

At last, it was happening: an appellate court was hearing the appeal of Kevin Barry Artt, thirty-seven years after Basil Kelly had stonily pronounced him guilty of an IRA murder.

Clerks had loaded the bench with three-ring binders. Hundreds of Post-it notes protruded from the reams of paper stuffed into them. Felt-tip markers of several different colors littered the bench. The Justices had done their homework.

A sense of gravity pervaded the courtroom. At the counsel tables, the barristers took their places and exchanged friendly greetings with one another.

All stand, please.

The Justices strode to their places on the bench. From right to left sat the men who now held Kevin Barry Artt's future in their hands—Bernard McCloskey, Ben Stephens, and Adrian Colton.

Stephens was the Senior Lord Justice of the court. He had a reputation as a wild card, a man with an independent streak and a powerful intellect.

Stephens had been educated in England, at Manchester University. He became a lawyer in Northern Ireland in

1977, then "took silk," attaining the honored status of Queen's Counsel, in 1996. In 2007, he had been knighted, as was customary for jurists obtaining an appointment to the High Court. His thinning gray hair was combed over a shiny dome of a head. When relaxed, he could display a winning smile.

Today he was all business. He spoke with a distinct English accent, not a Belfast dialect.

Fiona Doherty launched into her opening. Short, draped in her black robe, gripping the lectern in front of her, she addressed the court in a strong voice that conveyed command, confidence, mastery of the record of the case. The entire appeal boiled down to one thing, she told the Justices.

"Are these convictions safe? These convictions are not safe."

Doherty added a note of humanity. "We do not forget," she said, "behind this appeal is the terrible murder of Mr. Albert Miles and the bereavement of his family."

The Justices nodded. Each man was taking notes, paying close attention.

In thirty-two years of practicing law, I'd seen every sign on the juristic spectrum of body language—somnolence, boredom, half-listening, annoyance, anger, fatigue, amusement, puzzlement, scorn, eager engagement. These men were eagerly engaged. They were doing aerobic listening.

For most of the next two hours, Doherty addressed the .38 caliber Colt revolver recovered at Northwick Drive on January 5, 1979.

The gun, she said, raised two pivotal issues. The first was its color—polished blue, nearly black, directly undermining the color ascribed to it by Kevin while under interrogation. The second was the Crown's deliberate withholding of it from the defense at trial. Had Basil Kelly only seen it, she argued, and compared it with Alan Miles' description of the weapon as "dark" in color, the inconsistency could have planted a doubt in his mind about the reliability of Kevin's confession. Depriving Kevin of it in 1982 had denied him a fair trial.

Stephens looked at Simpson.

"Why is it that you think the prosecutor didn't disclose the .38 revolver to the defence in 1982?"

Simpson rose from his seat. His response barely rose above a half-hearted mumble. Again, his manner was sheepish. I wondered whether his heart was in it.

"This may not have been disclosed because it couldn't be linked to the Miles shooting," Simpson said.

Stephens looked back at Fiona Doherty.

"Is it your contention the .38 could be linked to the Miles shooting?"

"There are very good circumstantial reasons for this court to conclude it was, my lord," she said.

The .38 had been found with the same .45 conclusively linked to Miles, and less than a mile from Evelyn Gardens, Doherty said. Having test-fired it and compared the samples against the slugs found at Evelyn Gardens, the RUC had shown that it suspected it had been used to shoot Miles. And now, in 2020, because they had destroyed the weapon, there was no way for Kevin's team or anybody else to do any more test-fires.

Stephens challenged Simpson again, asking him whether he could rule it out as being a Miles murder weapon.

"You couldn't exclude it, my lord," Simpson said, meekly.

The Crown's behavior concerning the .38 gave off a malodorous air in other ways.

The RUC had redacted from the records the physical description of the weapon's finish, preventing a reader from knowing whether the detective who filled out the form had written that the gun was nickel-plated ("silver-coloured") or dark blue. It had taken the detective work of Kevin Barry

Artt himself to yield the truth of the matter from the Colt Manufacturing Company in 2020: the weapon had a dark, *polished-blue* finish, a four-inch-long barrel, and a date of manufacture of 1929. In 1982 and 1983, Ronnie Appleton could have made it available to anyone who wanted to look at it, but he hadn't.

"It wasn't a silver colour," said Doherty, firmly. "It was the blued."

From the bench, Bernard McCloskey jumped in, his mobile eyebrows arched above his glasses.

"It all comes down to the color of the weapon, doesn't it?"

"Yes," Doherty answered.

Stephens interrupted.

"Absent any other issue on this appeal, you say that the gun issue should warrant quashing the conviction?"

"Yes," Doherty answered. "This is about the credibility of Mr. Artt versus the credibility of the police officers." Depriving Kevin of the .38 at his trial had prevented him from planting doubt about the credibility of detectives who had gotten him to say he had used a .38 that was "silver-coloured," Doherty said. And that doubt could have been the difference between guilty and not guilty.

SEVENTY-THREE

If the Notes Are Cast Into Doubt

The hearing resumed the next morning, on March 6, 2020. It was ESDA day—an examination of whether Kevin Barry Artt's inquisitors had tampered with the notes they and Basil Kelly had used against him at the Black trial in 1983. McCloskey asked Doherty for a "nutshell" version of the two document examiners' reports. Was it the case, he asked, that the detectives had altered original notes of their interviews of Kevin Barry Artt in 1981?

"Yes," Fiona answered.

What made it worse, she said, was the detectives' testimony that they hadn't done that very thing.

The false testimony was no mere detail. It related to documents which the detectives had used to refresh their recollections in order to testify at the Black trial, months after Kevin had given up the ghost in Castlereagh. Their accounts of having created their original notes contemporaneously and not changed them afterward went straight to the credibility of the key trial witnesses against Kevin: RUC detectives Armour Hill, Norman McLaughlin, and Robert Turner, who had conducted the critical interviews of November 30 and December 1, 1981, and written up Kevin's confession. Kevin's sworn accounts of what had happened during his time with them clashed sharply with theirs. But between

Kevin and the police, only one had any notes to stand on to refresh recollection—the police.

If they'd lied to Basil Kelly about what went on in the interviews, what reason was there to exalt their testimony over Kevin's?

"If the notes are cast into doubt," said Doherty, "then so too should the testimony which is predicated on them."

The text of the alterations wasn't a game-changer. No detective had written, "I know Artt is innocent, but we will break his will," "We know Gilvarry shot Miles," or, "Make sure defence doesn't learn of .38 impounded at Northwick Drive." But it mattered not. The issue was whether the officers had lied at trial when they said they made their notes contemporaneously.

If they had, said Stephens, then the issue was enough to create reasonable doubt and warrant quashing the convictions.

British justices were nodding in agreement with a lawyer for Kevin Barry Artt, who was urging them to throw out a rotten conviction that was 37 years old. To my right, a pair of prosecutors sat meekly, timid and silent, scarcely rising or addressing the court except when asked to do so, and then giving terse, half-hearted answers. The prosecutors didn't look low-energy; they looked down, resigned, half-embarrassed to even be there, *beaten*.

If only Kevin could be here to see it! I thought.

The Justices would convene in one more hearing, on March 30, to hear from Gerry Simpson of the Crown, and then issue a ruling. But soon afterward, the coronavirus epidemic triggered a closure of the Royal Courts of Justice. There would be more delay.

Finally, the Justices issued a terse order. The last hearing would take place via video conference, on May 6, 2020.

SEVENTY-FOUR

Conviction Squashed More to Follow

On the night of May 5 in San Francisco, Kevin told his daughter, Odhran, to go upstairs and sleep with her mother, in Kevin's and Fiona's bed. The strange directive prompted a quizzical look from Odhran. Kevin gave her an excuse and told her he was expecting an early morning call. In truth, he didn't want to disturb Fiona with tossing and turning. Odhran kissed her dad goodnight and went upstairs.

Kevin tucked himself into Odhran's bed downstairs and turned out the light just after 10 p.m. The house was dark and silent. Kevin tried to relax but couldn't.

By 3 a.m., Kevin gave up on trying to sleep. He arose bleary, jittery, full of adrenaline, a bundle of nerves. He brewed some coffee, puttered around the kitchen, fidgeted, checked his phone, tried not to make too much noise. A couple of hours passed. The morning newspaper hit the driveway at about 5:30. Kevin retrieved it and brought it inside. At the kitchen table, he tried to read it, but couldn't keep his mind on it.

In Belfast, just before 2 p.m., Fearghal Shiels sat in his office at Madden & Finucane, staring at the screen of his computer monitor. A gallery of nine faces appeared. There were the three Justices, Stephens, McCloskey, and Colton. Each wore his scarlet robe and white wig. Only Stephens was in the courtroom. There, the gallery was empty, except for a journalist, Alan Erwin. There were the faces of Crown's lawyers, Gerald Simpson, Robin Steer, and Joelle Black. The countenances of Fiona Doherty, Andrew Moriarty, and Shiels filled out the rest of the screen.

Kevin had asked if the court would allow him to tune in from his home computer. The answer was no.

At last, the moment they had all waited for had arrived.

It had been over three years in the making since Kevin had first resurrected his appeal in 2017. The lawyers had briefed, argued, and submitted every point. Every legal stone that could be turned over—the .38 at Northwick Drive, Kevin's psychological state inside Castlereagh, the detectives' notes—had been. The Justices had pored over everything.

Stephens got down to business. In his measured, clipped tone, he started reading. Occasionally, he looked up at the camera.

"On 4 August 1983 Kevin Barry John Artt and Charles McKiernan were convicted in a non-jury trial by Kelly J of the murder at around 8:25 p.m. on Sunday 26 November 1978 of Albert Myles [sic], the Deputy Governor of HM Prison Maze, in the hallway of his home in front of his wife and son," he began.

He went on for thirty minutes.

There was nothing cinematic about it.

There would be no public reading of the court's ruling from the bench below the Great Seal of the Realm in the grand courtroom at the Royal Courts of Justice, no mourning or celebrating together in the grand marble foyer outside the courtroom afterward, no client to console or pound on the back, no throng of family and giddy well-wishers on the steps outside, no gaggle of photographers. There was only a computer monitor, a collection of images of faces, and the disembodied voice of Ben Stephens as he read to the camera.

At home in San Diego, I rose and got downstairs at around 6:45 a.m. In Belfast, it was eight hours later, 2:45 p.m. Since 1992, there had been many days when I'd waited on pins and needles for one court ruling or another—from Judge Legge, from the Ninth Circuit, from the Northern Ireland Court of Appeal. There had been good news, no news, bad news, elation, anti-climax, crushing disappointment, and chronic lengthy delays in between all of them.

On the night Albert Miles bled to death on the floor of his foyer in Belfast, Kevin Barry Artt had been a boy, a nineteen-year-old virgin with movie star good looks. Today he was a balding, graying, sixty-year-old grandfather. What reason was there to suppose this day might end the serpentine saga of his case once and for all?

I fixed breakfast, read the paper, tried to take my mind off it. When I had first heard the name of Kevin Barry Artt, it had been 1992, when I was a lightly-experienced, thirty-year-old lawyer who knew practically nothing about Northern Ireland or the Troubles.

At home in San Francisco, Kevin couldn't contain himself. He dialed Fearghal Shiels' cell phone number at 7 a.m. Shiels didn't pick up. He texted that they were still in court. He promised to call Kevin as soon as they were through.

Kevin's cell phone rang fifteen minutes later, at 7:15 a.m. In Belfast, it was 3:15 p.m.

The steady voice of Fiona Doherty's was the first Kevin heard. She was using a speaker phone. Kevin could hear the other lawyers in the background.

Fiona spoke evenly and firmly.

"There's been a ruling," she said. "The judges have quashed the conviction. It's over."

Kevin felt a rush of adrenaline surge through him like liquefied natural gas. He started crying, the phone pressed to his ear, his shoulders heaving up and down. Fiona and the kids were upstairs. Inside his cells in the Maze and the

Crumlin Road Jail, he had been alone. Hiding from British Army troops during his escape from the Maze, he had been alone. And now he was alone again.

"I learned to bottle up emotion being on the run," Kevin said later. "Having zero contact with loved ones, or anyone from my life . . . I got really good at it." During the late eighties, a girlfriend in San Diego had told him he was *emotionally sterile*.

Inwardly, Kevin felt a tsunami of forgotten, pent-up emotion. Now it all erupted in one beautiful moment.

"Kevin? Are you there?"

Kevin couldn't speak. He couldn't see through the river of tears coursing out of his eyes. He felt like his heart was going to explode with intense gratitude and pure joy.

Kevin thanked his lawyers and hung up. After taking a moment to compose himself he went upstairs. The kids were still asleep. Kevin told Fiona. She was overjoyed. The two shared a long embrace as they cried together.

My cell phone chimed at 7:21 a.m. It was a text from Kevin.

In the five words he had tapped out, he had managed to inject his usual wordplay, slightly mangling the legal jargon:

Conviction squashed more to follow.

I called Kevin right away. He didn't answer. I reckoned he was on the phone with the Irish lawyers or Jim Brosnahan.

Kevin called back twenty minutes later.

"What's going on?" I said.

"It's over, Dan," he said. "They overturned it. Stephens read it out from the bench."

There was a short pause. I took a deep breath. But I couldn't think of anything worthy to say.

"Did you call Brosnahan?" I asked.

"Just got off the line with him," Kevin replied. Then he excused himself, saying he had some more calls to make—to Carmen, Barry Paul, Maeve, Charlie McNutt.

Before we hung up, I tried a small joke.

"Who's gonna call Ronnie Appleton and tell him?"

Kevin laughed. "That prick!" he said.

On a day Lewis Carroll might have called *frabjous*, Kevin Barry Artt sounded numb. His voice was flat, with little inflection. There was no exultation, no jubilation that I could detect.

After thirty-nine years, it was over!

Kevin Barry Artt had beaten the British government twice in two rounds—once in San Francisco in 1996, and now in Belfast in 2020. He had managed the second victory *in absentia*, from five thousand miles away.

When it came to Irishmen resisting the British in the courts, it sure was something that didn't happen every day.

The news caught the attention of Seamus Deane, the venerable Irish historian and writer from Derry. His joy over the result was tempered with sadness. Today, the law had done the right thing. But that was still a relatively new phenomenon in the six counties, he wrote:

> This is surely good news but, along with it, the chilling realisation of what damage the police and politicians have designedly wrought, in the name of law. A parable for Northern Ireland. . . Kevin must be grateful but certainly must also be stunned. He did well to escape, at great cost, the jaws of the monster. The poor son of Albert Miles must remain, it seems, in the inferno.

SEVENTY-FIVE

A Significant Sense of Unease

"Is that Dan?" said Alan Miles. In England, where he was, it was about 6:20 p.m.

"I have some news, Alan," I began. "I wanted you to hear it from me and not from the media."

Alan stopped me.

"I've already heard, Dan," he said. "The court overturned it."

I reckoned someone in the PPS knew someone in the prison service or PSNI who was still in touch with Alan. One of them must have contacted him.

Alan sounded matter of fact, cheerful even.

"I know this decision has got to leave you with some mixed feelings," I said. "There's no closure in it for you. I hope you don't mind me asking how you're feeling right now."

"If Kevin's innocent, he's innocent," Alan replied. "And if he's guilty, he's guilty. There's no court ruling that can change that, one way or the other."

Before we hung up, Alan reminded me he still wanted to meet with Kevin in person.

"Please pass that on to him," he said. "It would be good for us to meet, to get together."

I promised I would.

By now it was 9:30 a.m. in San Diego. The sun was shining, the temperature on its way up to what would be a high of eighty-one degrees that day. Outside, it looked like a summer day.

I wanted to laugh, yell, open a bottle of champagne, jump on the next plane to San Francisco and then the next plane to Belfast, hug Kevin and Fiona and Andrew and Fearghal and Eamonn. But we were all miles apart. The coronavirus pandemic and stay-at-home orders prevented me from even seeing my secretary or any of my colleagues at the law firm where I worked. I was all alone, shut up in my house, banned from going to the office.

There was no one to celebrate with.

The email from Kevin arrived at 10:20 a.m. The subject line said it all: *Yea Yea Yea,* like the chorus to the Beatles song. The email attached a copy of the court's ruling.

At the top of page one appeared the case title, the words which captured what the entire case was all about in the first place. THE QUEEN *v KEVIN BARRY* John Artt. Ben Stephens had written the twenty-six pages of desiccated legal prose which followed.

Stephens recited the preliminaries quickly enough. Albert Miles had been murdered in 1978. The killers were Provisional IRA men. They had hijacked a Ford Cortina. The murderers had used it to drive to Evelyn Gardens. Florence Miles had heard a knock at the door at about 8:20 p.m. She heard a voice outside. It said, "Buller [sic] from across the road." She had cracked the door open. A man pushed his way in and put a gloved hand over her mouth. She heard bangs and saw flashes. "The gunman made off and Mrs. Myles saw her husband lying against the inner door . . ."

Four years later, Ronnie Appleton had stood in front of Basil Kelly and told him McKiernan was the man who had put his hand over Florence Miles' mouth and that Kevin had been "armed with the revolver and fired a number of shots through the door, at least one of which struck Mr Myles . . ." It was a single bullet fired from a .45 caliber pistol, fired through the back as Albert Miles lay prone, which had lacerated his heart, lung, and liver, causing a massive hemorrhage which killed him.

Scene of Crime Officers (SOCOs) had examined the scene, as well as the car, which officers recovered sixteen days later. They collected spent casings, took fingerprints and samples, and analyzed them. None could be traced to Kevin Barry Artt. Suspects were questioned and released. Among them was Kevin, whom the RUC released without charges after six fruitless days and nights of interrogation at Castlereagh.

On January 5, an explosion at Northwick Drive in Ardoyne had killed two IRA men, Lawrence Montgomery and Francis Donnelly, who died trying to transport their own improvised bomb into a car. In a raid which followed, police had found a cache of weapons. Among them were a .45 colt automatic pistol, serial no. 816045, and a Colt .38 revolver, whose color the court did not describe.

Stephens put to rest once and for all whether the .38 had been used to shoot Albert Miles:

> The [HET] Review Summary into the murder concluded that the Colt .38 revolver was the second weapon used in the murder though the bullet heads recovered after the murder were too badly damaged for comparison purposes. We agree with that conclusion given that the .38 was found in the same house as the weapon that was definitely used in the murder; the discovery of both weapons was within some 6 weeks of the murder; and both weapons were recovered some 1 mile from the scene of the murder.

The Crown had had in its hands, but neglected to produce to the defense, a key piece of evidence: the weapon

Kevin Barry Artt had supposedly fired, which happened not to match the description of it listed in his confession.

But that, said the Court, was beside the point. The pivotal issue, wrote Stephens, was the detectives' notes of their sessions with Kevin in November and December 1981. Each detective queried about his notes had said that he created them at the time he interrogated Kevin. Their testimony on this point had been unequivocal.

It had also been a pack of lies.

The lies had gone undetected at the trial. At the time, there had been no ESDA testing to expose them. Now both sides' experts agreed on what ESDA showed. The men of Castlereagh had tampered with their own notes.

The lying cops were Caskey, Whitehead, McLaughlin, and Turner. It was they who had taken notes of the most critical interviews with Kevin: on November 29 (when they had brought in McKiernan), November 30 (when Kevin finally broke and confessed), and December 1 (when Kevin described the .38 as "silver coloured"). The detectives had removed original notes they had made, destroyed them, and substituted other pages in their stead. Later, they had lied about it right in front of Basil Kelly, Ronnie Appleton, Kevin Barry Artt, and everybody else in the Christopher Black trial.

The ESDA issue was low-hanging fruit. The detectives had lied at the Black trial. Their testimony about what happened in the interview rooms, and the confession they had inveigled out of Kevin, was the only evidence of his guilt. It wasn't enough, Stephens wrote:

> In the absence of satisfactory explanations for the rewriting of interview notes we have a significant sense of unease as to whether the judge's conclusion would have been the same if the issue had been explored before him and therefore as to whether he would have admitted the statements in evidence. Those statements

were the only evidence against the appellant. It follows that we consider that the fresh evidence might have led to a different result in the case and we cannot regard the convictions as safe. We . . . quash the convictions.

SEVENTY-SIX

We Don't Know Who Yer Da Is

In the final scene of the movie "In The Name of the Father," the judge throws out the wrongful convictions of the Guildford Four—Gerry Conlon, Paul Hill, Paddy Armstrong, and Carole Richardson. As music swells, the four triumphantly exit the courthouse into the street. There, a joyous throng of family and supporters surround them as stone-faced bobbies stare sullenly from beneath the brims of their helmets. Photos of the moment suggest Hollywood's portrayal was not far from the truth.

In 2020, in California, there was no such moment for Kevin Barry Artt. He had won at last, beating Goliath again, once and for all. His victory was no less complete and astonishing than Gerry Conlon's had been thirty-one years earlier. But no journalist cared to call him up, no photographer wanted to take his picture, no motorcycle idled just off camera to whisk him away from the courthouse to a party where family and friends would kiss him and embrace him and toast him and pound him on the back.

It was over. Kevin's victory was total. His life would be different now. But the kids had homework to do. There was concrete to be poured in the morning.

The next day, the PSNI came calling at the homes of Carmen Artt and Barry Paul Artt in Belfast.

At around twelve-noon, a motorcade of twelve PSNI vehicles crowded into the narrow street in front of Carmen's tiny house, Marsden Terrace in north Belfast. Among them was an armored personnel carrier. Scowling constables alighted from the cars. Two of them approached the front door and appeared to make ready to kick it in. A startled neighbor who happened to be outside rushed to one of Carmen's windows. She knew Carmen was hard of hearing and might be inside, oblivious.

"Carmen, the police are here!" she shouted. "They're gonna kick the door in! Come on down and open up!"

Carmen rushed to the front door, peered through the peephole, cursed softly, and opened up.

The officers came piling in.

What are yese doing? she cried.

There was a search warrant, something about a pair of stun guns thought to have been purchased by someone associated with this address.

Search it, she said. *Ye'll find nothing.*

After forty-five minutes or so, the team of constables departed. They had confiscated one piece of contraband: a can of pepper spray, which Carmen kept in her purse for self-defense.

Their next stop was Barry Paul's house. The constables ransacked it. They came up with two stun guns. Barry Paul had ordered them on eBay and listed the delivery address as his mother's. Constables told him to put his hands behind his head and arrested him.

"What a coincidence," said the prisoner. "Yesterday, me da gets his conviction overturned. Today, here ye are."

We don't know who yer da is, sneered one of the constables.

Then they bundled him into the back seat of a PSNI sedan and drove him to the station for booking.

Kevin Barry Artt had beaten the British, twice, and embarrassed them in the process—and from five thousand miles away each time. Diplock, Kelly, and others were in their graves. But in 2020, with the Troubles long over, the British Army gone, and the surviving men of the IRA dead or in their un-pensioned dotage, some things were still the same.

SEVENTY-SEVEN

Cowards and Secrets

In 2019, men and women in the six counties continued to age out, sink into depression and addiction and dementia, and die without learning why their husbands, wives, brothers, sisters, children, and other loved ones were killed or imprisoned. The innocent dead are insensate, buried, gone. Their survivors wonder who killed their loved ones and who ought to pay. The men of the British government, RUC, IRA, and Loyalist paramilitary gangs say nothing. "Nobody learns the truth about their dirty war," Peter Heathwood told me in 2019.

Nobody learns the truth about their dirty war.

Proving Kevin Artt's innocence beyond doubt requires proving a negative, a logical impossibility. One cannot prove Kevin Barry Artt did not kill Albert Miles any more than one can prove that fairies do not exist. But one can test whether the proposition is plausible based on known facts.

A bundle of wires wrapped in a spiral combined to produce Kevin's conviction of the Miles murder. Each wire touched all the others, each was inseparable from the others.

The RUC's institutional hatred and suspicion for Kevin Barry Artt, manifested in two attempts on his life which bore hallmarks of RUC complicity.

Official eagerness to close the case of a high-profile murder which had gone unsolved for too long.

A trusted informant, cloaked in immunity for any crimes, who was known to be a murderer, a liar, and a betrayer of friends and colleagues.

Another informant, desperate to obtain immunity for his own crimes and facing an inevitable life prison term, who agreed to name whomever the police said he should name.

A young father and husband, who grew up without his biological parents, confronted by the second informant, susceptible to threats of destruction of his family by screaming men who held the power to carry out the threats.

A style of policing which decoupled the work of detectives in Castlereagh from the investigations of their colleagues in the field and emphasized confessions over the solving of crimes.

A court system designed to destroy the enemy with rules of procedure and evidence which removed the buffer of the jury from the process, encouraged and exalted confessions, trivialized the absence of other evidence in the face of those confessions, and lengthened the accused's odds of acquittal.

A bigoted trial judge who spent his career prosecuting Catholic defendants and sending them to prison.

A trial so unfair that not even Kelly's colleagues at the Court of Appeal could overlook its flaws.

Detectives conditioned to lie in court in order to achieve convictions.

The cowardice of a pitiless paramilitary organization, the IRA, which first boasted of the Miles murder and then stood silent as an innocent man went to prison for it and at least one of its men escaped punishment for it.

The men who murdered Albert Miles were not neophytes or young men auditioning for the IRA. They did not hesitate or flinch. Their actions on that night bespoke cunning, training, experience, and calm.

Of at least five rounds fired by the trailing gunman, who used a .38 caliber revolver, four hit Albert Miles. The round which missed ricocheted off the concrete pillar to the left of the front door. The man who fired it almost certainly aimed high and left in order to avoid hitting the lead man, who was struggling with Florence Miles in the vestibule—something a novice might not have had the presence of mind or skill to manage in a chaotic moment.

The .45 caliber bullet which killed Miles was fired into his back at point blank range as he lay prone on the floor. The man who fired it coolly aimed through an open space in the top half of the vestibule door. His movements were controlled, quick, economical. By the time the neighbors heard the shots and came out to see what was going on, the killers were back in the car and zooming out toward the Cavehill Road.

"Our evidence of the calibre of rank and file terrorists does not support the view that they are merely mindless hooligans drawn from the unemployed and unemployable," British Army general J.M. Glover, an intelligence expert, wrote in a secret report circulated in 1978. "PIRA now trains and uses its members with some care. The Active Service Units (ASUs) are for the most part manned by terrorists tempered by up to ten years of operational experience."

The IRA would never have entrusted an operation like the one at 8 Evelyn Gardens to a man like Kevin Barry Artt. Kevin had never held a firearm, much less aimed and fired one. He had no training, no indoctrination. The idea that the Provisionals would have asked him to assassinate a person like Albert Miles was absurd. They would have used an ASU which had the sort of background and skills that the situation demanded.

Acting on a tip from Maurice Gilvarry, the man who had himself hijacked the car used in the murder minutes before it happened, police swept up a gaggle of suspects in December

1978. The names we know for certain are Tommy Allsop, John Campbell, Frankie Steele, and Eamonn Sweeney. Declining to name himself as the one who had hijacked the car used to ferry the murderers to and from 8 Evelyn Gardens, Gilvarry gave them the name of Kevin Barry Artt instead. It was neat, convenient. Gilvarry disliked Kevin in the first place. Kevin had had the temerity to impregnate the girlfriend of Gilvarry's friend Jonah McClafferty while McClafferty was away doing time in the Maze.

Less than three months later, Gilvarry murdered a prison official and his wife, Patrick and Violet Mackin, after bursting into their home at night, in circumstances closely resembling those of the Miles murder. The Mackins were good friends of the Miles family. When interrogated about it afterward, Gilvarry named others, including at least one innocent, as the murderers. Detectives released him and never charged him. Later, in September 1979, Gilvarry had another stay at Castlereagh, where detectives questioned him about an unknown matter before again releasing him without charge. His reign of utter immunity stayed intact. Gilvarry didn't have a get-out-of-jail-free card. He had a state-issued license to kill.

Maurice Gilvarry had a powerful sponsor who shielded him from trouble and looked the other way when he shot someone dead. The sponsor valued their agent's delivery of intelligence above prosecuting him. Aware of his special status, the agent operated with impunity, even as the RUC investigated the killing of a man he had killed and took care not to charge him with it.

In 1981, detectives were nowhere on the Miles murder case, which was three years old. They had no leads. It was embarrassing. Miles was the most senior prison official killed by the IRA.

That was the setting in which police trapped a golden goose on November 21, 1981: IRA man Christopher Black, who had unwisely set up a roadblock in broad daylight in

Ardoyne. During an all-night, twelve-hour interview in Castlereagh two days later, Black made a deal for the ages: full immunity from prosecution for any and all crimes he had committed, taxpayer-funded support for himself and his wife and four young kids, and guaranteed personal safety under an alias abroad, in exchange for his promise to testify at a future trial against persons the RUC suspected of terrorist activity. Black was turned into a testifying machine, a human poleaxe that could be swung at the IRA in north Belfast, where it was strongest.

When detectives pointed at each hapless occupant of an interview room and asked whether Black recognized him as an accomplice, Black knew what the right answer was, *yes*. Black started naming names. One was Charles McKiernan's. Constables arrested McKiernan and escorted him to Castlereagh on November 24, 1981, the day after Black struck his deal.

McKiernan was in the soup and knew it. Black had implicated him in over thirty crimes, including the brutal murder of part-time UDR man Julian Connolly. Detectives dangled a dazzling deal before McKiernan: immunity, freedom, and a new life abroad on a government subsidy sounded better than life in prison. Before making it official, detectives wanted information, as a sign of McKiernan's reliability and good faith.

Detectives mixed encouragement with threats to arrest his mother and twenty-year-old wife Nancy, the mother of McKiernan's eight-month-old baby son. They gave McKiernan a list of names. McKiernan started nodding his head. Some belonged to men believed to be in the IRA but against whom the police lacked any evidence. Gerard Bradley, John Connolly, and Gerard McKee were among them. So was Kevin Barry Artt.

McKiernan, who still held out hope for his own deal of a lifetime, agreed to sign whatever they wanted. On November 26, he orally named Kevin as his accomplice in the Miles murder. That night, just before or just after midnight, McKiernan affixed his signature to a vaguely worded confession implicating himself and unnamed accomplices in the Miles murder.

The peelers had rousted Kevin from a drunken sleep in his flat in the early morning hours on November 28, drove him to Castlereagh, and started in on him.

During the early afternoon of November 29, detectives presented McKiernan to Kevin in an interview room. Then and there McKiernan said he had confessed to the Miles murder and named Kevin as his confederate. Kevin hotly denied it. After hustling McKiernan out, Kevin's interrogators threatened him with the inevitability of life in prison and destruction of his family unless he cooperated.

Kevin had heard it all before, in 1978. But he had not then been married or father to a toddler. His circumstances had changed.

Exhausted and in despair, Kevin agreed to confess. McKiernan signed a vaguely worded confession the same night. The next day, detectives typed up another vaguely worded confession for Kevin to sign. They neglected to include details which could have been known only to the actual murderers of Albert Miles. They did not bother trying to reconcile discrepancies between McKiernan's confession and Kevin's.

Kevin signed at 9:10 p.m. on the night of November 30, 1981.

Case closed.

Nothing would have prevented a lineup. During it, Florence and Alan Miles could have either pointed out Kevin as a killer or told police they did not recognize him. Kevin immediately agreed to do it when detectives floated the idea to him, saying, "it's no problem." Later, no detective ever offered a reason for skipping the exercise.

But the reason is not hard to imagine. A lineup in which Albert Miles' widow and son shook their heads when asked if anyone in it looked like someone they saw at 8 Evelyn Gardens would have handed Kevin a critical piece of evidence that he could use to defend himself. Not doing a lineup at all eliminated that possibility. So no lineup was done.

Gilvarry became unavailable. The IRA's nutting squad had seen to that, in January 1981, torturing him, shooting him in the back of the head, and dumping his body by the side of a road in south Armagh. McKiernan had to have been acutely aware of that particular execution, as every other IRA man was. A year later, aided by a lawyer known for representing IRA men, Pat Finucane, McKiernan did as he was told. He recanted one statement that implicated IRA men and stood on another which protected them. Saving Gerard Bradley, Sean Connolly, and Gerard McKee, and sacrificing Kevin Barry Artt, accomplished McKiernan's dual purpose: protecting the organization and protecting himself, all at the same time.

What followed at the Belfast Crown Court in 1982 and 1983 was a pageant, like a Soviet show trial during one of Stalin's purges in the 1930s. It played out in a courtroom whose atmosphere was one of thinly concealed official hysteria. The prosecutors' mission was not learning whether the defendants were truly guilty or whether unduly coercive techniques had produced their confessions. It was to get convictions. The police had the murder weapons in their possession. The .38 caliber revolver recovered at Northwick Drive in January 1979 was dark blue, not "silver-coloured." But, at the Black trial, no one got to see for themselves. Ronnie Appleton and the RUC saw to that, by keeping the Colt .38 Police Positive revolver out of the courtroom and neglecting to tell Kelly or the defense lawyers the RUC had it in the first place, taking a nice argument away from the defense.

The trial judge, Basil Kelly, was as ardent an agent of the Orange State as one could imagine: a Unionist, a former attorney general, a member of the Orange Order, who wore his bowler and sash proudly on the high holy days of Protestant triumphalism. He hated the IRA with a passion. He harbored a low opinion of Irish nationalism and those who believed in it. Before the first witness testified, he saw, heard, and felt things that were extraordinary: British Army helicopters hovering over the courthouse, RUC men armed with rifles glaring at the Irishmen in the dock, the weight of a bulletproof vest under his robe. Kelly was human, as liable to be affected by such things as anyone else.

McKiernan sat in the dock for nine months, never offering a word in his own defense, declining to testify or call any witnesses, and never challenging his confession, fortifying in Kelly's mind what seemed an obvious truth: McKiernan had murdered Miles.

Kevin challenged his confession as the product of coercion, the sort which has been proven again and again to result in false confession by innocent persons in police custody. But Kelly disbelieved everything said by Kevin and by his alibi witness, Lorraine Keenan. Keenan had made the mistake of telling the truth when asked what regard she had for the security forces who patrolled her neighborhood. There was no way Kelly would take the word of a young Catholic woman from New Lodge, especially when it provided a defense to murder. He took it as his duty to safeguard the community from a swarm of terrorists who had gone crazy in the summer and fall of 1981, when riot after riot convulsed Ardoyne and the Bone and other Catholic ghettoes which lay within a few miles of the courthouse.

That Kelly found Kevin Artt and everyone else guilty of virtually all but a few negligible charges was unsurprising to nearly everyone except the naïve young taxi driver.

Charles McKiernan murdered Albert Miles on the night of November 26, 1978. Maurice Gilvarry drove him there and helped him do it. Both men are dead today, one,

McKiernan, of natural causes, and the other, Gilvarry, of an unnatural cause, a bullet to the back of the head delivered in south Armagh in January 1981. Other IRA men ordered them to do it, supplied the weapons, helped them get away afterward, and celebrated at the news of Miles' death. You won't hear any of that from those alive today who could confirm it, British or Irish. A person who came forward to name them, even in death, might put his life and limb at risk. He would be a *tout*, the very worst thing a person in Northern Ireland could be called. And there is more than just social opprobrium for those who tell the truths of atrocities committed in the name of the Irish Republican Army.

In 1997, a publisher released the tell-all memoir of former IRA intelligence officer Eamon Collins, *Killing Rage*, a regret-laced, name-naming recital of IRA killings which Collins had aided and abetted. Two years later, in 1999, he went out early one morning to walk his dogs near his home in Newry. Unknown assailants ambushed him, bashed in his skull with a blunt object, stabbed him, ran him over with a car, and left his dead body lying in the road.

Denis Donaldson, an IRA man turned British informant, outed himself too, in 2005. Later he went into hiding in rural Donegal. In 2006, the men enraged by his treachery found him, smashed their way into his small cottage, and killed him with a shotgun blast to the head.

Those who might tell the truth of Albert Miles' murder know what happened to Eamon Collins and Denis Donaldson. And so they stay silent, even as the players in the Albert Miles murder case age out, retire, succumb to old age and dementia and alcoholism, or die of natural causes. Donaldson and Collins showed courage. To their families and friends today, that is cold comfort, if it is any comfort at all.

SEVENTY-EIGHT

Alan and Kevin

In 2019, Alan Miles, age sixty-two, was employed in a logistics company in England. He remained haunted by the sudden loss of his father. He still wondered who took his dad from him.

He was not alone in his sorrow. In September 2018, a memorial garden for prison service personnel killed in the Troubles opened in Alrewas, England. Alan attended the opening ceremony. Among the attendees were survivors of attacks on prison service officers by the IRA.

"I sat next to a lady whose mother and father were shot at their home by the IRA," Alan said. "They were friends of my mum and dad. He had retired two years early."

The father was killed. The mother survived. Forty years later, she remains afraid of the dark and answering the door of her home.

Sitting a row away from Alan was an elderly woman and her grown son. The son had been four years old when IRA men killed his father.

"He couldn't remember his dad," said Alan.

The names of another couple, Paddy and Vi Macken, are engraved in stone at the memorial garden. Maurice Gilvarry shot them dead as they sat watching television in their living room one night in February 1979.

In 2011, Alan tracked Kevin down and sent him an email.

Kevin replied. The subject line of his email read, "your Father."

"Dear Alan," Kevin wrote, "how really sad it is you had to experience what you did, no one should have to go through that, I can only imagine it is a terrible terrible thing. I feel it is only fair to point out in no uncertain terms that I did not kill your father, it was not I you seen [sic] on that fateful evening. I know you were convinced that I am the murderer, but I can honestly tell you I have never killed anyone, let alone your dad.

"I do remember seeing you in the courthouse, you seemed like a nice person, I am sorry that my name has got intermingled in your life, and probably the source of much anger and hatred.

"I too questioned why your father was murdered and all I was ever told by an ira prisoner in the Maze, that your dad permitted the beating and torture of ira prisoners in the Maze. Believe me Alan I have been kept in the dark about the facts of your father's murder, and that is about all I know, I wish I could help you more. I really hope and pray you can find some sort of closure, and I mean that most sincerely, Kevin Artt."

Alan responded in a reply email sent minutes later.

Many thanks for your reply i appreciate it
33 years on all i am seeking is closure
i am not bitter not angry not seeking revenge not seeking publicity just seeking some answers that are better face to face rather than by email
i know to some extent you are in a no win situation if you were guilty then you are hardly going to admit it in an open environment though i am sure you would want closure on it
if you are not guilty then you are in a living nightmare

*on the evening in question i was on the phone in
the hallway when the knock came to the door
my mother answered the door i saw the 2 people
at the door one clearly the other not so clearly
i believed if not you someone very like you was
the one i saw clearly all be it [sic] for a very
short time as i dived into the side door
if you didnt do what i think you did i apologise
for causing you any more grief if however you
feel it is worthwhile us meeting up to get closure
on both sides then i am available
in your evidence you said you held your hand
over my mother mouth [sic]⁹ the words you used
suggested someone with a conscience
on a separate [sic] subject can i ask did you
work for hartes headstone people a rumour
doing the rounds way back was that you worked
on engraving my fathers headstone
my mother is still alive and i really want to get
closure for her as well as at 85 she is getting on
in years*

Kevin replied eleven days later.

"Hi Alan, look I didn't kill your daddy," he wrote. "I have been laughed at and ridiculed for signing a confession admitting to a crime I did not commit, if I had been in any way responsible I would tell you Alan I would have nothing to lose.

"Its pretty fucked up I lost my family and friends, I was running and living another life for almost ten years, besides being in the maze and told I was going to die by alleged friends of your dad.

"The only reason I was asked if I wanted to escape was because of the notoriety of the Christopher Black supergrass

---

9. Kevin's confession did not say this. Charles McKiernan's confession said he had been the one to put his hand over Florence Miles' mouth.

trial. My son Barry is 31 this month I have maybe spent 4 weeks with him in 29 years. His mum was dating a guy by the name of Jona McClafferty who was in jail for killing a jail warden. His best friend Morrice Gilvary [sic] was an informant and was somehow involved with getting the car I think that was used for your dads murder.

"It was him who said I was involved with your dads murder, which is absolute fucking lies, that is one of many I hope roast in hell.

"I looked at current events in northern Ireland and I can't help wonder why so many had to suffer.

"As far as Harte's [sic] Bob Harte [sic] was a good friend of my dads John Artt who was a well respected businessman in whitehouse, my grandfather was an ric policeman, I am a well rounded decent man from a good family much like yourself Alan, think I mounted your fathers headstone that's what I did for Harte, little did I know I would be accused and convicted of his murder[.]

"It's a wild f'in life alan, the only thing you know is you don't know whats around the corner.

"The only good thing that has come of this I am out of that shithole belfast and getting on with trying to have some normalcy, I really wish you luck and a good life, you should not have experienced what you did, sincerely Kevin B."

At this writing, Alan and Kevin plan to meet in person in the U.S. Each is a victim of what happened at 8 Evelyn Gardens on the night of November 26, 1978. I wonder what words will pass between them when they first meet. I want to be there when it happens.

SEVENTY-NINE

Truth and Reconciliation

The Belfast of 2020 bore little resemblance to the city I recalled from my visits in the 1990s.

The murals, the memorial gardens, the peace walls, and other relics of the thirty-year war were still visible here and there. The once-ubiquitous British Army patrols and RUC checkpoints, the baby-faced soldiers using their telescopic sights on automatic rifles to peer down city streets, the sprawling fortified barracks with their colossal radio antennae climbing skyward were long gone. Watchtowers and barracks sat rotting, boarded-up, some still enveloped in rusting, '80s-era bomb mesh screens, relics of a garrison state of which children and teenagers lack any memory.

At night, instead of being deserted, the sidewalks and streets in the city center were jammed with people. There were women in town for an abortion rights rally, theatergoers swarming the Grand Opera House for a performance of "The Kite Runner," soccer fans thronging the pubs and jockeying for position to watch World Cup games on flat screens. The Europa Hotel was still there but no longer barricaded with sandbags. Other hotels were under construction, the crews going on their shifts before 7 a.m., jackhammers rat-a-tatting early on Saturday morning.

Nearby were McDonalds, Subways, Burger Kings, Mexican fast food, Starbucks, restaurants offering Kurdish food. A few blocks away, near the Royal Courts of Justice, stood a shiny ultra-modern shopping center, Victoria Square. In design and amenities, it put to shame any shopping mall I had seen in San Diego. On a walk to visit it, a couple of buskers could be seen on the street, offering amplified versions of Frankie Valli's "Can't Take My Eyes Off You" and "Hava Nagila." Uber drivers and hotel managers relished the prospect of the upcoming prequel to the "Game of Thrones" TV series, which HBO would soon produce in a new studio nearby, further boosting an already-thriving local economy. Buses ferried throngs of the show's obsessive fans north, to the Giant's Causeway on the Antrim coast.

The old courthouse on Crumlin Road was boarded-up, derelict. No one fixed its broken windows. After its closure, a real estate developer promised to develop the property into a luxury hotel. He persuaded county authorities into selling it to him for £1. Shortly afterward, a fire of unknown origin gutted the place.

In 2019, fourteen years after the IRA decommissioned over 150 tons of ammunition, rifles, machine guns, mortars, handguns, explosives, and other munitions and ten years after the UVF and UDA followed suit, Northern Ireland was mostly at peace.

But remnants of the Troubles remained. Belfast's peace walls, which started springing up in 1969, were even more numerous than they were during the seventies and eighties. Strict segregation between Catholic and Protestant communities continued in many neighborhoods and public housing. Ninety percent of all children in Northern Ireland still attended a school which was either exclusively Catholic or exclusively Protestant.

F. Scott Fitzgerald once wrote of people beating on against the current as they are borne back ceaselessly into the past. Was there any place, I wondered, where that phenomenon was more prevalent than in the north of Ireland? In Belfast City Cemetery, in Ballymurphy off the Falls Road, an underground wall, invisible from above, is said to divide the Catholic dead from the Protestant. In Milltown Cemetery, the Irish tricolor rises above the Republican plot. There lie the bones of Bobby Sands and other hunger strikers, not far from the site where the deranged Loyalist Michael Stone threw grenades and fired a handgun at Catholic mourners at a graveside service in 1988, killing three of them. Wandering the ground there in 2016, I wondered whether the generation born just after 1998 might be the first in the six counties in over 800 years in which religious denomination no longer fixed the chances, prospects, and outcomes of a life.

By the time the people in the six counties who are young today reach the age of sixty, they will think it absurd that being Catholic or Protestant ought to dictate where a person attended school, whether they were heckled and harassed on their way to that school, who they could ask out on a date and who they could not, whether they would have to elope if they chose a partner of the wrong religion or whether they could have a proper church wedding, what first names they could and could not give to their newborn children, whether they would grow up in adequate housing or a ghetto, what chances they had of getting a decent job in the civil service or winding up on the dole, who would ostracize them socially from age eight and who would not, which streets they could safely walk at night and which they had to avoid, whether a policeman would treat them with respect or humiliate them during a routine traffic stop, whether they would have to choose between misery at home and emigrating abroad, whether they would feel prideful rage or raging pride each twelfth of July when they heard beating drums and saw ranks of men clad in orange sashes and black bowlers marching down the street, whether they would hear or say words like *Taig, Fenian scum, Prod, Not an inch, Fuck the pope*, what section of the cemetery they could bury their parents in.

In 2018, Kevin Barry Artt's life had all the elements of the California Dream—a loving family, a house, a thriving business, a boat, a horse for his daughter.

On the morning of September 18, 2018, I called Kevin. It was his fifty-ninth birthday.

He answered his phone as he always has, a cheerful-sounding Irish voice that could belong to a twenty-year-old. He had just dropped off the kids at school. Being kids, they had forgotten it was their dad's birthday. I wished Kevin a happy birthday. I told him next year was the big one.

"The big six-oh," he replied with a chuckle.

"When you were twenty, did you ever expect to make it to sixty?"

"Hell no. I thought I'd be in Milltown Cemetery long before then."

"Look at you today. You're on top of the world."

"I'm on top of the *ground*. Every day above the ground is a good day."

Another day above the ground.

Kevin's good cheer was not always easy for me to understand.

I have spent hundreds of hours with Kevin Barry Artt. During those hours, I never saw him weep or display anything other than optimism and cheerfulness about his case, no matter what had been the latest discouraging ruling from Judge Legge or how distant his eventual release seemed. There were times when I succumbed to gloominess and grouchiness while fretting about family and law practice problems. They were all small potatoes, of course, compared to the enormity of Kevin's circumstances. None of my problems involved enemies who wished me dead or in prison. Kevin's problems were monumental, but he was buoyant and upbeat all the time. How was he able to do it?

When I asked him, his response was always the same, reflexive.

"I haven't any choice, Dan," he would say, matter-of-factly, as though that were an answer.

Of course, Kevin Barry Artt had a choice. He could have yielded to the despair, cynicism, fatigue, and bitterness that haunted his psyche from time to time. So far as I could tell, he did so only once, fleetingly.

I'm becoming bitter, he texted me one night in February 2019.

The text came on the heels of a suggestion by the Northern Ireland Court of Appeal that it might dismiss Kevin's appeal of his underlying convictions based on his supposed abandonment of it.

In trying to choose the right words for a reply, I struggled for a moment.

All I could muster was this:

> *You beat not one Goliath but two. The best revenge = living well. Which is what you are doing!*

His reply followed a moment later.

> *Still not 100% free though 38 years later*
> *I have grandkids I haven't met can you imagine grandkids*

Moments later, he had snapped out of it, or so it seemed:

> *I'm really blessed my kids are healthy and brilliant I have a good life . . . Someone pissed in my water boots this morning I guess*
> *Every now and then I get cynical*

Only every now and then.

Like Gerry Conlon before him, Kevin numbed himself with alcohol and drugs for a time. But he got straight, started a family, formed a successful business from scratch, and became a sort of Ward Cleaver. In 2019 as in 1990, he was the upright, always-reliable, firm-but-gentle dad, the friend who would help you move all your heavy furniture out of your apartment on a moment's notice and do it cheerfully, the kind of man you would like to have for a confidante, especially if you were in trouble.

My fondest hope for Kevin Artt is that he dies in bed decades from now while surrounded by his American and Irish families. Long before that day he will have flown to Shannon or Dublin and kissed the ground after getting off the plane. He will never have regained the six years and six months he spent wrongfully imprisoned for a murder committed by someone else. He will not have had the chance to address Basil Kelly, Charles McKiernan, Norman Cromie, Ronnie Appleton, Mark Zanides, Sara Criscitelli, Paul Hamlin, the men of the RUC who beat him and humiliated him and tried to kill him and ruin his life. He will have achieved something better: living well.

A secondary hope for Kevin is that those who tormented him will read of his gentle passing in the obituaries, and be reminded, one last time, that they lost, and he won.

EIGHTY

Kevin Barry

In 1920, during the Irish War of Independence, Kevin Barry was an eighteen-year-old medical student at University College Dublin. He had been born in Dublin and raised in a small town in County Carlow. His mother had moved the family there after his father died when Barry was six years old.

Barry joined the IRA at age fifteen. Three years later, the young medical student participated in the ambush of a British Army truck, aiming to capture weapons. The operation was scheduled to take place at 11 a.m., in time for Barry to complete the job and still make it to class for an exam scheduled for later that day.

The ambush went badly for the volunteers. After an exchange of gunfire, his comrades fled, leaving Barry behind, underneath the truck, where he dove after his gun jammed. One British soldier lay dead and two others badly wounded.

Barry's interrogators pressed him for the names of his accomplices. Even after they tortured him and promised to let him go if he cooperated, the prisoner refused to talk. The emergency laws prescribed trial by a court-martial composed of nine British Army officers. Barry refused to recognize the legitimacy of the court and declined to take the stand in his own defense. He went to the gallows on November 1, 1920, less than six weeks after the abortive ambush in Dublin.

To the British, Barry was just one more irksome rebel, an outlaw, to be dispatched fast and without fanfare. To the world press, Barry was a callow youngster whose execution represented the harshness of British justice in Ireland. To the Irish, Barry was a hero willing to give his life for Ireland rather than take the easy way out and betray his friends.

Thirty-nine years later, Maeve Artt christened her new adopted son Kevin Barry Artt, after the martyred young man whose name was a synonym to Catholic schoolchildren for courage in the face of British subjugation. By 2020, Kevin had fought the Crown's diplomats, police, and military to a standstill in an epic legal war that ended with that unlikeliest of events, a British whimper, and an Irish victory. The Maze prison, for years the symbol of the last vestiges of British oppression of Irish Republicanism, shut its doors without Kevin Barry Artt having seen the inside of it again.

In 1920, Kevin Barry's torment of the British occupiers was violent, brief and inconsequential, a failure in the end. His is one more sad Irish tale that ends with pallbearers carrying a dead man encased in a coffin draped in the Irish tricolor to a grave and a ballad that sets his story to music.

Kevin Barry Artt's torment of the British was peaceful, protracted, historic, and successful. Unlike the eighteen-year-old man from rural Carlow, Kevin Barry Artt sought no conflict with the British. They brought it to him. In that conflict, his achievement far exceeded Kevin Barry's.

A side-by-side comparison of photographs of the two men, unrelated by blood and separated by decades, reveals an eerie resemblance. The Kevin Barry of 1918, clad in a rugby shirt, looks into the camera. A slight smile turns his lips up at the corners, just barely. His eyes project a sort of bemused melancholy.

"Do you believe in reincarnation?" Kevin asked me after looking at the images.

In 2019, I met Charlie and Teresa McNutt in a pub in rural Fermanagh. Sixty-three years after meeting in the women's ward at Forster Green Hospital in 1956, the two were a happy couple enjoying their golden years together. The lighting inside the pub was low, the barmaid friendly, the atmosphere warm and friendly, and the Guinness perfect. I showed Teresa the image of the long-dead Kevin Barry on an iPhone, without telling her who it was.

"Tell me who it is," I said.

Teresa studied the picture closely.

"That's my son," she replied.

ACKNOWLEDGMENTS

Kevin Barry Artt had the courage to let his story be told. His fortitude and courage in the face of terrible odds and disastrous misfortune are an inspiration. Since 1992, the hundreds of hours I have spent with him and his honesty have been his greatest gifts to me.

John Artt, Maeve Artt, Therese Artt, Carmen Artt, and Barry Paul Artt all suffered terribly because of the suffering inflicted on Kevin. Several of them still suffer at the time of this writing. At every turn they showed me nothing but openness, hospitality, honesty, generosity and kindness.

For Alan Miles, the son of the late Albert Miles, our interviews cannot have been easy or pleasant. The calamity of his father's murder will always be with him and his mother, Florence. He could not have looked forward to our conversations and email exchanges. He was ever graceful, honest, and helpful as he helped me to understand exactly what happened at 8 Evelyn Gardens that night in 1978 and who his father was. In August 2018, Alan emailed me a photograph of his parents taken in happier times, when they were on vacation in England. The picture has been tacked up next to my computer monitor for the last fourteen months. I still look at it every day. His decision to share the British government's HET report with me in 2019 was unselfish and unsolicited. It resulted directly in the victory of Kevin Barry Artt in the Northern Ireland Court of Appeal in May 2020.

The testimony and information provided privately by scores of Irish interviewees and witnesses formed much of the basis for this book. Their names appear in the endnotes. Among them were Maze escapees and defendants in the Christopher Black trial, including Paul Kane, Gerry Kelly, and Brendan McFarlane. Many gave interviews or testified at personal risk to themselves and in the sole interest of telling the truth of their experiences. In a country where telling the truth can get one killed or imprisoned, there was nothing in it, and much to lose, for all of them. Each has my profound thanks.

An able team of research assistants comprised of Kent Easter and Gwenllian Kern-Allely tracked down hard-to-find articles and books, located photographs, and negotiated clearances and licenses for their use. In every hour of our collaboration, their talent, brilliance, and enthusiasm for the project shone through.

I am indebted to the Ulster University's Conflict Archive on the Internet (CAIN), whose website offered a treasure trove of databases, bibliographies, studies, records, and photographs on the Troubles and politics in Northern Ireland from 1968 to the present.

The generous and kind people of the Linen Hall Library opened their ample resources to me in the researching of this book. Each time I walked through the library's front door on Donegall Square in Belfast, I felt warmly welcomed. Several documents and ephemera which I found there in its Northern Ireland Political Collection could not have been found anywhere else. Had I not felt on a mission to complete this book, I would have liked to have wandered the library's stacks of local history, newspapers, fiction, plays and poetry, sat down, and lost myself in it all for a few days.

The National Archives in Kew and the National Library of Ireland also provided valuable source material from their archives, especially from the latter's collection of the papers of Sean O'Mahony.

Professors Michael Fryer and Jennifer Freeman of the Joan B. Kroc School of Peace Studies at the University of San Diego and Bonnie Weir of Yale University provided kind and thoughtful advice concerning the establishment of a truth and reconciliation commission in Northern Ireland.

Beth Bland of the Keough-Naughton Institute for Irish Studies at the University of Notre Dame kindly arranged for me to interview Irish historian and writer Seamus Deane, the Institute's founding dean, at O'Connell House in Dublin. Seamus gave me hours, memories, heartbreaking stories, and his wisdom. He has visited the Republican plot in the cemetery in Derry too many times. His insights about the Maze prison, the Diplock courts, and the emergency laws were indispensable.

My friends Saoirse O'Reilly and her mother, Fionnuala, shared their time and their family's history, helping to educate an American for whom the history of Ireland and the Troubles still defy easy understanding.

Ambassador Nancy Soderberg provided insight and recollections concerning the IRA cease-fire of 1998 and the Good Friday Agreement.

To Anthony McIntyre, the creator of *The Pensive Quill* weblog, I am thankful for his guidance and help.

The efforts of talented and dedicated lawyers and paralegals, both American and Irish, who made this book possible were essential to its composition.

The list of names of lawyers who have been killed for their clients' sake is a short one. One of the names on it belongs to the late Rosemary Nelson, murdered by Loyalists in her driveway in 1999. I treasure the memory of the two hours she spent with me in her office in Lurgan in 1995 and the interest she took in the case of Kevin Barry Artt. Her courage and commitment to her clients were unmatched by those of any lawyer I have ever met.

In Belfast, Fearghal Shiels, Peter Madden, Martin Finucane, Eamonn Rea, Fiona Doherty, Andrew Moriarty, and Aodhan McCavana worked skillfully and tirelessly on Kevin's behalf in trying to achieve a reversal of the Basil Kelly judgment in the Northern Ireland Court of Appeal during 2018 and 2019. I will always appreciate their patience and good cheer in responding to my inquiries about Kevin's appeal and their dedication to their client. Their offices were a friendly haven to me in 2018 and 2019.

The name of Pat Finucane, who was Peter Madden's law partner and Martin Finucane's brother, also graces the short list of lawyers who sacrificed their lives for their clients during the Troubles. After so many years of concealment and obfuscation, the British government must tell the Finucane family the whole truth of Pat's murder in 1989. Will it, can it do the right thing at long last?

In 1992, I was able to offer legal counsel to Kevin Barry Artt pro bono only because of two American lawyers. They are Carl Poirot, the former director of the San Diego Volunteer Lawyer Program, and Stephen F. Yunker, the coordinator of the pro bono program of the law firm where I then worked. It was Steve who unhesitatingly approved the law firm's investment of time and money into Kevin's asylum case. It was Carl who allowed Steve and me to help Kevin under the auspices of SDVLP, which matches private-bar lawyers with clients in need of free legal services.

In 2019, Steve was retired from the practice of law. I never knew a lawyer in private practice who provided more free legal work to people who needed it, at sacrifice to himself, than Steve. His friendship and bonhomie sustained me many times when I would have rather been at home in bed during our early-morning ocean swims at La Jolla Cove, especially in the winter months.

The lawyers of Devaney Pate Morris & Cameron LLP in San Diego showed their belief in this project by deferring rent while I worked nonstop on this book in their suite of offices in downtown San Diego for fourteen months. As a result, I had ample space for whiteboards, large maps, thousands of court records, and scores of notebooks stuffed with documents. I also had the peace and quiet that I needed to concentrate. The firm's partners and its managing partner, Leslie Devaney, and her husband, Judge Frank Devaney, believed in me and made this book possible. So did Heather L. Rosing, John D. Klinedinst, Susan Nahama, Scott Carr, and other colleagues and friends at Klinedinst PC.

I entered this project as a first-time author who needed guidance from experienced and successful writers. Several lent advice and wisdom in support of this book. They are Ryan Gattis, Alan Abrahamson, Major Garrett, Patrick Radden Keefe, Kevin Toolis, Rafa Fernandez, Jim Newton, Eric Nusbaum, and Joseph Wambaugh. George Klawitter, CSC, offered his keen eye for editing and sound advice about literary agents. Alan Dowty, Ph.D., of the University of Notre Dame, and Stuart Banner of the UCLA School of Law also gave thoughtful advice about book-writing. Judge Alex Kozinski contributed insight about the Ninth Circuit and sage counsel about editing. So did Bill Slomanson.

Writing can be a lonely and monastic experience. Self-doubt and the feeling you are your only friend come easily. The support and encouragement of loyal friends James Baker, Rico Bartolomei, Jeff Chine, Sean Curtis, Joleen Guckian, Marsha Herman, Mike Hird, Ralph Inzunza, Jr., Amita Sharma, Tim Katzman, Joseph Keith, Joe Kracht, Mary Lehman, Kathleen Malone, Charlotte and Daryl Lu, Ray Magnussen, Pennie McLaughlin, Ron Prager, Chris Saunders, Lorena Slomanson, Lisa Schall, Walter Scott, Sara Simpson, and Chris Yurcek kept me going. This book could not have been written without their friendship and support. Daryl, Ray, and Chris Saunders passed away before I could finish this book and share it with them.

During a time when few literary agents would deign to talk to a first-time author, Chip MacGregor took me on as a client, just before the coronavirus pandemic delivered a body blow to the publishing world. Through months of uncertainty and self-doubt his wise counsel, kindness, savvy, and loyalty encouraged me. Agent Paul Feldstein offered his kind and thoughtful counsel pro bono.

The professionals and service providers whose work enabled the research and writing of this book include the kind people of The Flint, the hotel which hosted me during two of my research trips to Belfast in 2016 and 2018; Kelly McLaurin, who built and provided technical support for my computer networks; Lone Star Legal, who scanned huge volumes of court records in San Francisco and made them word-searchable; Eric Peltola and his team at Copyscan, Inc., who provided scanning and copying services also; and photographer Michael Brennan, who licensed several of his photographs at a deep discount once he heard what the book was about. They all contributed greatly also. I am sure there are others whom I have forgotten. To them, I apologize.

Kelly Anastay has been this book's most unwavering and steadfast private supporter. Since 2017 she has served as an unpaid editor, *consigliere*, devil's advocate, chef, driver, and listener. Her companionship, love, good humor, utter unselfishness, and belief in the project were steady and unwavering throughout. She is the love of my life.

Because the venue of Kevin Barry Artt's extradition case was San Francisco, I traveled to that city many times during the last twenty-seven years. Nearly every time, I stayed in the home of my dear cousin Pattie Lawton, who put me up, fed me, listened to me, counseled me, and gave her unconditional support at all times. She was careful to offer candid advice only when asked, and then, always and only, gave it gently. This book could not have been written without her. My brothers, aunts, uncles, and cousins, particularly Ted Lawton, Rich Lawton, Tony Lawton, Matthew Lawton, Mark Lawton, Lisa Palmer, Michael and Setsuko Lawton, Robert Lawton, Patricia "Gussie" Lawton, Tom Lawton, Peggy Lawton, Jon Lawton, and Patty Ducey, all provided inspiration and encouragement as well.

To my parents, Joanna and Joseph, who recently celebrated their sixty-second wedding anniversary, I owe, simply, everything. This book is dedicated to them.

Steve Jackson, Michael Cordova, Stephanie Johnson Lawson, Jazzminn Morecraft, and Elijah Toten of WildBlue Press believed in this book, and they stuck by me when the going got rough at the last minute. Any writer would be blessed to receive the gifts of the professionalism, skill, and care they gave me in bringing this story to you.

APPENDIX

MAZE ESCAPEES

Name/ place of origin	Sentence	Fate	Location ca. 2013 if known	Comments
Artt, Kevin Barry / Belfast	Life	Escaped capture until 1992; moved to California, became one of "H-Block 4"	Bay Area, California	
Brennan, Pol/Bel-fast	16 years	Escaped capture until 1992 (arrested in California), became one of "H-Block 4"; resisted extradition; deported to Ireland 2009	Donegal	
Burns, Jimmy J./Belfast	Life	Captured same day; released 1993 after serving 17 years of life sentence	Belfast	

Name/ place of origin	Sentence	Fate	Location ca. 2013 if known	Comments
Campbell, Seamus "Spanner" / Tyrone	14 years	One of only 3 escapees never captured	Co. Galway	One of only 3 escapees never captured
Clarke, Jim P.	18 years	Captured 12-3-84; freed 3-13-90	Donegal	
Clarke, Seamus J.	Life	Captured 1987 in Dublin	Dublin	
Cleaky / Belfast		Sentenced to 7 years in Portlaoise, released March 1993		
Corey, Joe H. / South Derry	Life	Arrested on the Tuesday after the escape, released 1992	Co. Derry	
Cummings, Dennis / Tyrone	Life	Captured same day; served 16 years afterward; rereleased 1993	Co. Tyrone	

Name/ place of origin	Sentence	Fate	Location ca. 2013 if known	Comments
Donnelly, Jimmy G. / Belfast	15 years	Captured same day; jumped bail after Black case collapsed on appeal in 1986; arrested Belfast 1989; sentenced to 5 years on escape-related charges; released 1990 b/c of time already served on remand	Ardoyne, n. Belfast	Was in car that crashed front gate; knocked unconscious by collision
Finucane, Dermot / Belfast	18 years	Re-arrested Nov. 1987 in Grannard, Co. Longford, post-Eksund incident; held for 2 ½ years afterward in Portlaoise on extradition warrants; brother Pat shot dead in 1989; released after Irish Supreme Court refused to uphold his extradition, on 3-13-90	Co. Meath	

Name/ place of origin	Sentence	Fate	Location ca. 2013 if known	Comments
Fleming, Kiernan G. "Hush Hush" / Derry (d.)	BSOSP / Life	Drowned in River Bannagh 12-2-84 after gun battle with BA	N/A	Deceased
Fryers, Gerard J. "Rinty" / Belfast	20 years	Evaded capture; returned to struggle in the border area	Co. Monaghan	1 of 3 escapees never captured
Gorman, Billy G./ Belfast	BSOSP/ life	Recaptured same day; served 14 years of life sentence; released 1993; convictions overturned on appeal in 1999	Belfast	
Hamilton, Peter C. "Skeet"/ Belfast (d.)	Life	Recaptured same day while hiding in River Lagan; beaten savagely and thrown into punishment block; released April 1993 and returned to struggle; died February 2011 (cancer)	N/A	Deceased

Name/ place of origin	Sentence	Fate	Location ca. 2013 if known	Comments
Kane, Paul A./ Belfast	18 years	Arrested in Co. Down on Monday after escape along with Brendy Mead; released on bail 1986 after Black convictions quashed by the NICOA; jumped bail; arrested in Grannard, Co. Longford (with Finucane) Nov. 1987; released for defective extradition warrants; re-arrested same day so new warrants could be served; extradited back to north in April 1989; released 1989 for time served	Ardoyne, n. Belfast	

Name/ place of origin	Sentence	Fate	Location ca. 2013 if known	Comments
Kelly, Tony 'Spazzer' / Derry	BSOP/ Life	Arrested July 1985 in Killybegs, Donegal; jumped bail; re-arrested in Dublin 11-2-6-87 along with Clarke; sentenced to 7 years in Portlaoise; released 4-1-93	Donegal	
Kelly, Gerry/ Belfast	Life	Returned to Republican activity in Armagh border area; arrested along with McFarlane in Amsterdam Jan. 1986; extradited and returned to Crumlin Road Jail as remand prisoner; sentenced to 5 years in 1988; released June 1989 after serving 17 mos. On remand; joined Sinn Fein; participated in GFA negotiations as part of Sinn Fein negotiating team; elected in Forum Elections of 1996 and then as member of new Legislative Assembly; reelected MLA for n. Belfast every election since; since 2011, Policing spokesperson for Sinn Fein and their lead on Policing Board	Belfast	

Name/ place of origin	Sentence	Fate	Location ca. 2013 if known	Comments
Kerr, Rab/Belfast	Life	Recaptured on grounds of prison while holding off guards in Tally Lodge; released 1995; author of several books and historical pamphlets	Outskirts of Belfast	
Kirby, Terry/ Belfast	Life	Lammed to California, became one of "H-Block 4"; resisted extradition	San Francisco	
McAllister, Tony "Tank" / Befast (d.)	Life	Left the country; lammmed to San Francisco Bay area where he married and died of natural causes under an assumed name; had "loving wife and children."	N/A	Deceased. Only 1 of the 38 escapees who never appeared in the public eye again

Name/ place of origin	Sentence	Fate	Location ca. 2013 if known	Comments
McCann, Jim P. "Jaz" / Belfast (d.)	25 years	Recaptured same day on the Bog Road by British soldier close to the prison; released 1994 after earning Open University First Class BA (Hons.) degree in Humanities	Belfast	
McDon-nell, Gery P. "Blute" / Belfast	16 years	Recaptured in Glasgow, Scotland June 1985; sentenced to life imprisonment for conspiracy to cause explosions; released	Belfast	Carved the wooden replica of a handgun which was necessary to the escape
McIl-waine, Seamus T. / Monagh-an (d.)	Life	Ambushed by BA 4-26-86; shot to death by BA after having been wounded and resisting interrogation	N/A	Deceased (shot to death by British Army)

Name/ place of origin	Sentence	Fate	Location ca. 2013 if known	Comments
McFarlane, Brendan J. "Bik" / Belfast	Life	Walked to south Armagh; escaped to Netherlands; arrested there along with Gerry Kelly. January 1986; extradited in December 1986; sentenced to additional 5 years; released; now musician and singer	Ardoyne, Belfast	
McGlinchey, Sean 'Chinkey' / south Derry	Life	Recaptured same day after serving as part of Tally Lodge team and hiding in River Lagan; served 16 years; released December 1990; reorganized and strengthened Sinn Fein in Derry; elected Sinn Fein Councillor and first Sinn Fein Mayor of Limavady Council		

Name/ place of origin	Sentence	Fate	Location ca. 2013 if known	Comments
McIntyre, Paddy J./Donegal	15 years	Recaptured 2 days after escape in Co. Down; given pre-released parole in 1986; re-arrested in Killybegs, Co. Donegal, Jan. 1987; ordered released 5-7-87 by Judge Gannon; remained OTR	Donegal	
McKearney, Padraig O./Tyrone (d.)	14 years	Returned to active service; involved in attacks in Tyrone and Armagh; ambushed Loughgall Barracks 5-8-87	N/A	deceased
McManus, Marty G./ Belfast	15 Years	Recaptured on A1 dual carriageway at Banbridge; released Sept. 1989	In "rural setting," Co. Down	
Mead, Brendan/ Belfast	Life	Recaptured next day near Castlewellan, Co. Down; released	w. Belfast	

Name/ place of origin	Sentence	Fate	Location ca. 2013 if known	Comments
McNally, Dermot J. /Armagh	Life	Returned to struggle and went OTR; lived under assumed name; charged under assumed name for salmon poaching; denied false identity	Sligo	
Murray, Harry H./ Belfast	Life	Shot by BA solder from watchtower after shooting guard in the leg during escape; tried and sentenced for escape (1988); released	Andersontown, Belfast	Drew longest sentence at escape trial in 1988
Murray, Marcus L/Fermanagh	20 years	Recaptured at Banbridge; beaten by guards; released 1991	Sligo	
O'Connor, Eddie J./Armagh	Life	Recaptured after serving on Tally Lodge tea m with Kerr and Cummings for crucial minutes; beaten "black and blue" and to unconsciousness	Keady, Co. Armagh	

Name/ place of origin	Sentence	Fate	Location ca. 2013 if known	Comments
Roberts, Gary J./Belfast	BSOSP/ life	Recaptured night of escape by Scottish soldiers; became fluent in Irish while incarcerated; released 1989 after serving 14 years; became school principal and taught Irish	Belfast	
Russell, Robert P. "Goose"/ Belfast	20 years	Returned to struggle; re-arrested in Dublin 5-26-84; sent to Portlaoise Prison; caught trying to escape 1985; extradited to north in 1988 after serving 3-year sentence for attempted escape; underlying conviction overturned on appeal after he had already served all but 3 weeks of his full sentence (including extra 5 years for escape); released 1992	Bally-murphy, Belfast	

Name/place of origin	Sentence	Fate	Location ca. 2013 if known	Comments
Simpson, Joe/Belfast	20 years	One of four escapees recaptured in River Lagan (same day); released 1993 after serving 13 years	Andersontown, w. Belfast	
Smyth, James Joseph/Belfast	20 years	Escaped to California, became one of "H-Block 4"; won extradition trial but lost at 9th Circuit; extradited; released	Cork City, Ireland	
Storey, Bobby/Belfast	18 years	Recaptured; sentenced to another 7 years for escape-related convictions; released 1994; re-arrested and charged Nov. 1996 (acquitted 1998); became chairperson of Sinn Fein in Belfast and advocate of peace process	Belfast	

SELECTED BIBLIOGRAPHY

Beresford, David. *Ten Men Dead: The Story of the 1981 Irish Hunger Strike.* New York, NY: The Atlantic Monthly Press, 1987.

Bonner, David. *Emergency Powers in Peacetime.* London: Sweet & Maxwell, 1985.

Bonner, David. *Combating Terrorism: Supergrass Trials in Northern Ireland.* 51 Mod. L. Rev., January 1988.

Boyd, Andrew. *The Informers: A Chilling Account of the Supergrasses in Northern Ireland.* Dublin and Cork, Ireland: The Mercier Press Limited, 1984.

Boyle, Kevin, Hadden, Tom, and Hillyard, Paddy. *Ten Years On in Northern Ireland: The Legal Control of Political Violence.* Great Britain: The Cobden Trust, 1980.

Collins, Eamon, with McGovern, Mick. *Killing Rage.* London: Granta Books, 1997.

Coogan, Tim Pat. *On The Blanket: The H-Block Story.* London: Head of Zeus, 1980.

Coogan, Tim Pat. *The Troubles: Ireland's Ordeal 1966-1996 and the Search for Peace.* Boulder, Colorado: Roberts Rinehart Publishers, 1996.

Deane, Seamus (ed.) *The Field Day Anthology of Irish Writing.* Derry, Northern Ireland: Field Day Publications, 1991.

Diplock, William. *Report of the Commission to Consider Legal Procedures to Deal with Terrorist Activities in*

Northern Ireland. London: Her Majesty's Stationery Office, 1972.

Drizin, Steven, and Leo, Richard. *The Problem of False Confessions in the Post-DNA World.* 82 N.C. L. Rev. 891, 2004.

Dunne, Derek. Out of the Maze: The True Story of the Biggest Jail Escape Since the War. Dublin, Ireland: Gill and MacMillan, Ltd., 1988.

Farrell, Michael. *Northern Ireland: The Orange State.* London: Pluto Press, 1976.

Foster, R.F. *Modern Ireland 1600-1972.* London: Penguin Books, 1988.

Gardiner, Gerald. Report of a Committee to Consider, in the Context of Civil Liberties and Human Rights, Measures to Deal with Terrorism in Northern Ireland. London: Her Majesty's Stationery Office, 1975.

Greer, D.S. *Admissibility of Confessions and the Common Law in Times of Emergency.* 24 N. Ir. L. Q. 199, 1973.

Greer, S.C., and White, A. *Abolishing The Diplock Courts.* London: The Cobden Trust, 1986.

Gudjonsson, Gisli. *The Psychology of Interrogations, Confessions and Testimony.* West Sussex, Great Britain: John Wiley & Sons Ltd., 1992.

Hoan, Gerard, and Walker, Clive. *Political Violence and the Law in Ireland.* Manchester, England, and New York, NY: Manchester University Press, 1989.

Irish Republican Army. *Irish Republican Army Manual of Guerrilla Warfare: Strategies for Offensive & Defensive Maneuvers.* Los Angeles, California: Mikazuki Publishing House, 2013.

Jackson, John, and Doran, Sean. *Judge Without Jury: Diplock Trials in the Adversary System.* Oxford, Great Britain: Oxford University Press, 1995.

Keefe, Patrick Radden. *Say Nothing: A True Story of Murder and Memory in Northern Ireland.* New York, NY: Doubleday, 2019.

Kelly, Gerry. *The Escape: The Inside Story of the 1983 Escape from Long Kesh Prison.* Belfast, Northern Ireland: M&G Publications, 2013.

Kitson, Frank. *Low Intensity Operations: Subversion, Insurgency and Peacekeeping.* London: Faber and Faber Ltd., 1971.

Korff, Douwe. *The Diplock Courts in Northern Ireland: A Fair Trial?* Utrecht, the Netherlands: Netherlands Institute of Human Rights, 1982.

McKeown, Laurence. *Out of Time: Irish Republican Prisoners Long Kesh 1972-2000.* Belfast, Northern Ireland: BTP Publications Ltd., 2001.

Mitchell, George. *Making Peace: The Behind-the-Scenes Story of the Negotiations that Culminated in the Signing of the Northern Ireland Peace Accord, Told by the American Senator Who Served as Independent Chairman of the Talks.* New York, NY: Alfred A. Knopf, 1999.

Murtagh, Tom. *The Maze Prison: A Hidden Story of Chaos, Anarchy and Politics.* East Sussex, Great Britain: Waterside Press, 2018.

O'Hearn, Denis. *Nothing But an Unfinished Song: Bobby Sands, the Irish Hunger Striker Who Ignited A Generation.* New York, NY: Nation Books, 2006.

The Stop the Show Trials Committee. *Victims of the "Supergrass" System: 4000 Years on the word of*

Christopher Black. Belfast, Northern Ireland: The Stop the Show Trials Committee, 1985.

Taylor, Peter. *Brits: The War Against the IRA.* London: Bloomsbury Publishing Plc, 2001.

Toolis, Kevin. *Rebel Hearts: Journeys within the IRA's Soul.* New York, NY: St. Martin's Press, 1995.

Walsh, Dermot P.J. *The Use and Abuse of Emergency Legislation in Northern Ireland.* Great Britain: The Cobden Trust, 1983.

For More News About Dan Lawton,
Signup For Our Newsletter:

http://wbp.bz/newsletter

Word-of-mouth is critical to an author's long-
term success. If you appreciated this book please
leave a review on the Amazon sales page:

http://wbp.bz/atg

INDEX

A

B

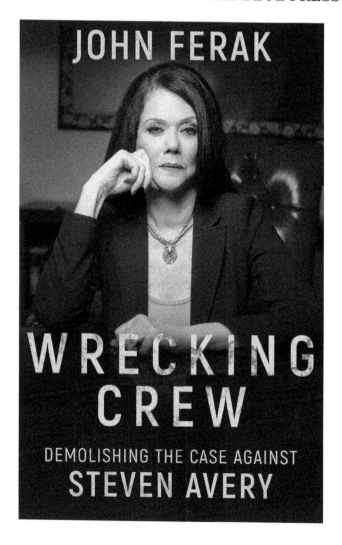

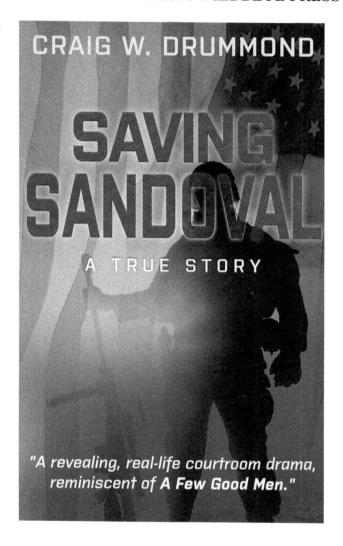

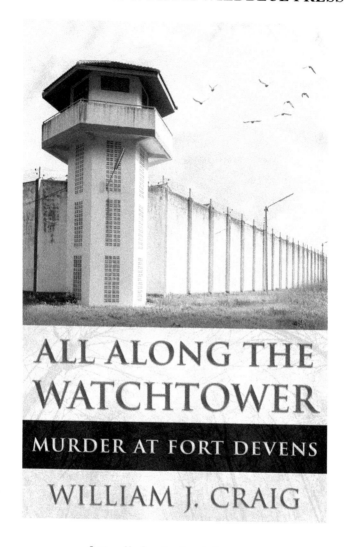

ALL ALONG THE
WATCHTOWER

MURDER AT FORT DEVENS

WILLIAM J. CRAIG

http://wbp.bz/watchtower

The controversy around the case of a former Green Beret's murder of his wife shows the lengths the government will go to to keep its secrets hidden.

Printed in the USA
CPSIA information can be obtained
at www.ICGtesting.com
LVHW011637220823
755987LV00037B/442